LIBERALISM
AND
CONSERVATISM

The Nature and Structure of Social Attitudes

BASIC STUDIES IN HUMAN BEHAVIOR

A series of monographs, texts, and treatises edited by
ANTHONY G. GREENWALD and ROBERT M. KRAUSS
Ohio State University   Columbia University

Kerlinger • *Liberalism and Conservatism: The Nature and Structure of Social Attitudes*

LIBERALISM
AND
CONSERVATISM

The Nature and Structure of Social Attitudes

Fred N. Kerlinger
University of Oregon

LEA LAWRENCE ERLBAUM ASSOCIATES, PUBLISHERS
1984   Hillsdale, New Jersey   London

Lawrence Erlbaum Associates, Inc., Publishers
365 Broadway
Hillsdale, New Jersey 07642

Library of Congress Cataloging in Publication Data

Kerlinger, Fred N. (Fred Nichols), 1910–
    Liberalism and conservatism.

    Includes bibliographical references and indexes.
    1. Attitude (Psychology)   2. Liberalism—Psychological
aspects.   3. Conservatism—Psychological aspects.
4. Psychology—Research.   5. Social psychology—
Research.   I. Title.
BF323.C5K47   1984   303.3′8   84-10217
ISBN 0-89859-377-8

Printed in the United States of America
10 9 8 7 6 5 4 3 2 1

This book is dedicated to my former colleagues of the Methodology Department, Psychology Laboratory, University of Amsterdam, The Netherlands

Contents

Preface

This book proposes a structural theory of social attitudes, presents the empirical evidence for the theory, and defines and explores liberalism and conservatism and the justification for associating social attitudes with these terms. The core ideas are that the structure of social attitudes, those sets of beliefs about social "objects" or referents shared by many or most people of a society, is basically dualistic rather than bipolar, and that the referents of social attitudes are differentially criterial to individuals and groups of individuals. The commonly held belief that social attitudes are polarized, with liberal beliefs at one end of a continuum and conservative beliefs at the other end, is questioned. Instead, liberalism and conservatism are conceived as separate and independent sets of beliefs. The book will elaborate and explain these statements and bring evidence to bear on their empirical validity.

Most of the research described in the book was conceived to test aspects of the above theoretical ideas. Its results, however, may have independent value. It describes, for example, factors of social attitudes that can be used in psychological and sociological research with other variables. It also suggests that social attitudes can be measured using what I call the referents (objects) of social attitudes as items, for example, *profits, religion, private property, equality, blacks,* and *labor unions.* Scales using such referents as items have been found to be reliable and factorially valid. Moreover, the factors formed by the referents—Economic Conservatism and Sexual Freedom, for instance—may be important attitude variables. The research also shows that the well-known rubrics liberalism and conservatism have empirical meaning in the sense that social attitude factors are usually clearly identifiable as liberal or conservative (but not both). Therefore the research may have scientific and practical value apart from the criterial referents theory.

An overview of the organization and contents of the book may be helpful. The book begins with a general discussion of social attitudes and their theoretical and practical importance in the context of Fleming's conception of "attitude man." In addition, the questions to which research answers are sought are also asked in Chapter 1.

In Chapter 2, liberalism and conservatism, the book's chief concepts or latent variables, are defined and explained. The treatment is historical and psychological: both are conceived to be larger ideologies of social attitudes and values that have evolved in modern times and that underlie many or most social attitudes. Attempts to measure them are briefly examined and the difficulty with the presumed continuum from liberal to conservative—liberalism *versus* conservatism—is studied, and an alternative conception of duality, or the relative independence of the two latent variables, is presented. The definition and nature of radicalism, especially vis à vis liberalism and conservatism, are also outlined. Finally, the educational attitudes progressivism and traditionalism are discussed.

The third chapter describes the criterial referents theory of attitudes, the theory to which the book is addressed, and the research needed to test the theory. Particular emphasis is given to the notion of attitude referents, the "objects" toward which attitudes are directed, the ideas and stuff of our beliefs and opinions.

One of the difficult problems in writing the book was the presentation of technical and methodological details. Because readers will want to assess the validity of the conclusions arrived at on the basis of the evidence, I present fairly complete accounts of what was done to collect and analyze the data. But certain aspects of the analytic methodology, particularly the factor analysis and the analysis of covariance structures, may not be familiar to all readers. While it was assumed that most readers would have sufficient statistical background to follow the discussion, other readers may not have such background. For example, while ordinarily factor analysis is probably well-understood, second-order factor analysis, a vitally important part of the analysis, seems not to be widely known and understood.

To cope with this problem, I have devoted Chapter 4 to the methodology used in the research. In addition, Appendix A discusses factor analysis. Other analytic procedures that are not well-known are explained in the text when the need arises. For example, analysis of covariance structures, a new multivariate procedure for testing complex hypotheses, is explained in Chapters 4 and 10. While the explanations are by no means complete, they should be sufficient to enable readers to understand the testing of the alternative duality and bipolarity hypotheses.

Chapter 5 critically reviews the measurement of liberalism and conservatism in the literature. It is found wanting mainly because it has been dominated by what I call the bipolarity assumption. More adequate measurement of these important constructs is suggested.

Chapters 6 through 9 are the research core of the book. They describe most of the studies that were done, the results, and the bearing of the results on the theory. Chapter 10 is, in a sense, an analytic summary of the major portion of the researches since it takes the factor analytic results of the research studies described in Chapter 6 through 9 and, using an analysis of covariance structures approach, tests them for their congruence with the alternative duality and bipolarity hypotheses.

Researches done by others specifically to test the theory are summarized in Chapter 11, as well as researches in other psychological areas and with variables other than attitude variables. Finally, Chapter 12 summarizes the conclusions arrived at on the basis of the evidence and discusses the presumed empirical validity of the theory.

Three appendices supplement the book. In Appendix A, those aspects of factor analysis pertinent to its use in the analysis of the data are explained so that readers only peripherally familiar with factor analysis may grasp the essentials of the approach. Appendix B contains the main statement and referent social and educational attitude scales used in the research. They may be useful to other researchers. Finally, Appendix C is a brief account of research done to assess the possible vulnerability of the main statement and referent scales to response set bias.

I am indebted to many people for various kinds of help with the research and the thinking behind the research. First, my thanks to the many students and the people outside the university who responded to attitude scales and Q sorts. Without their cooperation the whole enterprise would have collapsed. Second, a number of colleagues in other universities have administered scales to samples of subjects in New York, Texas, North Carolina, Virginia, and Michigan: Professors R. Sommerfeld, G. Kowitz, K. Gezi, R. McClintock, C. Helwig, and P. Echandia. I am most grateful for their help. Again, without this help the research could not have been done. Dr. G. Schild of the Netherlands Institute of Public Opinion is entitled to special thanks for having a lengthy attitude scale administered to a random sample of Dutch adults.

I want to thank Professors E. Pedhazur, E. Kaya, I. Smith, A. Klein, and Dr. A. Paranjpe for invaluable help with the earlier research. Computer work is today indispensable, as are the people who work at computer centers and who help researchers get their data analyzed. I express my gratitude to the following individuals who have helped me in New York and Amsterdam: E. Kolchin, R. Buhler, B. Holland, C. van de Wijgaart, and L. Störm.

In the cross-cultural study described in Chapters 8 and 9, my colleagues in the research were Professors J. Amón and C. Middendorp. I am indebted to them for working with me on the study and for their excellent and critical contributions over and above the difficult task of "transforming" a referents attitude scale into Spanish and Dutch. Although the scale was also translated into German and administered to students in West Germany by Professor L. Eckensberger, whom I thank, it was not possible to include the results in the first published report. Some of the results are given in Chapter 9. It should be noted that these individuals had reservations about my conclusions. Mention of their names and participation in the research, therefore, should not be interpreted as support of the conclusions.

Although our attempts to test aspects of the theory experimentally did not end satisfactorily, I want to thank Dr. B. Meuffels for working with me on the experimental research described in Chapter 12 as a failure. While the project did not succeed in the way we wished it to succeed, it was interesting and exciting work—and great fun! The frustration of failure—for me, anyway—was compensated by gaining a friend and many insights into Dutch society and the Dutch language.

In 1976 I decided that my knowledge of psychology had to be updated, and I had a vague idea that cognitive psychology was what I should study. Professor R. Glaser, in a discussion we had at the time, suggested that I try to apply the ideas of cognitive psychology to theory and research in attitudes. Although I don't think I succeeded too well, I have spent many interesting hours trying to follow his suggestion. I record here my gratitude to him.

The analyses of Chapter 10 and a new perspective on testing complex hypotheses are due to the work and help of three men. I am grateful to the superb achievement of Professor K. Jöreskog in developing his version of analysis of covariance structures and the computer program LISREL (with D. Sörbom). The influence of his work will be profound and deep, I think. And I am grateful to my former colleague in Amsterdam, Professor G. Mellenbergh, for stimulating me to study, learn, and use the system and then helping me with it. Mellenbergh also read and criticized Chapter 10. Thus my indebtedness to him is large. Those of us who studied and used LISREL in Amsterdam know that we all owe much to Professor W. Saris. He helped us constructively and unstintingly. I wish to express my thanks to him for the very considerable help he gave me.

My former colleagues and friends of the Psychology Laboratory, University of Amsterdam, may not know how much they helped me. Most of the writing and some of the research and the analyses were done during my six years in The Netherlands. I am grateful not only for the intellectual stimulation and the friendship they gave me, but also for the privilege of working with them. I express my gratitude by dedicating the book to them. I must in addition express my appreciation of a great country and society whose cultural and humane values and whose rational and tolerant coping with contemporary social problems I learned to admire and respect.

Professor T. M. Newcomb read and criticized the entire first draft of the book. I have followed many or most of his suggestions and am deeply grateful for his valuable contribution. I am also indebted to the late Professor J. Nunnally for his enlightened and detailed criticism of the book. Indeed, he stimulated me to make a number of important changes that I feel have improved the book.

Finally, I express my appreciation to an astute and perspicacious reviewer of the book, whose criticisms and suggestions were so cogent that I had to listen carefully and act upon almost all of them. Although he was, as my Dutch colleagues would say, Roomser dan de Paus (More Roman than the Pope), he clearly brought out the conceptual, methodological, and scientific weaknesses of the research and the exposition. Would that all reviewers were so helpful!

Financial support for the research was given by the School of Education, New York University, over a number of years, and by the Psychology Laboratory, University of Amsterdam, The Netherlands, from 1976 through 1980. In addition, both institutions gave me computer time to do the many analyses necessary. I am grateful to them for this support. I am also grateful for the generosity of the College of Education of the University of Oregon for making it possible for me to use one of the university's computers to do certain supplementary analyses. I here express my thanks for an enlightened policy and to the individuals who administered the policy.

As she has done in the past, my wife has had to put up with the vagaries, doubts, and frustrations I have experienced while writing this book. Moreover, she coped with the burdens and complexities of two overseas moves before the book was done. I record here my gratitude and appreciation for her support.

Eugene, Oregon   **Fred N. Kerlinger**
May, 1984

LIBERALISM
AND
CONSERVATISM
The Nature and Structure of Social Attitudes

1 Attitudes and "Attitude Man"

"Social attitude" expresses the psychological orientation of people to their social environment. Whether directed toward social issues, ethnic groups, or abstract ideas, attitudes are efficient psychological mechanisms that strongly influence social behavior. Voting, business and financial decisions, treatment of the opposite sex, judgments of national and international affairs, even relations of family members are influenced by social attitudes. They represent emotional, motivational, and cognitive reactions of people to the social "objects" of the environment and their predisposition to act toward those social objects. As William James said, attitudes "engender meaning on the environment." They are, in short, enduring psychological organizations that relate the individual to the environment.

Take a seemingly simple social object like "religion." Attitudes toward religion can be important influences on individual social behavior; they guide behavior in religious and religion-related situations. They give integrated and summary meaning to ideas and actions that have religious implications. They are, moreover, related to each other in predictable ways. Are one's attitudes toward religion, for example, related to one's attitude toward religion-related social objects? How? For instance, if people's attitudes toward "religion" are positive, will their attitudes toward "church," "Christian," "religious education," and "moral standards" also be positive?

A central question of this book is: What are the relations among the specific attitudes associated with attitude objects? If people react positively to an idea like "abortion," will they also react positively to ideas like "civil rights" and "sexual freedom"? Will they also react positively to ideas like "socialized medicine" and "collective bargaining"? What will their reactions be to people who espouse the cause of blacks or the cause of women?

Another central question is: Are attitudes polarized? Is the person who espouses conservative ideas and actions necessarily opposed to liberal ideas and actions? Does an individual who emphasizes the importance of private property oppose, say, socialized medicine? Does another individual for whom religion is high in value necessarily oppose liberalized abortion and birth control? Do belief systems have positive and negative ends as part of their "structure"? Most people seem to think of bipolarity—the technical term for this phenomenon of opposition of beliefs—as a natural and almost inevitable manifestation of human attitudinal thinking. If we are for some things, then we must be against certain other things. Is this so?

Writers of social attitude scales and researchers measuring social attitudes for the most part assume a continuum of attitudes from liberal through conservative. Even when they may not consciously assume that attitudes are bipolar, they classify their items and score them as though there were one bipolar continuum. The possibility that liberalism and conservatism are separate and different phenomena rather than the two ends of a polarized continuum is rarely considered. Furthermore, radicalism and radical themes, both left and right, are often conceived as extreme forms of liberalism and conservatism. The possibility that radicalism is separate, distinct, and quite different from liberalism and conservatism is also rarely considered.

ATTITUDE MAN

In a masterful and compelling essay on attitudes, Fleming (1967) has said that a revolution has taken place in our conception of ourselves, and this revolution has centered in the attitude concept. He even suggests that we are in the age of "attitude man." He points out that the age of attitude man has occurred quietly, unemphatically, especially in comparison to the "loud prophetic utterances of Marx and Freud." The individual has been envisioned by psychologists and sociologists—Fleming is tracing the history of the attitude concept—as learning and accumulating the psychological means of adjusting responses to the environment and preserving identity in the midst of social experiences. Human beings are seen to have persistent organized psychological tendencies from previous experience to react consistently to social objects. In other words, attitudes are a significant part of the personality. The adequately functioning person is one capable of forming and sustaining attitudes, and these attitudes focus the resources of the person on potential and actual responses to objects and concepts of the social environment.

Fleming accepted Goldstein's (1939) equation of the human with the attitudinal. People have been categorized as economic, religious, hedonic, rational, and irrational. Goldstein, however, felt that the essential humanness of people lay in their capacity to form and use attitudes. "Man was the supremely attitudinal organism" (Fleming, 1967, p. 320). This was a new definition of the human being. With the development of the scientific approach to attitudes as exemplified, say, by Thurstone, the attitude concept became central to psychology and sociology. Fleming's central point, which is implicitly a central point of the present book, is that the concept of attitude embodied a new conception, a revolutionary change in people's view of themselves and others.

If, indeed, we live in the age of attitude man, we face a central question: What is the nature and structure of social attitudes? Some of the problems involved were suggested in the beginning of this chapter when questions were raised about the relations among attitudinal concepts, for example, the relations among such concepts as "women's liberation," "racial equality," "free enterprise," and "competition." These questions were really structural questions because talking about relations implies structure. Structure can only be approached, at least empirically, through the relations among things. When we compare, for example, A to B to C, and we find that A is greater than B and C, we are defining a hierarchical structure based on size. Somewhat similarly we can compare responses to attitude objects and ideas and find, perhaps, a hierarchical structure or, more likely, more complex structures. A central task of the social scientist, then, is to discover the structure of attitudes.

Closely related to the question of the structure of attitudes is their nature or content. The example of "religion" as an attitude object suggests the content of such attitudes: "church," "priest," "religious education," and "Christian" contain some of the spelling of the content of religious attitudes. "Business," "private property," "capitalism," and "profits" spell some of the content of economic attitudes. "Children's interests," "pupil personality," "open admission to college," and "activity programs" spell some of the content of educational attitudes. The nature of attitude is of course more complex than these examples indicate. Another goal of this book is to explain some of the complexity of social attitudes. In doing so we find that structure and content are intertwined; if one talks about content one must at the same time talk about structure. For instance, when we discuss liberalism and conservatism below and later in the book and ask about their "reality," we will learn that the answer must involve both structure and content.

LIBERALISM AND CONSERVATISM

Two central concepts of this book are "liberalism" and "conservatism." As before, in dealing with these concepts there are questions to ask and, hopefully, answer. (For the present we will assume that we know what we are talking about when we use these terms. They will be defined in Chapter 2.) Some social scientists may decry using the terms. They can say that the words are reifications, constructs manufactured to mirror spuriously what is in people's minds. People are actually far too complex to be labeled in oversimplified ways; there are also too many inconsistencies— retired admirals who support women's liberation, Catholics who favor birth control, liberals who are anti-Semitic. Most important scientifically, continues the critic, the use of such concepts is not parsimonious: it is unnecessary multiplication of concepts. In effect, the critic is saying that there are no "entities" liberalism and conservatism. Such labeling of attitudes or constellations of attitudes is scientifically unsound. These criticisms are weighty and must be answered.

The main answer is empirical. Does research show, first, that the are clusters of people whose expressed attitudes can be accurately described as liberal and other clusters of people whose attitudes can be described as conservative, "liberal" and "conservative" being appropriately defined. It has been observed that conservatives emphasize the importance of religion, tradition, freedom (but not equality), private property, established institutions and conventions, stability, authority, and so on (Auerbach, 1959; Burke, 1955; Huntingdon, 1957; Kirk, 1960; Mannheim, 1953; McClosky, 1958; Nisbet, 1978; Rossiter, 1962, 1968; Viereck, 1962). Liberals, on the other hand, emphasize change, social reform, equality, the rights of minorities and women, human personality, internationalism, government aid, and so on (Girvetz, 1963; Hartz, 1955; Mill, 1975; Smith, 1968; Watkins, 1957). The question is not, then, do liberalism and conservatism exist? They do, at least in sociological, psychological, historical, and philosophical writings. The more pertinent question is: Do people systematically espouse doctrines and courses of action along liberal and conservative lines? And, can individuals and groups of individuals be reliably identified as "liberal" or "conservative" due to such doctrine espousal? These important questions and their answers will be discussed at considerable length in later chapters.

ATTITUDES, SOCIAL ATTITUDES, BELIEFS

There are many definitions of "attitude."[1] The definition given here is an eclectic combination of the ideas of Allport (1935), Krech and Crutchfield (1948), Newcomb (1950), and Rokeach (1960), with an additional emphasis on referents of attitudes. It must be emphasized that we are talking about, defining, and trying to explain *social attitudes*. We are not concerned with motor or postural attitudes, attitudes toward the self, or traits, feelings, motives, or so-called individual attitudes.

> *Attitudes* are enduring and organized structures of social beliefs that predispose individuals to think, feel, perceive, and behave selectively toward referents or "cognitive objects" of attitudes.

Like all definitions, this one can be criticized. It fits well, however, with the actual use and measurement of attitudes to be described later. But the definition needs explanation.

Attitudes endure; they go on through time, perhaps changing but usually not very much. If this were not so, then the psychological stability that attitudes give the individual—enabling consistent responses in different social situations—would be absent. People's attitudes toward economic matters, for example, stay with them over time. They supply a stable response background on economic problems and situations. If someone believes that taxes should be graduated, that every person has an inherent right to a minimum income, and that the unemployed are the responsibility of the state, then that individual is likely to have these beliefs for many years.

The definition says that attitudes are structures of social beliefs. So we need to know what beliefs and social beliefs are.

> *Beliefs* are statements or propositions that express presumed knowledge, faith, or opinion.

If I say "There are more Christians that Jews in the United States," I am stating a well-documented fact. But if I say "Christianity has built the

---

[1] For an overview of attitude definitions and related concepts, see Shaw and Wright (1967, Ch. 1). Fleming (1967) gives an excellent history of the attitude concept, including earlier views and uses. The classic definition is Allport's (1935, 1954): "An attitude is a mental and neural state of readiness, organized through experience, exerting a directive or dynamic influence upon the individual's response to all objects and situations with which it is related" (Allport, 1954, p. 45). McGuire (1969, pp. 142–149) has discussed in detail this definition, its implications, and related research.

Western world," I am stating a belief. I say that I "know" this to be true when it in fact may not be true. Similarly, I may state many beliefs as though they were factual knowledge: "Blacks are more musical than whites," "Women are bad drivers," "Capitalism is the only viable economic system." These are what we can call "knowledge" beliefs. A powerful part of prejudice consists of such beliefs—stereotypes we say—which attribute to members of certain groups characteristics peculiar to the group.

The second kind of belief is expressed in the statements "I believe in God," "I believe in the President," "Marxism (or capitalism) is the only answer to the world's problems." These are "faith" statements: they express the faith of the speaker in ideas or persons. usually they cannot be stated to be true or false because their truth or falsity cannot be empirically tested. "Knowledge" beliefs can, at least potentially, be shown to be correct or incorrect. "Faith" beliefs usually cannot be so checked. Nevertheless, they influence human behavior, probably more than "knowledge" beliefs do.

The third kind of belief can be called "opinion" beliefs. We may say "I think that women have stronger characters than men," "I believe that Chinese communism will ultimately triumph in the Far East," "I think that Bach is the greatest of all composers." Unlike knowledge and faith beliefs, the speaker here holds out the possibility of being wrong, even though he thinks he is right. Despite the differences between them, all three kinds of beliefs form the cores of attitudes. We can ask people what they know (or think they know) about religion, whether they believe in God and the Christian church, and what their opinion is on the problem of separation of church and state. We are well on our way to knowing their attitudes toward religion.

Strictly speaking, we should have used the term "social attitudes" instead of just "attitudes" in the definition given earlier. Henceforth, and by definition, the word "attitude" in this book means "social attitude." All attitudes are shared; if they are not held by many people they are not attitudes. It has been said that there are individual attitudes, and it does no great harm to talk as though an individual has individual attitudes. This is not quite correct, however, because if attitudes were not shared, they could not continue to exist and function as attitudes.

Beliefs require social reinforcement. The less evidence there is for the correctness of a belief the more it has to be reinforced, that is, the more the individual holding the belief has to know that other people, especially others important to the individual, also hold the belief. Without this shared reinforcement, this "social reality" (Festinger, 1954; Newcomb, 1947), beliefs and attitudes cannot exist. In other words, we "test" the "validity" of our beliefs and attitudes against those of other people—

including, of course, the products of other people, such as newspapers, books, radio, television. So social attitudes are shared; they must be.

The definition of attitudes given earlier states that attitudes are predispositions to think, feel, perceive, and behave selectively toward referents of attitudes. Attitudes are predispositions to behave (Newcomb, 1950). They are unobserved constructs, hypothetical entities, so-called intervening or latent variables. They are states of readiness for thinking, feeling, perceiving, and behaving in a selective manner. This means that they are triggered off, if at all, only by attitude-related situations, people, and ideas. The attitudes of some Americans and Europeans toward Jews, for instance, may be negative and strong. But they can be called into action only in situations or by people or ideas related to Jews, or, of course, perceived to be related to Jews. To put it succinctly, we may have negative attitudes toward Jews, but it is possible (though perhaps not likely) that we may never act in an anti-Semitic way.

The thinking, feeling, perceiving, and behaving part of the definition indicates that attitudes have cognitive, emotional, and motivational components (Krech & Crutchfield, 1948). The cognitive component includes knowing and perceiving, the emotional component feeling, and the motivational component the tendency to approach or withdraw from the cognitive objects of attitudes. These components influence each other; the emotional component especially influences the other components, giving attitudes a charged dynamic quality. Beliefs are conceived as the knowing and perceiving parts of attitudes (the cognitive component); they have a more static quality.

The last part of the definition of attitudes is central to a main theme of this book: "behave selectively toward referents or cognitive objects of attitudes." Attitudes are always focused on objects in the environment— groups of people, institutions, abstract concepts. Examples of such objects are *private property, socialized medicine, discipline, racial equality, love, birth control, corporate industry, sexual freedom.* A more general, and perhaps more appropriate, term is "referents," which is discussed in Chapter 3.

STRUCTURES AND FACTORS

Attitudes, then, are complex learned entities that can be conceived as structures in two senses. First, they exist in some form in the long-term memories of individuals. This cognitive psychological sense of structure is more explicitly dealt with in a later chapter. Second, attitude structures exist in large numbers of individuals, as suggested earlier. A substantial portion of this book is devoted to discussion of these "large" structures, and a theory of such structures is outlined in the next chapter.

The two senses of structure suggest different kinds of theories and different kinds of research. It would be scientifically more satisfying if only one theory could be used to explain both the responses of many individuals to attitude instruments and the structure of these responses and the presumed attitude structures "in the heads" of individuals. Cognitive psychological theory can be a bridge between the structure of attitudes found through factor analysis of the responses of many individuals to attitude instruments and the presumed structure of attitudes in the memories of individuals. The results of large-scale factor analytic research tell us a good deal about how aspects of social attitudes cluster. Social attitudes can be characterized as attitudes whose referents have shared general societal relevance in economic, political, religious, educational, ethnic, and other social areas. This means that large numbers of individuals share similar views on important social issues and problems. Religious people, for example, tend to have similar views on such issues as religious instruction and moral standards. Business people tend to have similar outlooks on corporate enterprise, money, and profits.

The attitudes themselves are of course not the same within a group. There are always individual differences. There will be sufficient similarity, however, among many people to produce systematic relations among the referents of the attitudes. These relations among referents can be analyzed to indicate what the factors are that underlie the attitude responses. If the above disquisition is correct, then we can expect to be able to identify common sources of similarities of attitudes. Instead of speculating that there are religious and economic attitudes, or sexual freedom and civil rights attitudes, for instance, we can determine empirically whether there are such factors of attitudes.

Even if we are able to successfully study and identify such attitude factors, they are still far from what is "in the head" of the individual. We can talk only of the structure of attitudes over many individuals: abstractions of abstractions, so to speak. Can we understand the structure of attitudes in the individual? Never, really. But we can approach closer to the individual's attitudes. One way to do this, through so-called Q methodology, helps us learn something of the individual's social attitude structure. But, as we will later find out, this can only be done by studying the relations between the particular individual's responses to rather elaborate instruments and the responses of other individuals to the same instruments. The methodology is powerful and does get closer to the individual's attitudes, but it will never tell us precisely the attitude content and structure in the individual's memory.

Another approach that helps us get closer to the individual's attitudes is the structural approach of cognitive psychology. Cognitive psychologists, like gestalt psychologists earlier in the century, believe that there are mental "structures" that are innate or are acquired through learning and experience. (We assume that attitudes are acquired.) Such structures are encased in memory and influence other psychological processes and behavior. Memory, perhaps the most important concept of cognitive psychology, is conceived to be organized. That is, we do not remember just associations, but structures or relations among elements. Recall is better, for example, when elements that "belong together" by some principle of grouping are learned using that principle (Bower, 1970).

Two other important preoccupations of cognitive psychology are categorization and prototypes (Rosch, 1973, 1975, 1977; Rosch & Lloyd, 1978). In research on categorization, cognitive psychologists ask, for example, whether certain categories are more easily learned than others and what such categories are. Perhaps more pertinent to attitude study, it is asked whether certain categories of attitudes are more central than others and whether the attitude structures of individuals reflect this centrality. Similarly, if certain referents of attitudes are more central in attitude structure, are they, for example, better remembered than other referents that are less central or peripheral? Are such referents as *human warmth, social change,* and *equality,* for instance, more central than such referents as *international cooperation, teachers,* and *civilization?* Are these central structures and referents more likely to influence attitude-related behavior than less central structures and referents?

While we may not be able to answer such questions definitively, we will at least approach the general problem of structure. In so doing, we will learn a good deal about the nature or content of social attitudes. We will find, for instance, that certain first-order factors appear in most samples, that these factors are either liberal or conservative but not both, that bipolarity is not a central characteristic of social attitudes as commonly supposed, and that two (sometimes three) second-order factors emerge from factor analysis of the correlations among the first-order factors, and these two factors correspond closely to liberal and conservative conceptions of social issues and actions. This is the large-scale approach to structure in which attitude structure is ascertained from the responses of many individuals to attitude measurement instruments.

There is much less evidence to support the notion that liberal and conservative attitude structures exist in individuals. In two studies inspired by the work of cognitive psychologists on memory, a Dutch colleague and I manipulated liberal and conservative attitude content experimentally. In so doing we hoped to demonstrate the existence of attitude structure in the individual by showing the influence on memory of the content manipulation. Unfortunately, the research was a failure because we did not really test the hypothesis crucial to the theory under test. Our disappointment and frustration, however, were somewhat ameliorated by the consistent finding that when liberal attitude concepts and conservative attitude concepts, both of which had been found to have high factor loadings on separate liberal and conservative factors in the large sample research, were presented *separately* to the subjects in the experimental sessions, they were remembered better than attitudinally neutral or mixed liberal and conservative concepts, which were also presented in the experimental sessions. That is, liberal concepts presented together and conservative concepts presented together were better remembered than concepts not clearly liberal and not clearly conservative, or liberal and conservative concepts mixed.

While the research failed to demonstrate a relation between, on the one hand, liberal and conservative concepts as determined in large-scale factor analytic research and, on the other hand, the liberalism and conservatism of the experimental subjects—a relation crucial to the criterial referents theory under test—it did show the existence of a relation between liberal and conservative concepts and recall and recognition memory. A more extended account of the research and its essential failure to test the theory underlying the research reported in this book, as well as its possible demonstration of structure in individuals, is given in Chapter 12.

LIBERALISM, CONSERVATISM, AND ATTITUDE MAN

Fleming had profound insight. The new conception of "attitude man" is remarkably appropriate. While no single conception of man can ever be complete, the conception of "attitude man" seems appropriate because attitudes are the psychological bridge between people and their complex environment: they provide psychological means to cope with many aspects of what is an extremely diverse and perplexing social environment. Much of this environment cannot be experienced and known directly. Yet we have to cope with it; we have to react to people and events about which we are only partly informed. Attitudes help us do so.

Much of our lives, then, is influenced by our social attitudes; we are, so to speak, "attitude people." When we judge others and their behavior, our attitudes influence the judgments, whether we know it or not. Do attitudes have anything to do with the varied and highly charged judgments of Israeli actions we read and hear almost every week? Evidently they do. Israeli actions appear to be judged by standards different from those applied to other nations. Actions that would be ignored or accepted if taken by other nations are vigorously condemned when taken by Israel. Is it possible that attitudes held by many people of the Western world have anything to do with such judgments?

Before concluding this general introductory chapter, I want to emphasize the importance of the concepts liberalism and conservatism and to
assert them as complex memory-embedded structures and processes that
are related to the notion of "attitude man." They *are* attitudes—and probably values.[2] They are general cognitive processes intimately tied to our
social lives. They are, however, more abstract, general and remote, say,
than the specific attitudes that make them up, and are therefore harder to
recognize as research variables. Nevertheless, they underlie much of the
theory and research reported later. As attitudinal generalizations, they
help to explain complex social thinking. When a country has a change of
government from, say, liberal to conservative, we can expect changes of
social outlook and social policy. Although it has been said that there is no
real difference between the policies and behaviors of Republicans and
Democrats in the United States, there are actual and deep differences,
especially in policies that affect the conduct of business and the social
welfare of people. Such differences spring, at least in part, from ideological concerns that are reflected in liberal and conservative attitudes.

A good example is the change of government of The Netherlands a few
years ago from long-dominant socialist to conservative. During the period
of predominant socialist power, a number of liberal policies were made
law. Every person who reaches the age of 65, for instance, has the legal
right to a government pension. No Dutch person should be destitute, and
so on. While the change to a conservative government cannot wipe out
the fundamental benefits instituted by a liberal government, there can be
shifts to less liberal policies. And that is what happened in 1980. For
instance, the socialists wanted to liberalize the abortion law, but did not
succeed in getting it on the books before they relinquished government.
The conservatives were then faced with producing an abortion law; they
could not avoid it. But they tried to alter the proposed law to one more
conservative than the earlier proposed law.[3]

If the notion of "attitude man" is valid, then can we talk of "conserva-

----

[2]Values are important and should be discussed. Actually, many of the attitude referents
we work with are probably value referents. For example, more abstract social ideas, like
equality, freedom, love, morality, civil rights, probably express values rather than attitudes.
The more social cognitive processes are directed toward specific objects or ideas, the more
likely they are to be attitudes. The more abstract they are, the more likely they are to be
values.

[3]The liberals (socialists) strongly opposed the government's proposal. They insisted on
the free right of women to choose whether or not to have an abortion. The government's
proposal limited the choice in certain important respects. For example, the proposal still
made abortion a punishable offense, required agreement of a woman's physician, and also
required a five-day "thinking over" period.

tive attitude man" and "liberal attitude man" as the general prototypes of Western democratic societies? To answer Yes would seem to go too far. Yet the attempt to answer the question, or at least to consider it, should stimulate social attitude theory and research. To return to an earlier assertion: Attitudes enable us to adjust to and simplify our complex environment. They operate as efficient cognitive processes that assure our social psychological continuity and that stabilize us by providing us with more or less ready-made reactions to people, events, and social issues and problems. I think this is part of what Goldstein and Fleming meant by "attitude man." The function of the book, then, is to understand and to explain the nature and structure of social attitudes and thus to some extent the nature of "attitude man" in contemporary Western society.[4]

---

[4]An important distinction in the conception and measurement of social attitudes should be mentioned. Later, in Chapter 3, the distinction will be elaborated. The usual approach to the study of attitudes is directed to beliefs and feelings about single attitude "objects," or referents as we shall call them. People are asked to respond to a set of statements about attitude objects like United Nations, birth control, Jews, militarism, church. The set of statements is scored in some appropriate way and each respondent receives a score. This score represents that person's attitude toward the psychological object. The approach, then, usually focuses on the single psychological object and the items of the attitude scale all express beliefs or sentiments about that object. (See Thurstone, 1959, Chs. 19 and 20.)

The approach of this book to the conceptualization and measurement of attitudes is different. Its focus is on respondents' reactions to many attitude objects. The items of the scales used contain many different attitude objects: religion, business, blacks, equality, discipline, private property, civil rights, and so on. The main reason for the difference is that liberalism and conservatism can only be empirically studied and measured through the responses of many individuals to many attitude objects, to many statements involving various social issues and attitude objects. Keeping this distinction in mind will help us resolve certain theoretical and measurement points that arise later.

2 Liberalism and Conservatism

An ideology is a set of coherent concepts and beliefs centered around a general idea or concept that usually commits believers of the ideology to behavior consistent with the beliefs of the ideology. Apparent examples are Catholic ideology, communist ideology, and capitalist ideology. Although "ideology" has often been used in a negative sense to mean a body of beliefs that has something irrational about it, irrationality is not a necessary condition of ideology.

Among the ideologies that influence social belief and behavior, two of the most important in the Western world are liberalism and conservatism: they are general systematic sets of related concepts and beliefs about social ideas, issues, and behavior, particularly in religious, economic, political, ethnic, educational, and what I will call general social areas.

Ideologies are broad and general, pervade wide areas of belief and behavior, and give core meaning to many issues of human concern. They unify thought and action. Catholic ideology pervades most areas of life for many Catholics. So does communist ideology for communists. There are of course varying degrees of commitment to ideologies, but there is always the explicit or implicit assumption of the wide pervasiveness of the ideologies, and the dedication of followers of the ideologies to their purposes and teachings. Liberalism and conservatism, while perhaps not as strong as religious and political ideologies, nevertheless pervade many areas of thinking and behaving, especially social problem areas. Mention "abortion," "women's rights," "social welfare," "capitalism," "religious teaching in schools," or "corporate profits" and we evoke the larger ideologies of liberalism and conservatism.

The purpose of this chapter is to define and describe liberalism and conservatism and to outline their relation to social attitudes. In a book that emphasizes these general and somewhat abstract words, we must try to know what we are talking about. Fortunately, there are good, even excellent, treatises on both outlooks.[1] These treatises are, for the most part, historical, sociological, and political. Unfortunately, there has been little psychological theory and research on liberalism and conservatism, though the terms have been used in their hyphenated bipolar form in a number of discussions and studies.

Another purpose of the chapter is to define and describe, if only briefly, the educational philosophies of progressivism and traditionalism[2] Since these educational ideologies are conceived as subsets of liberalism and conservatism, and since a substantial portion of the research to be reported later is on educational attitudes, they require definition and explanation. Finally, the phenomenon of radicalism is explored because understanding its nature throws light on liberalism and conservatism. The term has often been used to mean the extreme of liberalism or the opposite of conservatism. But such uses are probably incorrect and misleading. Therefore, although it can be viewed as a digression, I think it is important to attempt to clarify what radicalism is and how it relates to liberalism and conservatism.

DEFINITIONS

All definitions are to some extent arbitrary, subject to the judgment of the definition writer. This is especially so with the definitions of complex and abstract concepts. "Liberalism" and "conservatism" are highly complex and abstract. Maybe they really elude precise definition. Certainly most writers have avoided direct definition. They are content with descriptions of a phenomenon and with its presumed origins and characteristics. Perhaps this is sufficient; perhaps attempts to define complex ideas like liberalism and conservatism cannot succeed. As Rossiter (1968) says about conservatism, ". . . a word whose usefulness is matched only by its capacity to confuse, distort, and irritate" (p. 290). (He also says elsewhere that "liberalism" is the stickiest word in the political dictionary [Rossiter, 1962, p. 12].)

---

[1]The treatises on which this chapter leans heavily are Girvetz (1950/1963), Mill (1859/1975), Laski (1962), Smith (1968), and Watkins (1957) on liberalism, and Burke (1790–1955), Huntington (1957), Kirk (1960), McClosky (1958), and Rossiter (1962) on conservatism.

[2]The following references are valuable guides to progressivism and traditionalism in education: Beale, 1936; Brubacher, 1962; Cremin, 1961; Curti, 1935; Dewey, 1902, 1916; Dupuis, 1966; Henry, 1942; Morris, 1961.

Despite the difficulty and danger, we now offer formal definitions. At the least, such definitions focus discussion and force concentration on the meaning of the concepts being defined. They are attempts to extract from the writings of a number of authors the main aspects, emphases, or characteristics of the two ideologies. In considering these definitions—and others elsewhere in the book—it should be clearly understood that there is no intention of laying down absolute meanings. They are, as just indicated, attempts to focus and give meaning to the discussion. While I have tried to some extent to base definitions on systematic discussions in the philosophical, historical, political, and social scientific literature, the definitions are of course limited by my own perspective.

Liberalism

> *Liberalism* is set of political, economic, religious, educational, and other social beliefs that emphasizes freedom of the individual, constitutional participatory government and democracy, the rule of law, free negotiation, discussion and tolerance of different views, constructive social progress and change, egalitarianism and the rights of minorities, secular rationality and rational approaches to social problems, and positive government action to remedy social deficiencies and to improve human welfare.

Experts agree that liberalism is a relatively modern phenomenon that has had great influence in the Western world—and, indeed, the whole world (Laski, 1962; Smith, 1968; Watkins, 1957). Laski (1962) even says, ". . . liberalism has been, in the last four centuries, the outstanding doctrine of Western civilization" (p. 9). Its greatest influence has been in England, the United States, and Western Europe, but in its "classic" form especially in England (Girvetz, 1963). It has even changed our view of ourselves. The individual early became the focus of attention and values; society and government were seen as subordinate to the individual's rights, aspirations, and efforts.

The above definition refers to contemporary liberalism. "Liberalism" has two meanings, two origins, however, and the two are easily confused. In the United States "liberal" is a word that more or less expresses the ideas of the above definition. To say a person is "liberal" means that he or she believes in the supremacy and rule of law, free discussion of issues, constitutional government, majority rule, tolerance, the rights of minorities, social progress and change, and positive government action to improve the social order and human welfare. In Europe, on the other hand, "Liberal" can mean "conservative," at least from the viewpoint, say, of socialists. In The Netherlands, for instance, the word "liberaal" is applied to a political party that is conservative on economic issues. The difficulty is resolved, at least partly, when we realize that the European use of the word goes back to what is known as "classic liberalism," the original great tradition of liberalism that grew and flourished in England in the eighteenth and nineteenth centuries.

The basic credo of classical liberalism was freedom and the rights of the individual—"individual" meaning people of substance and property— limitation of government within the framework of constitutional principle, and the sanctity of private property. It was a middle-class movement, strongly individualistic and capitalist in orientation, that sought to free business enterprise from the restraints of government. It made business and trade central in society. In so doing, it had the effect of strengthening constitutional democracy, individual rights, and capitalism. Smith (1968) says that classic liberalism was essentially negative: it wanted protection of individuals and groups *from* government. But in limiting government it emphasized the rule of law rather than the arbitrary rule of men or governments. Its basic postulate was laissez faire and the self-regulating market. As is well-known, it created untold human misery. But it also created, in effect, a great modern tradition and set of beliefs.

Classic liberalism, with modification, became the conservatism of today (Girvetz, 1963). It is probably more accurate to say that classic liberalism was both a stimulus and support of modern conservatism rather than that it "became" conservatism. (Conservatism is considerably more.) It provided a good bit of the foundation of economic conservatism—it exalted the successful man of business, wealth, and property— but it also provided part of the foundation of modern liberalism in its emphasis on freedom (but not equality), constitutional principle, the fundamental rights of the individual (even though the privileged individual), and the rule of law. In time, liberals split into two groups. One group clung to the ideas of non-intervention of government and free trade. The other group, the precursors of the modern liberal, argued for the remedy of abuses other than those of the state. They "assigned greater importance to the social environment within which liberty had to be realized" (Smith, 1968, p. 281).

Henceforth, when we say "liberalism" and "liberal," we mean modern or contemporary liberalism. The results of the research to be reported in later chapters show that modern liberalism is the set of beliefs and the doctrine expressed in our earlier definition, infused with ideas and practices of contemporary non-Marxist socialism.

Conservatism

Conservatism is a set of political, economic, religious, educational, and other social beliefs characterized by emphasis on the status quo and social stability, religion and morality, liberty and freedom, the natural inequality of men, the uncertainty of progress, and the weakness of human reason. It is further characterized by distrust of popular democracy and majority rule and by support of individualism and individual initiative, the sanctity of private property, and the central importance of business and industry in the society.

In addition to these larger social concerns or themes, conservatives espouse certain virtues or characteristics: prudence, justice, wisdom, moderation, self-discipline, frugality, industry, piety, honesty, obedience to and respect for authority, duty (Rossiter, 1962, pp. 25–26). Ignorance, intemperance, laziness, luxury, selfishness, disobedience, and bad manners must be shunned.

Two other important aspects of conservatism are its anti-speculative, anti-theoretical stance and its espousal of some form of aristocracy. As Rossiter has said, the conservative would not find it easy to write a Conservative Manifesto! Theory is for liberals and radicals. Political and social theory is even a sign of an ill-conducted state. The conservative, then, tends to mistrust theoretical answers to problems, preferring the test of time and history. The conservative tends also to mistrust intellectuals, especially liberal and radical ones.

More important is the conservative's position on liberty and equality. Liberty is insisted upon; equality, however, does not exist nor can it exist. As Burke (1955, pp. 55–56) said, with his customary eloquence, levelers, acting for equality, change and pervert the natural order of things: "In this you think you are combating prejudice, but you are at war with nature" (p. 56). This is perhaps the single most significant difference between the conservative and the modern liberal (and the socialist). The latter would make all people equal; the former insists that it is not possible, even if it were desirable.

Modern conservatives strongly and positively prize freedom, as do liberals, and they acquiesce to policies and programs of equality because it is necessary or politically expedient to do so. Whereas conservatives of an earlier age actively opposed egalitarian ideas, modern conservatives, while maintaining skepticism about the validity of such ideas, bow, if they bow at all, to what they see as a powerful contemporary force. It may even be said that modern liberals actively espouse equality, whereas modern conservatives actively espouse freedom and liberty and leave equality to liberals. This is speculation, however. Rokeach (1973) has found sharp differences. Hobhouse (n.d.) has argued that liberty "is also, when pushed through, a struggle for equality" (p. 32). Indeed, one of the basic themes of his book on liberalism is the close connection between freedom and equality. One argument, for example, is that the parties to a contract have to be equal if the contract is a true contract. Be this as it may, there is certainly opportunity for further theory development and research on these two concepts.

The above definitions are based on the writings of liberal and conservative thinkers. They are distillations of the historical, philosophical, and political studies and writings of Burke, Locke, Mill, Kirk, Laski, Huntington, Rossiter, Smith, and others. One can also define liberalism and conservatism empirically and operationally. Although the purpose of this book is not basically to define liberalism and conservatism, definitions, even though not explicit, are always implied. Later, when we present factor analytic evidence on liberal and conservative factors, we are, at least implicitly, defining the terms. These "implicit" definitions are in effect "empirical" or operational definitions, though the term "operational definition" is here a bit stretched. Liberal factors such as "Sexual Freedom" and "Social Welfare," for example, or conservative factors such as "Religiosity" and "Economic Conservatism" yield more differentiated pictures or "definitions" of liberalism and conservatism. And they have the virtue of being grounded in empirical evidence as well as in theory. In other words, I present in this chapter broad definitions of liberalism and conservatism based on the large literature of the subject, and in later chapters I present more differentiated "definitions" that emerge from empirical factor analytic evidence.

RADICALISM

Little attempt to study radicalism has been made in the research reported later in this book. The reason is both theoretical and practical. Although radicalism is of course related to liberalism and conservatism, it is a separate, distinct, and different phenomenon. I consider it here briefly for two reasons, one positive and one negative. Consideration of radicalism as a social phenomenon will help us understand better the nature of liberalism and conservatism. The negative reason stems from questionable word usage. It has sometimes been assumed that radicalism is a phenomenon of the extreme left and that it is the polar opposite of conservatism. Although part of the essence of radicalism is opposition and destruction (Bittner, 1968)—the Marxist radical violently opposes bourgeois capitalism and seeks its destruction, for instance—this does not mean that radicalism and conservatism are opposite ends of a belief continuum.

Nor is radicalism an extreme form of liberalism. In some people's minds, push liberalism to its logical extreme and you have radicalism. Not so: radicals of the left or the right have little use for liberalism, just as most liberals have little use for radicalism. Liberalism is opposed to limitation of freedom or liberty in any form, except the legal or constitutional limitations necessary to protect essential freedoms. As Mill (1859/1975) said, ". . . liberty of thought and feeling; absolute freedom of opinion and sentiment on all subjects, practical or speculative, scientific, moral, or theological" (p. 13).

We attempt a definition:

> *Radicalism* is any set of beliefs, but usually beliefs of the extreme right and extreme left, that is centered in opposition to existing sets of beliefs, institutions, governments, economic, political, and moral systems, or existing traditions; it espouses drastic thoroughgoing, revolutionary, even violent change and the ultimate supplanting of existing beliefs, institutions, and systems with government, institutions, and systems advocated by the radicals.

The existing system is seen by radicals as diseased, corrupt, and oppressive. It is incurable and must be rooted out completely. Values and beliefs anchored in the corrupt system must also be rooted out and be supplanted by healthy "correct" values and beliefs. To attain a just, honest, and fair life, people must be shown the wickedness, even horror, of the old system and the goodness and purity of the new. Reason and persuasion should be used, but if they are ineffectual—old reactionary ways die hard; they are rooted in sick privilege—then force and compulsion must be used. The new dream must survive at any cost. People must be saved despite themselves.

In one of the few published statements on the general nature of radicalism, Bittner (1968) outlines several characteristics of radical movements. (1) The members have charismatic fellowship which reinforces their membership in the radical group. (2) The radical creed and program are distinct from the rest of the world. This is often accomplished by associating it with a revered leader, prophet, or magic helper—Marx, Lenin, Hitler, Jones, Malcolm X, Khomeini. (3) Radicals have a sustained concern for purity of belief and conduct. Self-criticism, people's courts, and purges are devices used for purification. (4) The radical doctrine is "diffusely comprehensive"; it completely dominates the lives of the followers, and it also neatly annuls the significance of external sources of sanctions. The law of the society is nonsense, an abomination; the police are pigs; the faculty is authoritarian and oppressive.

(5) The movement monopolizes the commitments of the members. Nothing is as important as the movement. All other loyalties and commitments are secondary. The members are deindividualized; they become absorbed in the movement's ideas and ideals. (6) Suffering and martyr-

dom must be accepted by the members. And (7) The movement uses and exploits opposition to its own advantage: its members are compromised and thus their bridges are burned behind them. Summarizing much of the above, "In radicalism the ideal is the supreme taskmaster" (Bittner, 1968, p. 299).

There is some common ideological ground between liberalism and conservatism. Liberals have faith in democratic methods and in freedom. While conservatives may not have great faith in democratic institutions and methods—the rule of the majority and constitutional representative government, among other things—they support them, nevertheless, mainly because they can't be escaped and because the alternatives are worse. They also usually believe in freedom of the individual. Radicals, however, will ordinarily not believe in democracy and democratic institutions as they have been known in the Western world. They are cloaks for oppression. Even if they weren't, they must be swept away and replaced by true and correct governmental and social systems, systems that work rapidly and thoroughly to establish the new order. Freedom, for example, is illusory. Freedom is the freedom of the establishment to forward its own ends. The individual is not important; individualism is a myth of decadence. The new society is what is important. The people cannot have freedom to do as they wish; they must be led to a greater happiness, a greater tomorrow.

It is possible to say that conservatism looks to the past, liberalism looks to the present and the future, while radicalism looks only to the future. This futurism of the radical helps to justify the means used to achieve the ideal future system. And these means have to be rapid, drastic, and hard if the future ideal is to be achieved. The gradual change of liberalism and conservatism is eschewed. Indeed, gradual change can never be fundamental; it cannot achieve the radical and thorough transformation of men and systems required. Not reform, but abolition and rebirth! Not evolutionary! Revolutionary!

Modern liberalism espouses equality, especially equality of opportunity. Radicalism may preach equality—though radicalism of the right does not—but practices it only on the surface. Radical governments are governments of the elite. Here radicalism and conservatism are alike. The difference is that conservative fear of change, especially sudden change, softens the elite tendency. The ways of Western democracy are safer.

The laboriously built-up rule of law of liberalism is sacrificed by radicalism. It is too slow and too easily perverted by the power system. To accomplish radical goals requires the rule of men, the rule of the dedicated and completely convinced elite, the group of individuals who, armed with truth and righteous purpose, can lead the people efficiently, quickly, and ruthlessly to the desired solutions of social and other problems.

Because of the loss of freedom and of the rule of law and constitutional democracy, the deemphasis of the importance of the individual, and the conscious, even systematic, use of violence, radicalism leads to totalitarianism and tyranny. They seem to be inescapable concomitants of radicalism. Democracy, certainly in its constitutional, majority rule, and protection of rights of minority form, is of course absent. After all, how can there be elections among competing candidates? Competing on what basis? How can there be freedom of the individual and free discussion of political and other issues? There is one truth, whether it be Marxian, Hitlerian, or Khomeinian. Minority rights? But there are no minorities; all are one. Freedom of the individual, the rule of law and constitutional participatory democracy, those great but vulnerable "inventions" or "discoveries" of liberalism, are antithetical to radicalism.

It is important to be aware that radicalism is not being equated to any particular set of beliefs, Marxist, fascist, or other. Radical movements, after revolution and successful takeover, must of course ultimately settle down to stable government and routine administration. They can even become conservative! They are less likely, however, to become liberal because the fundamental precepts of liberalism are incompatible with the rapid, radical, and violent changes required by radical movements. Not only is radicalism as a phenomenon not being equated to particular sets of beliefs; it is not being identified as always revolutionary, though revolution is frequently a concomitant of radicalism. What is meant is that revolutions are not necessarily always carried out by radicals. A revolution can be carried out by citizens outraged by a tyrannical government—the American Revolution is a case in point. The citizens are not radicals, however. They do not want to destroy the government and societal institutions. They want only to escape what they see as arbitrary and unbearable tyranny. Some radicals of the right, too, do not want to destroy societal institutions. Rather, they want to restore older institutions or to escape the communist menace or the blunders and bumbling of liberalism (Forster & Epstein, 1964).

The point of this digression is not so much to define and characterize radicalism as it is to throw more light on liberalism and conservatism and, most important for our purpose, to show that radicalism is not on the same level of discourse as liberalism and conservatism, except from the point of view of radicals. What does this enigmatic statement mean? It is true that radicals of the left will be strongly opposed to "establishment" values and systems, and that this may seem to put their beliefs on the same continuum. But this negativism is "total"; they want to destroy the existing system completely. It is not, in other words, like you disagreeing with me on, say, abortion or desegregation or private property. It is the total rejection of all ideas espoused by any part of the existing order. The existing order is rotten. All of it must go. This is not the same as disagreement. It is complete and uncompromising rejection.

To say "radicalism-conservatism" or "radicalism-liberalism" is mistaken verbal usage. The implication of a continuum is erroneous. To say that the radical is anti-conservative or that the radical is an extreme liberal is misleading. Such expressions miss the essentially different nature of radicalism as a phenomenon. Somewhat oversimply put, liberalism stands for a certain positive set of beliefs and conservatism stands for another certain positive set of beliefs that are different from the liberal beliefs, but that are also on the same level of discourse. Radicalism, on the other hand, is largely negative. As such, it is not on the same ideological or belief system level of discourse as liberalism and conservatism.

Another important area of difference among liberalism, conservatism, and radicalism is values, but especially values associated with human rights. The main origin of concern for human rights—the right of the individual to disagree with authority, the rights of women and minorities, the rights of children, religious freedom, and so on—has been liberalism. "Moderate" socialism borrowed its emphasis on human rights from liberalism. Conservatism has had little concern with human rights as a doctrine. Its contemporary espousal of such rights seems to me to be more acquiescence in strong trends than enthusiastic espousal, as indicated earlier. Radicalism evidently has little or no concern for human rights, if one judges from actual behavior. Radicals of the left (not of the right) may talk a good deal about human rights, but it seems that they mean the rights only of those in their favor—reminiscent of classic liberalism with its espousal of the freedom and rights of men of property and wealth. This follows from radical logic: What is important is the overthrow of the existing order and the establishment of the new. In this way all will ultimately benefit, even though some get hurt on the way, especially if they question the new establishment.

ATTITUDES TOWARD EDUCATION: PROGRESSIVISM AND TRADITIONALISM

The research reported in this book started with Q studies of attitudes toward education, and the results of these early studies stimulated interest in the structure of attitudes both over many people and within the individual. These results are reported in Chapter 6. In this chapter we discuss progressivism and traditionalism in general.

Educational attitudes are here conceived as subsets of the broader sets of beliefs, liberalism and conservatism. That is, we can talk about educational attitudes on the same level as economic, political, religious, and other social attitudes. Research evidence to support this assertion is available (Kerlinger, 1972c; Smith, 1963). In any case, we define and briefly discuss progressivism and traditionalism.

Progressivism

> *Progressivism* is a set of educational beliefs that is characterized by emphasis on the needs and interests of the child, the freedom of the child and the teacher, permissiveness, life experiences as educative, quality of teacher and student, democratic citizenship, and physical, emotional, and social development and thus education of the "whole child."

Although Dupuis (1966, Ch. V) traces progressivism, or educational liberalism as he calls it, back to earlier centuries, I think we can safely say that its intellectual and moral ancestory was liberalism, especially modern liberalism. The key words are freedom, the individual, and democracy. The emphasis of progressivism is on the child and his needs, interests, and experiences. This is where the curriculum originates. To attain the objective of educating the mature democratic citizen, as much freedom as possible must be given both teacher and student. Permissiveness is thus necessary. So is education and teaching that are child-centered and not teacher- or subject-centered. Even with this brief discussion the close relation between liberalism and progressivism should be obvious.

Traditionalism

> *Traditionalism* is a set of educational beliefs that focuses on ultimate truths and principles, the intellectual aspects and standards of education, subject matter, spiritual and moral values, tradition, discipline and the authority of the teacher, and education as preparation for further education and for life.

While we view traditional attitudes toward education as a subset of general social attitudes, it does not seem possible to say that traditionalism arose out of modern conservatism. Traditionalism in education is much older than modern conservatism; indeed, it goes back to Plato.

The central emphases are the intellect, tradition, moral values, subject matter, and authority and discipline. The traditionalist believes that education must be aimed at the person's intellectual growth and achievement, at factual knowledge of fundamental subjects, at sound moral development and moral character, and at adequate preparation for later education and life. Man is conceived as rational, and children have to be taught respect for reason, how to reason, and the stuff with which to reason. Abstraction is important because students must learn to deal with ideas—literary, mathematical, historical, and others. Deduction is also important. The student has to learn general principles. (The progressive educator emphasizes induction, that is, the student learns principles that are generalizations from experience.)

Implications for Educational Practice

Both schools of thought have had strong influence on the thinking and attitudes of educators and laymen (see Cremin, 1961, and NSSE, 1955). Most schools are varying mixtures of both sets of beliefs; it would be hard to find a purely traditional school or a purely progressive school. Traditional educational ideas have always been with us in education, and there is little doubt that they will continue to be with us. Progressive educational ideas, however, have had only a short life and have even waned, at least in outward manifestations. Nevertheless, some of progressivism's core principles have sunk deep into modern educational thinking and practice, perhaps because they have been reflections of modern liberalism and are commensurate with democracy. Even though the influence of progressive education has waned—the journal *Progressive Education* discontinued publication long ago, for instance—there is no doubt of its former power, influence, and vitality. It literally transformed elementary and, to a lesser extent, secondary education in the United States. It has also had considerable influence in Western Europe and the Soviet Union. It even penetrated the university classroom, especially in the 1950s in connection with the group dynamics movement (Kerlinger, 1956b).

If one is traditional in educational matters, one would worry about the teaching of subject matter, and especially subject matter of substantial intellectual content: literature, mathematics, history, foreign languages. One would be less than enthralled with subjects like social studies, swimming, human relations, art appreciation. A traditionalist would also be concerned with discipline and order. The classroom of the traditional teacher will (ideally) be quiet, orderly, and work-oriented. The authority of the teacher will be stressed. Students are expected to be polite, respectful, obedient.

If one is a progressive in education, one would stress the importance of democracy in school as well as in life. The school should be a microcosm of the world outside. But it should be more: it should be an agent of social change. Any signs of authoritarianism—and to a progressive, traditional ideas are undemocratic, even autocratic—must be eliminated from schools. Permissiveness is a prevailing norm of the progressive school. Relationships between students, between teachers and administrators, and between students and teachers should be egalitarian. The curriculum and teaching should be based on children's needs and interests. Some subjects are of course necessary, but their teaching must be alive, dynamic, and meaningful to the student. Group methods that involve students actively in interaction with each other as well as with the teacher are important to use. Children should be helped to discover answers and to solve problems for themselves rather than have answers and solutions given in lectures or books.

The above examples are only a part of the manifestation of the differences; there are of course others. Our interest is that progressivism and traditionalism are broad constellations of attitudes: toward children and their learning, toward schools and their organization and even their physical attributes and appearance, toward teaching, toward the community, and, of course, toward the whole society.

In Chapter 6 we examine empirical evidence on the nature and structure of educational attitudes, and we will see, among other things, that progressivism and traditionalism are congeries of attitudes toward aspects of education, each with its separate and distinct character reflecting the larger social attitudes of liberalism and conservatism. Technically put, progressivism and traditionalism are relatively independent second-order factors of educational attitudes, each characterized by two or more first-order attitude factors, each of which is progressive or traditional, but not both.

3 The Criterial Referents Theory of Attitudes

A theory is a systematic explanation of natural phenomena. It states the relations among the phenomena and how and (hopefully) why they occur. The phenomena explained by a theory are often, perhaps usually, dependent variables. A theory of prejudice, for example, attempts to explain prejudice by stating the relations between prejudice and certain psychological and sociological variables, such as economic circumstances, education, social class, frustration, authoritarianism. Similarly, there can be theories of juvenile delinquency, school achievement, aggression, memory, and so on.

There are theories, however, that focus more on what appear to be independent variables. An example is the theory of cognitive dissonance (Festinger, 1957), which is an attempt to explain a wide variety of human behavior by invoking psychological "dissonance," a mental state produced by incongruent psychological elements. Another similar psychological theory in which the emphasis is on the independent variable side is the theory of reinforcement in which the effects on behavior of reinforcing responses are predicted.

The criterial referents theory of social attitudes, which is the subject of this chapter, is still different. It seeks to explain how social attitudes are structured—and why they are so structured.[1] With this kind of theory

---

[1] The rather difficult words "structure" and "factor" are used liberally in this book. A definition and an explanation of structure is given in the next chapter. For now, conceive structure as "organization" or "configuration." A structure is actually a set of relations. For

there is little concern for independent and dependent variables. One is not, at least immediately, concerned with saying that a structure is produced by a set of independent variables. The "causes," for example, may be a combination of the economic system, the historical and ideological background, and the social problems of the immediate past and the present. With this kind of theory, however, one puts aside—for now at least—the "causes" of the structure. One seeks to determine the structure without systematic regard for either the determinants or the effects of the structure. Perhaps an example from a more familiar area of structural research will help us to understand what is meant.

Psychologists now know a great deal about human intelligence in large part due to what can be called structural research. Such research has sought to "discover" the various components of intelligence mostly through factor analysis. After European pioneering in such theory and research (Guilford, 1967, Ch. 1), psychological researchers pursued structural investigations in attempts to learn the factors behind measured intelligence. Thurstone (1938; Thurstone & Thurstone, 1941) made a substantial advance by establishing the "existence" of seven primary ability factors behind the mental test scores of many children. Thurstone forever altered the idea that there is one "intelligence," and made an excellent start toward defining a "structure" of intelligence. He found, for instance, that verbal, numerical, spatial, perceptual, memory, and reasoning abilities were separate and distinct factors, even though positively correlated. The factors he repeatedly found form a "theory" of intelligence. They "explain" intelligence structurally and substantively. Such theory and investigation, while different from the two kinds of theory mentioned above, are highly important parts of modern behavioral research.

The "theory" of this book is an attempt to formulate a structural explanation of social attitudes in the factor analytic tradition of the search for structure, analogous to the search for factors of human intelligence. It

---

example, if four items of an attitude scale are positively and substantially correlated, they will probably form an attitude factor. The factor itself, the underlying entity behind the four items, is determined or named from whatever is common to the four items, say Economic Conservatism, or Social Welfare, or Sexual Freedom. This factor, then, is part of the factor structure of the attitude scale. "Structural research" is some form of investigation that uses various kinds of multidimensional analysis, primarily factor analysis, aimed at determining the attitude factors and the relations among the factors. For our purpose, a structural theory is an explanation that specifies how attitude elements—scales or items—are related to form factors, and how the factors, the underlying entities, are themselves related to form what are called higher order factors. A "factor" is a hypothetical entity that underlies tests, scales, measures. It would be helpful at this point for the reader to study Appendix A on factor analysis.

seeks to explain the structure of such attitudes by specifying the factors behind the responses to attitude scales and items and also specifying the relations among the factors. Some of the ideas behind the theory and the approach were discussed in Chapter 1. Now we must be more specific and more general. We must explain what the theory is and what it explains. In doing so, we assume that attitudes, like intelligence and virtually all human psychological attributes and characteristics, are multidimensional. We assume that there is some finite number of attitude factors that underlie the varied responses of many individuals to attitudinal stimuli. We further assume—more shakily, to be sure—that there are systematic relations among the factors found in factor analysis of the responses of many people to attitude stimuli and what is in the minds of individuals. If we find, for instance, a factor that can validly be labeled "Conservatism," we assume that something like a conservative attitude structure exists in the minds of many individuals.

An important caveat must be mentioned before we proceed. Although I use the term "theory" liberally throughout this chapter and, indeed, the whole book, it should be understood as a factor analytic "explanation" of the structure of social attitudes, together with a hypothesized reason, the criteriality of attitude referents, for the underlying structure and the latent variables of the social attitudes. Moreover, the various discussions of attitudes are to be understood to be limited to social attitudes as defined (see below). There does not appear to be a more modest word, except, perhaps "hypothesis." And "hypothesis" seems to be too restricted in the context of the general discussion. So I use "theory" in the limited sense of meaning explanation of the factor structure of social attitudes, recognizing that it is not a theory in the general and usual sense of the word.

GENERAL BACKGROUND

The measurement of social attitudes and the search for attitude organization and structure go back four decades. Many scales were written and administered to thousands of individuals. The reader can find generous selections of them in the valuable scale anthologies of Robinson, Rusk, and Head (1968), Robinson and Shaver (1969), and Shaw and Wright (1967). These books also contain brief descriptions of the research behind the scales—or the lack of it—and critical assessments of the reliability, validity, and usefulness of the scales.

One of the most important assumptions behind the measurement of social attitudes has been and is what I will call the assumption of bipolarity. This has been mentioned before, but it needs repeating. It is assumed, usually without empirical evidence, that attitudes are for and against things. The assumption has two or three important implications. One of these applies to people's beliefs and attitudes. For example, if a person is for free enterprise and competition, then he is against income leveling and labor unions. In sum, if an individual is conservative in social attitudes, then he must be anti-liberal. Such reasoning springs from the bipolarity assumption: Whenever there is a positive set of beliefs there must also be an opposite negative set of beliefs. This is the most general implication.

A second implication affects the measurement of attitudes. If a researcher seeks to measure attitudes, then there must be two poles of measurement, positive and negative. If one were measuring attitudes toward education, for instance, one might have the following two items in a scale to measure such attitudes:

Learning is essentially a process of increasing one's store of information about the various fields of knowledge.

The goals of education should be dictated by children's interests and needs, as well as by the larger demands of society.

These two items, though not logical opposites, are based on quite different philosophies of education. The first expresses a traditional view of education, whereas the second expresses what has been called a progressive view. It has been found (Kerlinger, 1967b) that the two items are expressions of separate and distinct attitudes toward education, which means that people who support one of them do not necessarily oppose the other. A view of education and educational attitudes that is dominated by the bipolarity assumption, however, would see the two items as expressing opposing views. If the items were both included in an attitude scale, they would be scored by some investigators in opposite directions. If a person agreeing with the first item is scored positively, a person agreeing with the second items would be scored negatively.

The above items were deliberately chosen for the subtlety of the difference between them and because empirical research has shown them to measure quite different things. Take more obvious examples:

The well-being of a nation depends on its business and industry.

Large fortunes should be taxed fairly heavily over and above income taxes.

The first item reflects a conservative attitude and the second a liberal attitude (Kerlinger, 1970a). It is unlikely that a person agreeing with the first item would agree with the second. The bipolarity assumption would put them at opposite sides of a presumed liberal-conservative continuum and score them, accordingly, positively and negatively on one continuum.

Much of the earlier and later research on social attitudes reflects the power of the bipolarity assumption. Items of attitude scales are scored in ways similar to that just described.[2] In a relatively sophisticated study, Hicks and Wright (1970) used five liberalism-conservatism scales. They say, "The L-C scales were keyed to have conservatism reflected by high scale scores and liberalism reflected by low scale scores" (p. 115). A much-used and evidently influential scale to measure conservatism— though it contains liberal items—is the C Scale of Wilson and Patterson (1968). The scale consists of 50 items, with presumably conservative and liberal items presented alternately. "Yes" responses to odd-numbered items (usually conservative) and "No" responses to even-numbered items (usually liberal) were scored 2. Responses that were not "Yes" or "No" were scored 1. This procedure provides scores that are on the presumed dimension of conservatism. (For a critique of the Wilson-Patterson scale, see Pedhazur, 1978.)

Part of the purpose of this book is to challenge the bald and uncritical acceptance of the bipolarity assumption. Research evidence is presented that shakes the assumption, and an attempt is made to specify the conditions that can and do produce bipolarity of attitudes. Bipolarity of attitudes *does* exist. But is it a major attitudinal phenomen, as commonly assumed, or is it a relatively minor phenomenon? When does it occur? What are the conditions that produce it?

---

[2] A lovely example of the power of the bipolarity assumption is in an anthology of attitude scales (Shaw & Wright, 1967). Two of my scales were included in the book. Each scale is supposed to yield two scores. For example, the social attitudes scale yields two scores for each individual, a liberal score and a conservative score. (The reasons are given later in the chapter.) The editors of the book, however, affixed asterisks to the conservative items and inserted the following footnote at the bottom of the scale: "These are conservative items whose weights should be reversed for scoring purposes. All unmarked items are liberal" (*ibid.*, p. 323). This instruction is similarly reinforced in their discussion of the scale, which includes: "Higher scores are indicative of liberalism." The implication of a single bipolar continuum is clear. In fact, in their comments on my early educational attitudes which they included in the book, they comment: "It seems to us, however, that the scale is measuring a single continuum ranging from highly favorable to highly unfavorable attitudes toward progressive practices in education, or conversely, highly unfavorable to highly favorable attitudes toward traditional practices in education" (*ibid.*, p. 84). The bipolarity assumption can hardly be better expressed!

THE THEORY[3]

Definitions

Recall that attitudes are defined as sets of beliefs that are directed toward "objects" in the environment. These objects are what we will call "referents." A *referent,* like a name, is a category (Brown, 1958, pp. 7–10). It applies to all classes of phenomena: physical objects, events, behaviors, constructs. As Brown says, any sort of recurrence in the nonlinguistic world can become the referent of a name. We extend this idea to attitudes: Any social recurrence can be the referent of an attitude. More generally, a referent is any object or construct of psychological regard. Applied to attitudes, it is a set of things toward which an attitude can be directed. We have had a number of examples of referents in Chapter 1: *private property, corporate industry, moral standards, money, business, profits, blacks, labor unions, Soviet Union, equality, birth control, sexual freedom, women's liberation.* Note that referents are names of more or less specific "objects"—*money, labor unions, Soviet Union*—or designations of abstract ideas, even principles—*women's liberation, sexual freedom, private property.*

"Criterion" means a test, a rule, a standard that is used to help make a judgment or a decision. "Criteriality" means the relevance, significance, pertinence, or importance of something in helping to make a judgment or a decision. A *criterial referent* of an attitude is a construct that is the "object," the focus of an attitude, that is significant, salient, and relevant for an individual or for groups or individuals. For example, if I have a positive attitude toward the United Nations, then the referent *United Nations* is criterial for me. On the other hand, I may be relatively indifferent to the United Nations. I may even know little or nothing about it. It is therefore not criterial for me, though it may well be criterial for many other people. The expression "criterial referents of attitudes" is a central concept of the theory and of this book.[4]

---

[3]Many of the ideas and some of the discussion of this section and subsequent sections were first elaborated in Kerlinger (1967a).

[4]I am indebted to Bruner, Goodnow, and Austin (1956, Chs. 1 and 2) and to Brown (1958) for the referent and criteriality notions. Brown, for instance, talks about attributes and attribute criteriality and about" . . . the relative 'criteriality' of an attribute for a category" (p. 10). He also makes it clear that referents are categories, recurrences (p. 8). Bruner, Goodnow, and Austin discuss and make the important observation that objects have criterial attributes and degrees of criteriality: "Obviously the extent to which an attribute's values affect the likelihood of categorization is a measure of its *degree of criteriality*" (p. 31). "Criteriality" is akin to Newcomb, Turner, and Converse's (1965) notion of the "centrality" of attitudes. They mean, I think, the central salience of attitude objects or referents, which is of course like "criteriality" as used in this book.

Criterial Referents, Shared Predispositions, and the Positivity Principle

Referents of attitudes are differently criterial for individuals and groups of individuals. For businessmen, for instance, it is likely that the referents *business, money, profits, private property,* and *corporate industry* are criterial. It is less likely that these referents are criterial for teachers and scientists (though they may well be in many cases). For socialists, *public welfare, income equalization, labor unions, social equality,* and *minimum wage* are likely to be criterial. In other words, what is relevant or salient for one individual is not relevant or salient for another individual. What is attitudinally important for one group of individuals may not be important for other groups of individuals.

The criteriality of referents is shared by many individuals. While we may talk about the criteriality of certain referents for an individual, we really mean that the referents are similarly criterial for large sets of individuals. Referent criteriality is what binds the psychological stuff of attitudes together.

To illustrate what is meant, take attitudes toward education. Many years ago, John Dewey (1902) laid part of the foundation for understanding modern philosophies of education and attitudes toward education. He described two large and different views of educational thinking and philosophy, which were later expressed as progressivism and traditionalism. In the context of the present discussion, the duality of educational beliefs and attitudes can be expressed in part by educational attitude referents. For the traditionalist in education, for example, *subject matter, discipline, moral standards,* and related referents are criterial; they are the substance of his educational beliefs. Such referents as *children's needs, social learning,* and *individual differences,* on the other hand, are criterial to the educational progressive; they are part of the core of his educational beliefs. We must of course always be aware that such dualities are never complete and clean. They are general tendencies.

The point of crucial significance to the criterial referents theory is that what is criterial for one individual or group may not be criterial for another individual or group. If you and I both share traditional ideas and principles about educational practice—we both believe, for example, that education is basically intellectual training, that moral standards are important to teach, and that subject matter must always be emphasized— then many educational attitude referents will be similarly criterial for us. If you hold traditional beliefs and I progressive beliefs, however, then the set of attitude referents that is criterial for you is different from the set that is criterial for me.

The criteriality of attitude referents is shared but it is differentially shared. We can assume a continuum of relevance for any referent, in other words. For example, you and I may both approve and support the women's liberation movement, but you are, say, passionately committed to it, whereas I may approve it only mildly. The referents *women's liberation* and *equality of women* will then be highly important and relevant for you, but only marginally important and relevant for me. And to one of our mutual friends they may not be at all important and relevant. Although not opposed to women's liberation and equality of women, they do not really touch him. He is indifferent to them. Despite the difference in the degree to which you and I differ in our reactions to women's liberation, we share some common core of cognition and sentiment about women's liberation and related matters. We may, for instance, share more or less positive perceptions of related referents like civil rights, equality, and blacks. Our mutual friend, however, does not share positive (or necessarily negative) perceptions and sentiments about women's liberation—and about civil rights, equality, and blacks. They just do not mean much to him. Instead, other sets of referents may be relevant for him.

The emphasis above has been on positive reactions, on you and I and others sharing positive perceptions of a set of related referents. A key point of the criterial referents theory is just this: what is shared among large groups of individuals is their generally positive perceptions, sentiments, and reactions to attitude referents. Our friend, for whom women's liberation is not criterial, does not share our attitude. He is not necessarily negative to the women's cause; it is simply not important to him. It is of course possible that other individuals are negatively disposed to women's liberation. The theory, however, states that such negative predispositions are relatively infrequent. What is in general shared about attitudes are positive predispositions toward referents. This can be called an attitude positivity principle. Negative predispositions exist, of course—witness the prevalence of prejudiced attitudes—but they are usually less important than positive predispositions. They operate mostly under certain circumstances and with certain people. (For an important distinction between approaches to the measurement of liberalism and conservatism, see the addendum to this chapter.)

Guttman's (1976) "first law of attitudes" expresses a similar idea. The essence of what he says is that there are no negative correlations between attitude items. Formally stated, the "law" reads: If any two items are selected from the universe of attitude items towards a given object, and if the population observed is not selected artificially, then the population regression between these two items will be monotone and with positive or zero sign.

Duality and Orthogonality

One of the most difficult technical and substantive problems we face is polarity of beliefs and attitudes. In Chapter 1, we asked whether attitudes are polarized; whether the attitudes of conservatives, for instance, are necessarily the opposite of the attitudes of liberals. If we are for some things, are we then against other things? We also categorized this idea as bipolarity. We said that bipolarity of attitudes is generally assumed and accepted by both laymen and social scientists. In addition, we also suggested that the larger attitudinal constellations called liberalism and conservatism actually exist. We must now try to put more flesh on these statements by stating certain propositions and by defining and discussing duality and orthogonality, as well as bipolarity, in the context of the criterial referents theory.

An assumption of this book—later it will become a testable hypothesis—is that the aggregate structure of social attitudes is not bipolar; it is, rather, dualistic. There are, to be sure, liberals and conservatives (and radicals of both left and right) and liberal and conservative positions and statements. But liberal is not just the opposite of conservative, nor is conservative the opposite of liberal. Each is an attitude system in its own right, a system that is relatively orthogonal to the other system. This is what "duality" means. Social attitudes are dualistic and not bipolar: they have two broad general facets, liberalism and conservatism, that are relatively "independent" of each other.

The basic minimum of any large social attitude system, structurally speaking, is two relatively orthogonal dimensions. (The frequent use of the word "relatively", while tiresome, is necessary, as we will see in later chapters.) By a "large" system is meant any set or subset that includes a number of attitude referents that are criterial to many individuals. By "relatively orthogonal dimensions" is meant sets of attitudinal propositions, statements, or expressions that are minimally correlated with each other.

The duality-orthogonality-criteriality argument will perhaps be still clearer if we translate it into factor analytic terms with specific examples of social attitudes and their referents. We assume that many attitudinal objects are used in the measurement of attitudes. The usual measurement procedure is to use several or many items to measure one attitude object or idea. (For elaboration of this procedure, see the addendum to the chapter.) In order to study attitude structure, however, one must study the relations among the attitude objects or referents. To do so of course requires that the same subjects react to many attitude referents.

To clarify what is meant, we anticipate later measurement discussion with a miniature example of the main method of measuring social attitudes used in the research reported in this book. Suppose we have four attitude referent items, *private property, religion, civil rights,* and *social equality,* and we ask a large sample of people to record their feelings toward the four referents or items on a 7-point scale, 7 indicating a strong positive feeling and 1 a strong negative feeling, with gradations 2 through 6 in-between. (Naturally, we would use many more items than four.) According to the criterial referents theory we expect that many people will feel positively toward *private property* and *religion.* The responses of these same people to *civil rights* and *social equality,* however, will be unpredictable. In other words, *private property* and *religion* are criterial for them, but *civil rights* and *social equality* are not. Similarly, many other people will react positively to *civil rights* and *social equality* but their reactions to *private property* and *religion* are unpredictable. The former referents are criterial to them; the latter are not criterial to them. The correlations between *private property* and *religion* and between *civil rights* and *social equality,* calculated over the whole sample should be positive and substantial. The correlation between the two sets of items, however, should be low negative, close to zero.

Assume that we have the responses of many unselected individuals to a large number of heterogeneous social attitude items that include many attitudinal referents, and that we factor analyze the responses and rotate the factors obliquely to simple structure. Ordinarily, more than two factors will emerge, six to twelve or even more. Assuming that we are able to categorize the items as liberal and conservative—how this is done will be discussed later—each factor will have only liberal items or only conservative items, but not both. In general, negative loadings of the rotated factors will be low in value, not greater than $-.30$.[5] In addition, these factors, when rotated obliquely in order to estimate the correlations among the factors, will form two clusters, the factors of each cluster will be positively correlated and the two clusters will be orthogonal to each other, or more realistically, slightly negatively correlated. We are of course talking about first- and second-order factors.

Why should the larger attitudinal constellations, liberalism and conservatism, be orthogonal to each other? The orthogonality inheres in the criterial referents. It was said earlier that referents that are criterial for one individual or one group of individuals may not be criterial for another individual or group of individuals. Nevertheless, there must be sharing, "collective representation," so to speak, of the referents. To many Americans, for example, *private property* is criterial; to many others it is not

---

[5] A troublesome aspect of talking about negative loadings is that, strictly speaking, we should say "not lower than $-.30$," or "negative loadings not greater than .30." We will, however, say "not greater than $-.30$" meaning "not greater than $-.30$" in absolute value.

criterial. Many people share more or less the same sentiment about *civil rights;* many others do not hold the same sentiment. Many people think alike about *sexual freedom:* they may think that more of it is desirable. But many other people don't particularly care about *sexual freedom;* it is not relevant to them and their interests. I am not suggesting that this is an established law; other patterns emerge. These examples, though realistic, are idealized. Low positive correlations occur between liberal factors and between conservative factors, and negative correlations, especially low ones, occur between liberal and conservative factors.

The orthogonality of liberalism and conservatism is due to this differential positive sharing of the relevance of attitude referents. Take a rather obvious conservative example, religious attitudes. Many people of course have positive attitudes toward religion and religion-related referents. In the Western world, the dominant religion is Christianity. (Note, too, that Jews share the relevance of some of the Christian ethic because of common features of the Judaic and the Christian ethics.) Many or most people in the Western world will evaluate religious referents positively. Many others for whom religion is not important will be indifferent to them. Their evaluations would be mildly approving or mildly disapproving. Some few people evaluate religious referents negatively. But their numbers are comparatively small, usually insufficient to affect the basic relations among the referents.

Now, a more difficult example, this time a liberal one: referents related to notions of social equality. "Equality" is a key word in the modern world. Commager (1950, pp. 13ff.) traces equality ideas in America and their effects on American thinking and behavior. The differences between American and European manners, says Commager, are profound, and they are due to American notions of equality. Much earlier, de Tocqueville (1945, especially Vol. II, pp. 99–103) found American notions of equality and its importance a key element of American thought and behavior. Rokeach (1968; pp. 168–178; 1973, Chs. 10, 12) has focused a good deal of his values thinking and research on the related referents of *equality* and *freedom.* It is safe to say that *equality* and related referents and ideas are key elements of modern liberal doctrine.

Many people will endorse social equality as an important, even indispensable, human value. If we ask them, they will respond positively to referents like *equality, social equality, racial equality, equality of women, civil rights,* and *income leveling.* The correlations among such items are positive and often substantial. Factor analysis of these and other referents has shown that they form a separate factor distinct from other liberal factors, though positively correlated with them, and quite distinct from conservative factors (Kerlinger, Middendorp, & Amón, 1976). For example, in a factor analysis of data obtained in New York and Virginia, the correlations between a liberal factor called "Equality and Civil Rights" and two other liberal factors, "Human Warmth and Feeling" and "Social Welfare" were .53 and .31, whereas its correlations with two conservative factors, "Religiosity" and "Economic Conservatism," were .07 and − .08.

In sum, the theory asserts that social attitudes are dualistic: two large related clusters of attitudes, corresponding to what is called liberalism and conservatism, underlie most social attitudes and these two clusters are relatively orthogonal to each other. Liberalism and conservatism are not "opposite" doctrines or ideologies; they are different ways of approaching social problems, assessing them, and seeking solutions to them. What is a problem of importance to a liberal may not be important to a conservative—and vice versa. A liberal may be committed to the idea of the equality of blacks: equal education, equal job opportunity, and, in general, equal rights. A conservative is not necessarily opposed to equality of blacks; indeed, many conservatives may espouse such equality. Equality of blacks, however, is not as important to conservatives as it is to liberals, and it is not as important as other basic social problems. Conservatives are, generally speaking, not against black equality (though some may be); they are just not for it as liberals are.

Similarly, conservatives may strongly stress the importance of business, corporate industry, adequate profits, and "sound" money policy. Liberals are not necessarily against such conservative ideas; but they are usually not for them either. Conservative referents are, again generally speaking, not criterial for them.

Bipolarity

Although we have already discussed bipolarity, we must tackle it again. "Bipolarity" is really a technical term rather than a phenomenon. Nevertheless, since it refers to a phenomenon—the opposition of ideas and of people's opinions, attitudes, and values—we will use it as though it were a phenomenon. So, when we use the term "bipolarity," we mean both the technical idea of a continuum with two opposed ends and the opposition of ideas, beliefs, opinions, attitudes, and values. The statistical expression of bipolarity is positive and negative correlations among attitude items, clusters of items, and scales, and positive and negative first- and second-order factor loadings (on properly rotated factors).

Let us take an educational attitude example again. Let A be a set of educational referents criterial for a group of progressive educators and B a set of referents criterial for a group of traditionalists. (We assume that progressives and traditionalists can be independently identified—by competent judges, say.) The two sets, A and B, have no necessary relation to each other, except, of course, educational content which may imply relations between *A* and *B*. They are, in other words, assumed to represent independent and different ways of regarding educational "objects." It is also assumed that *A* and *B* are not both criterial for the same individuals. Common sense, of course, dictates otherwise. Common sense dictates bipolarity. It suggests that individuals who approve statements with *A* referents and connotations should disapprove statements with *B* referents and connotations. In other words, progressives are antitraditional and traditionalists are antiprogressive. We are saying that this is not a necessary conclusion. In fact it is probably not correct—or rather, it is correct only under certain conditions and circumstances.

Since attitudes are said to be based on the criteriality of referents, there is no basis for knowing and predicting how progressives will respond to *B* statements and referents, or how traditionalists will respond to *A* statements and referents. This means that progressives and traditionalists will respond heterogeneously, virtually at random, to statements that contain referents that are, for them, not criterial.

There are many adventitious sources of variance of the responses to any set of attitude items: social norms and values expressed in some of the items, knowledge and interest, response-set tendencies, confusion of issues, and so on. Criteriality of referents is the strongest source of variance. Therefore, when a set of referents is not criterial for a group of individuals, there is no main basis for systematic response that is strong enough to override these other sources of variance. Nevertheless, while the responses of progressives to *B* (traditional) statements will be heterogeneous, they will tend to be indifferent to or mildly opposed to some *B* statements. Even though the *B* referents will in general not be criterial for progressive individuals, the statements will now and then contain referents that have become negatively criterial for them. With extreme individuals and groups, this tendency to negative criteriality will be strong. Fervent followers of Nixon or Goldwater, fervent Marxists or Maoists, very fervent liberals, very fervent conservatives: Negative criteriality is strong for them. It is part of the stuff of bipolarity. (For further discussion of negative criteriality, see the addendum to the chapter.)

We should pause here and clearly state certain limitations on the argument on bipolarity. The above explanation of the relative lack of negative correlations between liberal and conservative items and factors, seems to be empirically justified, as we will see. The empirical results, however, were obtained with the research approach of this book: the use of many attitude objects, or referents, and the analysis and study of the relations among them. The criterial referents theory of social attitudes applies only with this approach and only when measuring liberalism and conservatism. The conventional approach to attitude measurement, the use of many positive and negative attitude statements with a single attitude object or referent, is excluded from consideration. Bipolarity as produced by negative correlations between items is a more likely outcome because one attitude object is considered with approximately equal numbers of positive and negative statements presented to subjects. Provided there is a wide variety of attitudes among the individuals of a sample, bipolarity is almost assured: the positive items will ordinarily correlate negatively with the negative items.

In short, I believe that bipolarity is not a necessary and general characteristic of attitudes when studied in the manner that I term the many attitude objects approach. To be sure, in the single object approach, in which all items are focused on a single referent, the probability of obtaining bipolarity is increased because respondents are given more opportunity—indeed, encouragement—to respond both positively and negatively to the items, and because the items express both positive and negative sentiments. Whether it is indeed so that bipolarity will or will not occur with the single attitude object approach is not known since it was unfortunately not studied.[6] The reader is urged at this point to read the addendum to the chapter. With this important distinction mentioned, let us continue the argument.

When many unselected individuals respond to *A* and *B* statements, the net outcome will be a low negative correlation between *A* and *B*. That is why we say that the two dimensions are "relatively orthogonal" or "relatively uncorrelated." It is, rather, a special characteristic that appears when an attitudinal referent is criterial for different sets of individuals, positively for one and negatively for the other. There are of course other conditions that will produce bipolarity—times of crisis and social and political situations when certain referents like *birth control, women's liberation,* and *Israelis* are highly charged concepts—but under "usual" conditions and circumstances and with most people there will be little bipolarity. Probably the most important specific condition that will produce bipolarity is the presence of substantial numbers of radicals of the right or the left in a sample whose attitudes are measured. Radicals are probably as much against doctrines and policies as they are for the doctrines and policies they themselves espouse. Indeed, many radicals have

---

[6]It must be confessed that until recently I was not aware of the two different approaches. And there seems to be little or nothing on it in the literature. The critical review of this book, and especially of this chapter, by an anonymous but astute reviewer forced me to rethink the argument on criteriality and bipolarity. In the process I became aware of the important difference between the single attitude object approach and the many attitude object approach. The above remarks and the addendum to the chapter resulted from this awareness.

little positive doctrine; their doctrine is negative, generally aimed at negating those ideas they oppose. In brief, the referents of the conservative *are* criterial for the Marxist—negatively. The referents of the liberal *are* criterial for the fascist—negatively. In fact, many radicals reject both liberal and conservative referents. Their basic approach to social issues is negative. The devout John Bircher hates the United Nations and civil liberties; so does the devout Communist (B'nai B'rith, 1955; Rokeach, 1960).

A RESEARCH EXAMPLE

The form and substance of an actual research study may help the reader understand what the theory says and implies. The study is typical of the many similar studies done to test the theory. Large numbers of individuals are given attitude scales, and the correlations among the scales or the items of a scale are factor analyzed to "discover" the factors or "dimensions" underlying the scales or items. The study to be summarized analyzes the items of a scale. The items in this case were attitude referents. (See Appendix A for an explanation of factor analysis.)

In Chapter 1 the intelligence studies of Thurstone were briefly described: a number of different kinds of intelligence tests were given to large numbers of school children. Each child had a score on each test. These scores were then intercorrelated and the resulting correlations among the tests factor analyzed. In other words, the many tests were reduced to the common factors underlying them. The method used in the present study was conceptually the same except that the correlations among items instead of the correlations among whole scales were analyzed. Just as Thurstone predicted the factors that would emerge from the correlations among his intelligence tests, one can predict how the items of a scale will correlate and how the results of factor analysis of the items will turn out. In other words, the criterial referents theory is tested by ascertaining the congruence of the factor analytic results with the predictions of the theory.

Among the study's four purposes one is relevant here: to test the criterial referents theory by intensive study, through factor analysis, of the structure of the relations among the items of a scale. If the criterial referents theory has empirical validity, then certain predictions should be supported. First, there should be a number of first-order factors, five, six, or more, and each of these factors, after rotation, should be characterized by either liberal items or conservative items, but not both. That is, each factor's substantial loadings should be associated with liberal items or with conservative items, and both kinds of items will not appear together on a single factor, either positively or negatively. This prediction springs, of course, from the duality argument presented earlier. It should also be clear that the prediction in effect denies the prevalence of bipolarity.

Second, factor analysis of the correlations among the factors—after oblique rotations—should result in two second-order factors, one of which will be characterized by liberal factors and the other by conservative factors. That is, second-order factor analysis of the correlations among the first-order factors should produce the basic dual structure dictated by the theory. This is a crucial and difficult test, difficult because of the "delicate" nature of second-order factor analysis. We will have much more to say about these matters later.

An unusual feature of this research, which has been a principal feature of the series of recent researches to be reported later, is the kind of items used. Most attitude research has used what can be called statement items, items in the form of sentences, propositions or statements about social issues. Here are two examples, the first a liberal statement and the second a conservative statement:

> All individuals who are intellectually capable of benefiting from it should get college education, at public expense if necessary.

> The well-being of a nation depends mainly on its business and industry.

In the present study, however, a new kind of item was tried and found to work well: items that were presumably the actual referents of attitudes. These were single words and short phrases that expressed either the actual "objects" of attitudes—*United Nations, Jews, money, church*—or "principles" of value or conduct—*civil rights, social security, free enterprise, private property*.[7] Such items have attractive advantages: they are brief, more reliable than statements, probably less ambiguous, better for cross-cultural research, and perhaps less subject to adventitious sources of variance. In any case, they were the items of the scale used in this study, Referents-I, or REF-I (Kerlinger, 1972c).

Some 400 possible attitude referents were collected from several liberal and conservative sources (Brubacher, 1962; Dewey, 1902; Dupuis, 1966; Hartz, 1955; Kirk, 1960; McClosky, 1958; Morris, 1961; Orton, 1945; Rossiter, 1962; Viereck, 1962) and from existing attitude scales (see

---

[7] At the time of the study, it was believed that this was the first time that referents had been used as items. Unknown to me, however, Wilson and Patterson (1968) had developed a single-word and short-phrase scale at about the same time. I will discuss the Wilson-Patterson scale at a more suitable time.

Robinson, Rusk, & Head, 1968; Robinson & Shaver, 1969; Shaw & Wright, 1967). In addition, a number of referents were culled from my own attitude scales and Q sorts, or were written from knowledge and experience. The 50 items of the scale resulted from the application of the criteria: representativeness of the social attitude domain (religious, political, economic, educational, and general social aspects), clarity of meaning, lack of redundancy, relative specificity, and generality of usage (in common speech or writing). There were difficulties in applying these criteria, however. First there were many more conservative than liberal referents, limiting the choice of liberal items. Second, many referents in the pool were really useless because of vagueness and ambiguity (e.g., *orders and classes, noble culture*). Nevertheless, the final scale seemed to have satisfactory psychometric properties.

A 50-item 7-point summated-rating (Likert) scale was used. Twenty-four items were liberal *(L)* and 24 were conservative *(C)*.[8] Two items were omitted from the analysis of Table 3.1. They were included for an extraneous purpose. All 50 items were used in the factory analysis. The instructions asked respondents to express degrees of positive and negative feelings toward each of the concepts, $+3$ expressing a very positive feeling, $+2$ a positive feeling, down through -3, which expressed a very negative feeling. Positive and negative designations were used to allow negative correlations between items to emerge if, indeed, there were such negative correlations.

REF-I was administered to three samples of teachers and graduate students of education in North Carolina ($N = 206$), Texas ($n = 277$), and New York, ($N = 263$) and to two smaller samples in North Carolina ($N = 270$), including 97 miscellaneous business people. We report here mostly the results of a combined North Carolina and Texas sample ($N = 530$). The New York results were highly similar. (The study actually included other measures, but we limit discussion at this time to the North Carolina and Texas sample data with REF-I.)

The psychometric properties of REF-I were satisfactory. The means,

---

[8]The critical reader may wonder how items were "known" to be liberal or conservative. There were two bases for such knowledge. First, items were explicitly dictated or implied by conservative or liberal social theory. Treatises on conservatism, for instance, emphasize the importance of business, authority, religion, and tradition. Treatises on liberalism emphasize the importance of equality, economic reform, civil rights, and social welfare. These and related ideas, therefore, were used in items. Second, the results of factor analyses of item intercorrelations had shown the relations among items and thus had provided indirect empirical evidence of the conservative and liberal nature of an item. If an item correlated positively and substantially with items either "known" or believed to be conservative, then it was reasonable to suppose that it was a conservative item. This problem of item identity will of course be discussed in more depth later.

TABLE 3.1
Referents Scale I (REF-I): Means, Standard Deviations,
Reliabilities, and Correlations Between L and C Subscales,
North Carolina, Texas, and New York Samples[a]

		N.C.		Texas	N.Y.
		206	97	227	263
M:	L	5.62	5.07	5.65	5.67
	C	5.79	5.84	5.47	5.57
s:					
	L	.63	.71	.60	.63
	C	.60	.59	.70	.78
r_{tt}:[b]					
	L	.83	.85	.85	.83
	C	.84	.87	.88	.89
r_{LC}:		-.15	-.01	-.07	-.21

[a] There were 24 items in each subscale.

[b] r_{tt}: alpha reliability coefficients.

standard devisions, and alpha reliability coefficients of the L (liberal) and C (conservative) subscales are given in Table 3.1, together with the correlations between the L and C subscales (last line of table). The statistics of the New York sample are also included for comparison purposes.) The means and standard deviations require no discussion except to say that the means are higher in level than comparable L and C means from statement scales (see original research report, p. 620). The standard deviations are a little lower than those of statement scales (about .10 to .20). The reliabilities (r_{tt}), however, are higher: about .07 to .10 higher. The comforting aspect of the table is the substantial level of the reliabilities: the middle .80's. (In later studies, the reliabilities of L and C subscales of referent instruments have been higher, especially the C subscales.) Evidently referents can form reliable scales. The last line of the table is important because it is a partial test of the theoretical predictions. Recall that when we discussed duality we said that the two underlying liberal and conservative dimensions of social attitudes were relatively orthogonal. The correlations between the L and C subscales of Table 3.1 show this to be so: they are low negative, with an average of $-.11$.

After extracting and rotating obliquely (and orthogonally) various numbers of factors from the 50-by-50 correlation matrix, a 6-factor solution was found to be best. The principal factors method (Harman, 1976) and Promax oblique rotations were used. (See Chapter 4 for technical discussion.) The factor arrays of the six factors, with the names of the factors are given in Table 3.2. The solution is clear and unambiguous. (Later we will see that this is not always so.) One can fairly easily grasp the nature of the factors. More important for our purpose, however, the theoretical predictions are clearly confirmed. The liberal and conservative items are loaded positively on different factors, with only two exceptions: an *L* referent *(scientific knowledge)* loaded positively on a *C* factor, and a *C* referent *(racial purity)* loaded negatively on an *L* factor. There is little evidence of bipolarity. Although there were negative loadings, they were for the most part small.

The correlations among the six oblique factors (Thurstone, 1947, Ch. XVII) were themselves factor analyzed and the two factors obtained were rotated orthogonally (Varimax method). The correlations are given in Tables 3.3, and the unrotated and rotated factors are given in Table 3.4.

There is some bipolarity in the correlation matrix: six negative *r*'s of $-.24$, $-.15$, $-.16$, -20, $-.03$, and $-.23$ among the 15 *r*'s. They are relatively small, however, especially when compared to the positive *r*'s. The rotated factor structure (right side of Table 3.4) make it clear that bipolarity is a minor characteristic of these data. There are four negative

TABLE 3.2
Factor Arrays of Oblique First-Order Factors,
Combined North Carolina and Texas Samples, $N = 530^a$

I. Religiosity	V. Educational Traditionalism	VI. Economic Conservatism
religion (.78)	subject matter (.59)	free enterprise (.62)
church (.73)	education as intellectual	real estate (.53)
faith in God (.72)	training (.52)	private property (.43)
Christian (.69)	school discipline (.44)	capitalism (.37)
religious education (.57)	homogeneous grouping (.30)	national sovereignty (.30)
teaching of spiritual values (.53)		(scientific knowledge (.30))
moral standards in educ- tion (.36)		
patriotism (.33)		

II. Civil Rights	III. Child-Centered Education	IV. Social Liberalism
Negroes (.60)	children's interests (.56)	Social Security (.53)
civil rights (.57)	child-centered curriculum (.54)	Supreme Court (.50)
racial integration (.57)	pupil personality (.54)	federal aid to education (.49)
Jews (.46)	children's needs (.52)	poverty program (.48)
desegregation (.43)	self-expression of children (.47)	socialized medicine (.47)
(racial purity (-.37))	pupil interaction (.44)	United Nations (.43)
	child freedom (.37)	

^{a} Factor loadings are given in parentheses. Loadings $>.30$ were considered significant. The two paren- thesized referents are one *L* item loaded on a *C* factor and one *C* item loaded on an *L* factor.

TABLE 3.3

Correlations Among Primary Factors,

Combined North Carolina and Texas Samples, $N = 530$[a]

	I	II	III	IV	V	VI	
I	1.00	-.24	.11	-.15	.57	.39	C
II		1.00	.39	.43	-.16	-.20	L
III			1.00	.37	.15	.09	L
IV				1.00	-.03	-.23	L
V					1.00	.55	C
VI						1.00	C

[a]II, III, IV: L factors; I, V, VI: C factors.

TABLE 3.4

Unrotated and Rotated Second-Order Factor Matrices,

Combined North Carolina and Texas Samples, $N = 530$[a]

	Unrotated Matrix		Rotated Matrix		Factor Type
I	.69	.19	*.71*	−.09	C
II	-.44	.51	-.22	*.64*	L
III	-.05	.64	.19	*.61*	L
IV	-.36	.55	-.13	*.65*	L
V	.70	.33	*.78*	.04	C
VI	.68	.14	*.68*	-.12	C

[a]Significant loadings ($\geqslant .35$) are italicized.

loadings in the matrix, and they are all less than .35, the criterion used for "significance." The crucial second-order factor analytic predictions are also supported. The first three eigenvalues were 1.76, 1.14, and .19, clearly indicating two factors. Evidently the structure of social attitudes of this sample and with REF-I is dualistic. There were two relatively independent factors underlying the responses to REF-I, one of which was associated with conservatism and the other with liberalism. The C factors loaded substantially on the first factor and the L factors on the second factor.

To depict the second-order factor analytic results clearly—and even a little dramatically—we plot the rotated factor loadings of Table 3.4 in Figure 3.1. We follow a convention that we will use throughout the book (whenever possible): we designate the abscissa as L and the ordinate as C. For example, the L and C loadings, respectively, of Factor I (first row of Table 3.4) are − .09 and .71. These loadings determine the placement of Factor I on the graph. It can be seen that there are two clusters: II, III, and IV high on L, and low on C, and I, V, and VI high on C and low on L. The dualistic and orthogonal structure of the social attitudes as expressed in the referent factors could hardly be clearer.

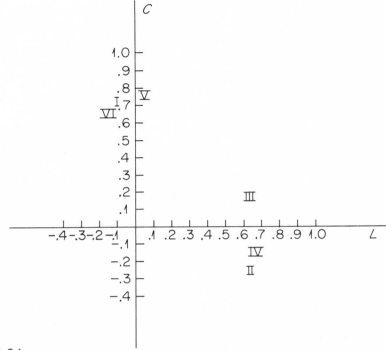

FIG. 3.1

The approach, methodology, and findings of this study are like those of a number of studies done both before and after the formulation of the criterial referents theory. The studies have in general supported the theory. And a number of studies done by others, two or three of which were also done to test the theory, also support it. This does not mean, of course, that the theory is "correct." There are always possibilities of alternative explanations of the data. The evidence can also be said to be one-sided. Perhaps most pertinent, there may have been defects in the methology used. To enable others to judge and assess the research evidence and the methology that produced it, we devote Chapter 4 to methodology and technical problems.

Methodology is of course always important in research. It is particularly important in the research reported in this book because it is both complex and controversial. It is easy to make technical mistakes—and to persist in making them. An example of probable improper scoring has already been given. Improper scoring is disastrous because it fouls all later analysis and interpretation of results. Using an inappropriate method of factor analysis, or an appropriate method inappropriately—for example, using principal components analysis when factor analysis is needed, or rotating too many or too few factors—can obscure results, even distort them. So we must be especially careful to describe the methodology used and to discuss its strengths and weaknesses so that readers can judge for themselves the empirical validity of the results.

THE THEORY AND THE INDIVIDUAL

We must be clearly aware of the level of discourse on which we are talking. In Chapter 1 we talked about two senses of structure: structure presumably in the long-term memories of individuals and structure that is a product of the responses of many individuals. Psychological theory is usually preoccupied with the first kind of structure: what is in the heads of single individuals. When Festinger (1957) talks about cognitive dissonance, he means the psychological dissonance in the head of an individual—even though research to determine the existence of cognitive dissonance and its causes and effects is done almost always with groups of individuals. Rosch (1973), in her theory and research on categorization, talks about the categorization processes of individuals. The criterial referents theory of attitudes, however, is a "large-group" theory. It attempts to explain the structure, the clustering, of attitudes exhibited in the responses of many individuals. In brief, what is attitudinally common to many individuals is the focus of theoretical and empirical attention.

Psychological scientists are always faced with what can be called the individual-group paradox. Psychologists often want to talk about the psychological processes operating in the individual: memory, perception, motivation, and so on. If I invoke attribution theory and want to study how people attribute causes to observed events, I assume that some sort of attribution process goes on in the heads of individuals and it is this process, in part, that produces the judgments of the individuals. Cognitive psychologists studying memory are interested in the memories of single individuals. To reach scientific conclusions about, say, the "structure" of memory they must of course study many individuals. But their discourse is often ensconced in an "individual memory." Baddeley (1976), for example, says, "What the subject acquires are fragments comprising a cluster of features" (p. 346). Elsewhere, to be sure, he says "subjects," but the central interest is the memory of the single individual, a generalized single individual, of course. In discussing categorization, Bruner, Goodnow, and Austin (1956) say, in one place, "What does the act of rendering things equivalent achieve for the organism?" (p. 11) Here the word "organism" generalizes the individual. The paradox centers in what can be called the "unit of speech." The unit of speech in science is the set, the group. But psychologists, naturally enough, often talk as though the unit of speech were the individual, and theories are often enunciated to explain the mental processes of the individual.

Even though it is difficult to make clear what is meant, I labor this point because of the two possible applications of the criterial referents theory. As already indicated, the theory's main preoccupation is with the attitudinal responses of groups of individuals. The preoccupation with the results of the factor analysis of the study summarized above was with the factors that emerged from the correlations among the items of an attitude scale calculated from the responses of many individuals. The factors do not refer, except very indirectly, to psychological processes in the heads of the responding individuals. If we label a factor "Economic Conservatism," we do so because items that presumably reflect conservative economic ideas correlate substantially with each other. And the substantial correlations are produced by the covarying of the responses of sets of individuals. The factors are group products and, strictly speaking, say little about the economic conservatism in the minds of the individuals who responded to the items.

We can certainly ask the question, however, whether there is some sort of relation between these group factors and what is in the minds of individuals. Is it possible, for example, that there are structures in the memories of individuals, structures that reflect or are in some way related to the "large" structures found among many individuals? Can we even be outrageous enough to ask whether "Economic Conservatism" is a significant part of an individual attitude structure? If conservatism and liberalism are reliable factors that emerge from the responses of many individuals, is it possible that they form some sort of attitudinal structure in the brain, some sort of organizing principle or process in memory? Such questions may be far out. Then, again, the pursuit of their answers may lead to productive research, research that may aid in understanding social attitudes.

We ask such questions and report one or two attempts to find answers to them. Although these concerns are only a small part of this book, I think they are an important part. It is possible that they open up a new sort of research on attitudes, a new approach that may link the "larger" factor analytic approach just described, to a cognitive psychological approach that studies, among other things, the relation between, on the one hand, the structure of "larger" factors and, on the other hand, the possible psychological structures of individuals, especially memory structures.

IMPLICATIONS FOR ATTITUDE RESEARCH AND MEASUREMENT

The implications of the criterial referents theory for attitude research and measurement are interesting but upsetting. First, the assumption behind much attitude research and thinking is that social attitudes are unidimensional and bipolar. When a scale is written to measure conservatism, for example, it often seems to be assumed that conservatism is a single dimension with positive and negative ends. Such scales are also "conservatism-radicalism," "radicalism-conservatism," or "liberalism-conservatism" (e.g., Adorno, Frenkel-Brunswik, Levinson, & Sanford, 1950; Comrey & Newmeyer, 1965; Hicks & Wright, 1970; Ladd & Lipset, 1972; Wilson & Patterson, 1968). Earlier, two examples (Hicks & Wright, 1970; Wilson & Patterson, 1968) were summarized. Let us look briefly at another and older example.

Long ago, Kerr (1946) assumed that there was no generalized liberalism-conservatism factor and provided, a priori, separate scales to measure five attitude areas: political, economic, religious, aesthetic, and social. Each scale, however, was believed to measure a different aspect of liberalism-conservatism. This is clear from the scoring, which assigns 1 to the most conservative response to 5 to the most liberal response. This assumes, of course, that each item measures both liberalism and conservatism, even though, for example, all the items of one whole subscale (economic) are liberal items (see Shaw & Wright, 1967, p. 320). Kerr's contribution, however, was substantial: by assuming multidimensionality, he was at least nearer the facts.

The unidimensional assumption is clearly incorrect. The available evidence indicates that several factors underlie both liberalism and conservatism (e.g., Kerlinger, 1970a, 1972c; Kerlinger et al., 1976). The evidence seems to indicate that liberalism and conservatism are separate and distinct dimensions that are relatively orthogonal to each other. If this is so, or even only approximately so, then the implications for social attitude measurement are clear. Two of them are obvious. (1) Liberalism and conservatism should be measured separately. That is, if both kinds of items are included in a scale, then each subject gets two scores, one L and one C. (2) Items should not be reversed on the assumption of a single continuum at one end of which are liberal items and at the other end conservative items. These assumptions and others and their implications will be discussed later in the book.

A second implication of the theory is that the correlations among attitude items should be mostly positive or near zero, with few substantial negative correlations. This means, of course, that rotated factor loadings will also be positive or near zero, with few substantial negative loadings. When substantial negative item intercorrelations and factor loadings occur, they are a function of "negative criteriality" (see Addendum, below), faulty item wording, improper scoring, "deviant" samples, or lack of adequate factoring and rotation.

There are of course other implications springing from the theory and from the above implications. They will be discussed in considerable detail, with examples and evidence, in several parts of this book. We will find that certain accepted ideas, such as most people having "no attitudes" (Campbell, Converse, Miller, & Stokes, 1960; Converse, 1964), are oversimplified, even erroneous, derived from questionable assumptions, improper measurement, or both. Positive suggestions for attitude research and measurement will also emerge from our review of the criterial referents theory and the research supporting it—and not supporting it.

ADDENDUM:
TWO APPROACHES TO ATTITUDE MEASUREMENT AND THE MEANING OF NEGATIVE CRITERIALITY AND BIPOLARITY

At the end of Chapter 1 (Footnote 4), we alerted the reader to an important distinction in the conception and measurement of social attitudes. We need to elaborate on that brief note because understanding the distinction will help us better understand the criterial referents theory and the arguments presented explaining the theory and its applications. It will also help us resolve certain theoretical and measurement problems that have already arisen and will continue to arise. The expressions "bipolarity of attitudes" and "negative criteriality" of attitude objects or referents may cause difficulty. So, in this addendum we try to make the distinction between the two approaches referred to and, in the context of the discussion, also try to show what bipolarity of attitudes and negative criteriality are and how they fit into the picture.

Attitudes are usually measured by asking people to respond to a number of statements about a single attitude object, which can be a relatively specific, denotable, concrete object, like *United Nations, blacks, the church,* or an abstract idea, principle, or concept like *birth control, capital punishment, private property.* The statements are designed to assess the respondent's beliefs and feelings about the attitude object. The respondent's responses to each of the statements or items is appropriately scored. This score represents the person's attitude toward the attitude object (Thurstone, 1959, Ch. 19). Note that *the approach focuses on a single attitude object or referent.* For example, a measure of attitude toward birth control is needed. A number of statements expressing positive and negative beliefs and feelings about birth control are included in an attitude scale. A sample of individuals responds to the items of the scale in some suitable manner, such as on a 5-point summated-rating scale of agreement-disagreement, or approval-disapproval. Each respondent's scale responses are scored according to the system used, and each member of the sample receives a score, perhaps the sum or mean of the responses to the scale items. This score represents the individual's attitude toward birth control. Again, note that all the items of the attitude instrument are focused on the single attitude object *birth control*.

The approach to the measurement of social attitudes used in the research reported in this book is different: it requires respondents to react to many attitude objects or referents. Respondents' reactions to the items of the scale may be the same or similar, *but the items of the scale contain several or many different attitude objects or referents.* In other words, a respondent reacts to many aspects of social attitudes and not just one: *private property, business, religion, civil rights, equality, blacks,* for instance. The reason for the difference is that one of the objectives of the research has been to study and measure liberalism and conservatism, and they can only be adequately studied and measured through analysis of the responses of many individuals to many attitude objects and thus to many statements involving multiple social issues and attitude objects. In order to ascertain the structure of the social attitude domain, the correlations among the attitude objects must be obtained.

When statements are made in this book about the predominance of positive correlations between attitude items and the relative lack of negative correlations, a technical way of talking about the positivity principle enunciated in this chapter, the statement applies to the many-object approach. That is, it is said that in general, attitude items are positively correlated and that bipolarity, which has to be a product of negative correlations between items or subsets of items, is a relatively minor phenomenon. This means that many items have to be responded to by subjects so that the correlations among items, which contain many different attitude objects, can be analyzed. Such items and the attitude objects they contain, reflect liberal and conservative ideologies, if the domain of social attitudes is studied. The usual conception of liberalism and conservatism is that they are polarized: acceptance of liberal issues, it is thought, implies rejection of conservative issues, and vice versa. If this generally accepted view is correct, then there has to be substantial negative correlations between liberal and conservative items and subsets of items. So the statements made about the theory of criterial referents and its implications apply only when measuring social attitudes with the multiple attitude object approach.

It may well be that the statements and claims made apply also to the traditional attitude measurement approach of many statements about single attitude objects, but no such claim is made. Indeed, it may be that bipolarity is a more conspicuous phenomenon with the single attitude object approach since respondents are virtually stimulated to provide responses to both positive and negative items. If investigators include among their items statements that express acceptance of the attitude object and other statements that express its rejection, then it is possible, perhaps probable, that there will be negative correlations between the acceptance and rejection items.

We must try to explain what "negative criteriality" means because it is the basis of bipolarity when using multiple attitude objects. In order for there to be bipolarity in the data as gathered in the studies reported in this book there must be negative correlations between the attitude items used. More specifically, the negative correlations must be between liberal items and conservative items since it is highly unlikely that liberal items correlate negatively or that conservative items correlate negatively. If, for instance, the referent *religion,* a conservative referent, and *legalized abortion,* a liberal referent, are substantially and negatively correlated, then there will be bipolarity in the data, especially if several similar liberal and conservative items correlate substantially and negatively. The criterial referents theory states, however, that in general liberalism and conservatism are independent of each other, meaning that on the average the correlations between liberal and conservative items are zero or close to zero. The theory also states that under particular circumstances certain referents may be negatively criterial for substantial numbers of individuals, or even for most individuals. While such circumstances are relatively rare, they *do* occur, as will subsequently be pointed out.

Negative criteriality means that an attitudinal object arouses strong feelings of repugnance, rejection, dislike in people. *Legalized abortion,* the referent just mentioned, is a good example. At present in the Western world the word *abortion* is repugnant to many people, especially people with Catholic or fundamentalist religious sentiments. For such people *legalized abortion* is negatively criterial. *Private property* is another example. For conservatives of the Western world *private property* is positively criterial: they hold it in high esteem, even venerate it. To communists, however, *private property* is negatively criterial. It and what it represents are strongly disapproved. Indeed, it must be destroyed, or at least converted to public property. If there is a substantial number of radicals of the left in a sample, then there will be negative correlations between *private property,* a conservative referent, and liberal referents like *socialized medicine, Social Security,* and *civil rights.*

Another condition that can produce legitimate negative criteriality and bipolarity is when social conditions are such as to make certain referents more criterial than they ordinarily may be. ("Legitimate" here means not artifactual, not due to ipsative measurement, reverse scoring, or other such procedure.) For example, a few years ago *busing, integration,* and *blacks* may have become more negatively criterial than usual for many Bostonians. *Abortion* is today probably such a referent in the U.S. and Western Europe. It has become negatively criterial for many people, especially people of fundamentalist beliefs, as indicated earlier. Other contemporary issues of high negative criteriality may be evolution, hereditary intelligence, testing, and equality. There are, however, few such issues and referents that become negatively criterial. For the most part people will respond positively to the referents that are criterial to them: liberals to liberal referents and conservatives to conservative referents. The occasions and circumstances for very high negative criteriality, in short, are rare—perhaps fortunately.

It is of course possible to combine the two approaches. An investigator can use a number of items expressing acceptance and rejection for each of several referents. Then each subject of a sample can conceivably receive scores on each of the referents. In such a case the probability of negative correlations between liberal and conservative referents may be greater than in the many attitude objects approach. The measurement method, however, would be cumbersome. Quite large numbers of items would be required, more items, perhaps, than can be conveniently handled. To my knowledge such an approach has not been used except with only a limited number of attitude objects or referents. And it is possible that even if it were feasible to use, the positivity principle would operate and substantial negative correlations would again appear only occasionally.

4 Methodology[1]

Why devote a chapter to methodology—"mere methodology," as some might say? There are two reasons. First, all research stands or falls on the adequacy of its methodology. Adequate methodology is, in other words, a necessary but not sufficient condition of the empirical validity of reported results and the value of the conclusions drawn from the results. The research reported in this book is particularly vulnerable to methodological inadequacies for reasons that will become apparent later. Readers will of course reach their own conclusions on the adequacy of the reported results and conclusions. In order to do so, they should have the methodological bases to help make their judgments.

Second, and closely related, the nature of the research and the research methodology are vulnerable and controversial. If one does an experiment and uses analysis of variance, F tests, and some measures of the magnitude of experimental effects, the method and analysis are fairly clear-cut—though of course not without pitfalls and controversial technical points. One usually tests one's results against the null hypothesis, or some other alternative hypothesis, and if the results are statistically significant and measures of relational magnitude are substantial enough, one can interpret the data with a fair degree of assurance. In most of the research of this book, however, the factor analytic methodology that must

---

[1] Some readers may find the methodological discussion of this chapter unappealing, even dull. If so, its reading can be omitted. But such omission may result in lack of clear understanding of what follows. I suggest, therefore, that the chapter at least be used selectively to help clear up points in later chapters.

be used to test the structural hypotheses lacks the relatively clear-cut quality of experimental research and its accompanying tight design and statistical tests. One is dealing with structural methods that have many complex facets that often elude the precision that one would like to have. This does not mean that they are wrong or unimportant. It simply means that they are more complex and harder to deal with.

When we have to "test," for example, the factors of an attitude item factor analysis for their conformity to the prescriptions of a theory, how do we do it? We specify the theoretical expectations and then examine the factors to determine their conformity to the expectations. But an uncomfortable amount of individual judgment has to be used, not always the best scientific way to test a theory. Nevertheless, it has to be done and done as objectively as possible. What does one do about errant factor loadings that, though minor, do not quite fit into the "pure" theoretical picture? There *are* answers. Replication, for example. If an errant factor loading does not appear in a replication, then its first appearance need not be taken too seriously. Fortunately, more objective methods of assessing the fit of factor analytic results to theoretical models have recently been devised. We discuss and apply one of the best of these, analysis of covariance structures, later and in Chapter 10.

Another methodological problem, though fortunately not as difficult a one, is the measurement of attitudes. Attitude measurement is one of the outstanding psychological accomplishments of the twentieth century, along with intelligence testing, projective testing, sociometry, and personality measurement. The remarkable progress made in the early years of attitude measurement has not always been equaled in its later applications. There has been marked lack of theoretical development and often unquestioning use of what may be questionable practices, both in measurement and analysis. The implications of the criterial referents theory require that measurement be at least such as to allow factors that may underlie attitude responses to emerge from obtained data. An ipsative method of measurement[2] and questionable scoring practice can both prejudice the results of factor analysis, because they can introduce artifactual and spurious (usually negative) correlation between the items of an attitude scale. Other methodological factor analytic difficulties in at-

---

[2] Ipsative measurement means that all individuals who have responded to a measure have the same mean and the same standard deviation. Rank-ordering a set of objects, for instance, is an ipsative procedure: no matter how the persons of a sample rank the set of objects, each person has the same mean and standard deviation. (See Kerlinger, 1973, pp. 508–509.) In general, ipsative procedures yield measures that are unsuitable for factor analysis because there are systematic dependencies among items and thus correlations due to the procedure itself.

titude study are interpreting unrotated factors (fortunately a dying practice), extracting too many factors, reporting all variables or items in a factor as negative when in fact predominantly negative signs in a factor are an artifact of the analytic rotation method, and neglecting to check factor solutions against the correlation matrix from which they came.

The purpose of this chapter, then, is to describe and discuss the methodology used to test the criterial referents theory. Most of the studies to be reported used similar observations and data analysis. We present the rationale and purpose of the methodology and also discuss certain difficulties that may affect the interpretation of the data.

An example alluded to above may help to clarify further the reason for devoting a chapter to methodology. In the early days of attitude study, especially in England, the factors yielded by factor analysis of attitude scales and items were reported and interpreted without rotation. It is of course possible to interpret factor analytic results in several ways. One can rotate factors or not rotate them: one solution is in a mathematical sense equivalent to any other solution. The same information is contained in a rotated or an unrotated matrix. The trouble is that rotated and unrotated matrices can usually be interpreted quite differently. More serious, unrotated solutions of factor analyses can lead to distorted conceptions of what the data of a study say.

The unrotated factors yielded by, say, the principal factors method (Harman, 1976, Ch. 8) are characterized by a large amount of variance of the correlation matrix extracted by the first factor, often much larger than that of any other factor, leading sometimes to the conclusion that this first factor is a "general factor." But the matrix of correlations may not contain a general factor, and interpretation of such a first factor in attitude study as a general factor may be quite incorrect. It amounts to interpreting a methodological artifact as a substantive finding. By definition, the first factor extracts the largest amount of variance. In some research circumstances, of course, it may be legitimate to interpret unrotated factors, but it is misleading to do so in the attitude research we are concerned with. After rotation, some substantial portion of the variance of the first factor will spread to other factors, hopefully in agreement with the factors that are actually inherent in the correlation matrix.

STRUCTURE

The basic purpose of the methodology to be discussed is of course to provide tests of aspects of the criterial referents theory. Since the theory is essentially structural, analytic methodology must be directed toward assessing predicted structures. Therefore we must sidetrack the discussion of methodology to grasp what "structure" is and to define it for our purpose.

"Structure" is a troublesome word because it is hard to define clearly and unambiguously. The "structure" of a building is easy to grasp: "the steel and concrete frame on which the various building parts are supported" is one way to characterize it. But something is missing, and it is the missing part that is really important: the relations among the constituent parts of the building. When we talk about the "structure" of psychological traits, of intelligence, or of attitudes, however, knowing what we mean is more difficult.

A *structure,* then, is a framework, a design, an organization, a configuration of elements related in some specifiable way. The essence of the concept is that a structure is defined by the relations among the parts of the structure. The structure of a building was just mentioned. A tree is a complex mixture of wood, bark, leaves, and sap. Its structure lies in the relations of the size, texture, shape, and mass of the parts. We can talk, even, of the "plan" of the tree, or its configuration, its scheme, all terms that seek to express "structure."

The most general and powerful way to express a structure is mathematical: through systems of equations. A set of equations and its terms more or less precisely describe the relations of a structure. One of the simplest of such structures is expressed in a regression equation in which, say, two independent variables, X_1 and X_2, predict a dependent variable, Y:

$$Y = a_1X_1 + a_2X_2$$

where a_1 and a_2 are so-called regression weights obtained from a regression analysis of the data of a number of individuals whose X_1 and X_2 scores (on two tests, say) have been obtained. The solved equation, for example, $Y = .60X_1 + .40X_2$, expresses the "structure" of the observed data, or the relations among the two independent variables and the dependent variable. The structure, in other words, is a system of relations.

Similarly, in factor analysis a set of simultaneous equations—many more than in the simple regression model above—in which the X's are measure of variables (tests, items) and the a's are factor loadings (see Appendix A), expresses the relations among the X's and thus the structure of the observed data. When it is possible to write a set of equations in some such manner, we have a structure. In factor analysis such a structure is naturally enough called a factor structure. The mathematical equations are a succinct way to express the relations of the factor analytic structure of the data. In Chapter 10 we use a rather complex approach, called analysis of covariance structures, that explicitly studies the structure of actual data by specifying the hypothesized relations in the data through systems of equations. The hypothesized structure, or set of relations implied by the criterial referents theory, is then tested against the structure yielded by actual data. We will hopefully make these abstract ideas more concrete and meaningful as we proceed.

The structure of attitudes is the relations among the elements of attitudes. What these elements are can be argued. In this book they are defined as the referents of attitudes. So the structure of attitudes is defined as the lower- and higher-order relations among social attitude referents. These relations are indicated by the correlations among referents themselves and among sets or clusters of referents. If the correlations among single referents were all close to zero, there would be, in effect, "no structure," or absence of structure. If the correlations break down into two sets of clusters, *A* and *B,* say, then there is a two-dimensional structure. A possible larger or second-order structure might in part be defined by the correlation between the *A* and *B* clusters.

In sum, then, the "structure of attitudes" means the relations among the basic elements of attitudes, and, in this book, the basic elements are attitude referents: *equality, women's liberation, civil rights, capitalism, law and order, religious education, morality,* for example. Actually, however, more is meant by structure, and in a later chapter this further meaning, the sense of "structure" in the minds of individuals, will be discussed. As we will see, it is an extension, or perhaps an elaboration, of the conception of structure discussed here, which is a conception derived from the responses of many individuals to many attitude stimuli (statements and referents). It is, in short, a conception of structure closely tied to factor analytic reasoning and method. That is, the "structure" is delineated by the factors or clusters of referents obtained from the factor analysis of attitude scales and items responded to by large numbers of individuals. The word "structure" will be used again and again in this book. In most of it, the meaning will be the rather lean meaning just given of sets of correlations among referents and sets of referents.

An Example of Structure

Let us get a better grip on "structure" with an example. The example will hopefully illustrate what is meant by structure and also serve as an introduction to the factor analytic methodology to be described later. Suppose that a number of individuals have responded to four attitude referents: *civil rights, socialized medicine, free enterprise,* and *private property.* The first two are liberal *(L)* referents and the second two, conservative *(C).* We wish to discover the "structure" behind these referents. Also suppose that the correlations among the four referents, calculated

TABLE 4.1
Correlations Among Four Social Attitude Referents

	civil rights	socialized medicine	free enterprise	private property
civil rights	1.00	.91	-.15	.04
socialized medicine		1.00	-.23	-.11
free enterprise			1.00	.81
private property				1.00

over the several subjects, are those given in Table 4.1.[3] Although we know that the structure probably consists of two factors, suppose further that we don't know this and wish to "discover" the structure.

The "structure" is immediately apparent. Since the first two items correlate highly with each other ($r = .91$) and not with the third and fourth items (mostly low negative r's), and since the third and fourth items also correlate highly with each other ($r = .81$) and not with the first and second items, there are two factors relatively orthogonal to each other. Factor analysis of the correlation matrix indeed shows this to be so. The rotated factor matrix is given in Table 4.2: *civil rights* and *socialized medicine* have high loadings (italicized) on Factor *A* and *free enterprise* and *private*

TABLE 4.2
Rotated Factor Matrix Obtained from Factor Analysis
of Correlation Matrix of Table 4.1

	Factors	
Items	A	B
civil rights	.94	.13
socialized medicine	.94	.00
free enterprise	-.25	.83
private property	-.10	.87

---

[3]The correlations are unrealistic. It is highly unlikely that we would obtain the high r's of .91 and .81 between attitude items, or even scales. They illustrate the points being made, however. It is also unlikely that the factors derived from these correlations would be so clearly orthogonal. We use the word "orthogonal" liberally in this book. It means at right angles, that is, factors *A* and *B* of Table 4.2 and Figure 4.1 are orthogonal to each other. If the plotted values of the factor loadings of the referents of *A* and *B*, for instance .94 and .13, as in Figure 4.1, cling closely to the two axes with few plotted points elsewhere, the factors are said to be orthogonal or uncorrelated. Of course, the axes are orthogonal or at right angles to each other—which means, too, that the correlation between them is zero. Factors can also be "oblique." This means roughly that axes through their plotted points are less than or more than 90 degrees. In this case the correlations between the factors are greater than or less than zero. For a more detailed but relatively simple explanation of these matters, see Kerlinger (1979, Ch. 12).

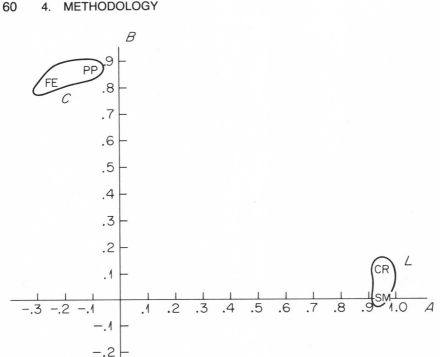

FIG. 4.1

property have high loadings on Factor *B*. The remaining loadings (− .25 and − .10 on *A* and .13 and .00 on *B*) are quite low and can be discounted, though not ignored. We also plot the results of Table 4.2 in Figure 4.1 by using two orthogonal axes labeled *A* and *B* and plotting the ordered pairs of factor loadings. (The initials of the referents are used in the figure.)

The two tables and the graph of this hypothetical example tell the same structural story. They are also much like the tables and graph obtained from actual data given in Chapter 3. The correlation matrix talks directly to the issue: the *r*'s express all the relations among all four referents. In this fictitious example it is easy to see the structure because the pattern of the *r*'s is clear. In actual correlation matrices, however, it is rarely this clear, and it is almost always necessary to determine the structure through factor analysis. The factor matrix also expresses the relations among the referents. (It is possible to recover an approximation of the correlation matrix from the factor matrix.) It tells us that the first two referents are high on Factor *A* and low on Factor *B*, and the opposite for the third and fourth referents. The relations are here expressed in a more succinct and interpretable form than in the correlation matrix.

The relations are also expressed in Figure 4.1; the ordered pairs of Table 4.2 plotted on the two axes show the structure. Although the graph expresses the same relations that are in the correlation matrix of Table 4.1 and the rotated factor matrix of Table 4.2, it does so in a way that makes the relation between the structure of the attitudes and the correlations among the four items quite clear. *Civil rights* (CR) and *socialized medicine* (SM) are close together high on axis *A* and low on *B,* and *free enterprise* (FE) and *private property* (PP) are close together high on axis *B* and low on *A*. The two sets, call them *L* and *C* because of the liberal and conservative nature of the referents associated with them, are far apart from each other close to orthogonal axes *A* and *B*. The whole plot, in short, expresses the underlying structure of the correlations of Table 4.1.

This is the major sense in which "structure" is used in this book. It means sets of relations among the correlations of attitude items or scales. To be sure, the structures we will talk about will be more complex, almost always more complex than the structure of Figure 4.1. Nevertheless, they are all relations among the attitudinal elements under study—statement items, referent items, scales, even factors themselves. Structures can thus be succinctly described as systematic relations among the elements and sets of elements under study. Obviously we can't study just any relations and any structures. We even impose the structure, in a sense. We test the deduced implications of theory structurally by choosing and using appropriate methodology. The ultimate criterion of both the empirical validity of the theory we're testing *and* the methodology is the correspondence between the deduced or predicted structures and the structures produced by the data. This, then, is the core of the factor analytic methodology.

ROUTINE PSYCHOMETRIC ANALYSIS

General Statistics, Reliabilities, and *L - C* Correlations

In most of the studies to be reported certain analyses of the data were routinely done. The means and standard deviations of all items used were calculated, as were the means and standard deviations of the liberalism *(L)* and conservatism *(C)* subscales (see below). In published reports only the statistics of the subscales have been reported. In addition, three, sometimes four, different kinds of reliability estimates were calculated. The four kinds of coefficients were: odd-even, average *r* (Guilford, 1954, pp. 359–360), Cronbach's (1951) alpha, and repeat reliabilities. Alpha coefficients have usually been reported in published studies. When we talk about the reliability of attitude scales in this book we usually mean the reliability reflected by the internal consistency coefficient estimate alpha. Occasionally, however, repeat reliability estimates are reported. They will be specifically designated as such. The correlations between the *L* and *C* subscales were also calculated and reported. (An example was given in Table 3.1, Chapter 3.)

The reasons for calculating and reporting these routine statistics are obvious and, with one exception, need not be discussed here. The exception is the correlation between the *L* and *C* subscales. One of the "demands" of the criterial referents theory is that there should be a close-to-zero correlation between *L* and *C* since the theory says that the two dimensions are relatively orthogonal. If the theory is "correct," then the *L - C* correlations should be low and usually negative.

Item Analysis

The analysis of items was also routine, but more complex. Item-total correlations were always calculated, *L* items with *L* totals and *C* items with *C* totals. What is the justification for using the separate *L* and *C* totals? Why not the totals of all the items? Since it has been found in a number of research studies that *L* and *C* are virtually independent dimensions or factors, it is reasonable to calculate item-total correlations separately for the two dimensions. But how does one know the *L* and *C* character of the items? Most of the referent items were obtained from or suggested by a variety of references on liberalism and conservatism (see below for references), from political speeches, editorials, existing attitude scales, and knowledge of liberal and conservative social issues. The criterion used for labeling an item-total correlation satisfactory was .35. In most of the studies the item-total correlations were fortunately greater than .40. When a study is summarized and nothing is said about item-total correlations, it means that they were all, or almost all, satisfactory. When item-total *r*'s were not satisfactory, this will be indicated.

SCALES, ITEMS, AND ITEM SELECTION AND WRITING

The items used in the scales and *Q* sorts of the studies were of two kinds: statements and referents. A statement item is the usual kind of declarative sentence in which an attitude-relevant proposition or statement is given to which subjects can respond with varying degrees of approval or disapproval, support or no support, positive feeling or negative feeling. Here are two examples, the first a conservative item and the second a liberal item:

The well-being of a nation depends mainly on its business and industry.

Society should be quicker to throw out old ideas and traditions and to adopt new thinking and customs.

Statement items have been used in most published research.[4] Their worth has been well-demonstrated.

A new type of item has been used in several of the studies to be discussed and in the research of Wilson (1973). This is the referent item. As pointed out in Chapter 3, referents are single attitude-related words— *religion, capitalism, desegregation,* for example—or attitude-related short phrases or expressions—*teaching of spiritual values, children's needs, economic reform.* Judging from the available evidence, they are reliable and valid. They are certainly economical. Many more referent items than statement items can be administered in a given time period.

A difficult question is the interpretability or ambiguity of such items. It can be said, for instance, that responses to items like *competition, profits,* and *civil rights* cannot be consistent because such items can be variously interpreted and depend on the contexts in which they appear. Even more specific items, such as *blacks, labor unions,* and *money,* also depend on context. True. But the answer is fortunately simple, pragmatic, and statistical. They work and they work well. The reliabilities and item-total correlations have been mostly satisfactory, even highly satisfactory. Evidently there is considerable consensus of subject interpretation (over many people) of such items. If there were no common core of meaning in the referents, that is, if respondents did indeed interpret the referents in different and idiosyncratic ways, then systematic relations among them could not emerge. In short, the intercorrelations among them would be virtually zero, reliabilities would be low, and consistent factors could not emerge. We will see that this is far from the case.

Items were of course written or selected for each study separately, though many of the same items were used in several studies. We describe here the principles used in writing and selecting items and the criteria used for inclusion of items in scales and *Q* sorts.

---

[4]The interested reader can find many attitude scales and items in the anthologies of Robinson, Rusk, and Head (1968), Robinson and Shaver (1969), and Shaw and Wright (1967). These authors also provide the backgrounds of the scales and the research evidence on their reliability and validity.

In the beginning of research on educational attitudes (Kerlinger, 1956a), a collection of some 250 statements on educational philosophy and practice were written based on study of books and articles on the philosophy of education, educational practice, and related fields (Beale, 1936; Brubacher, 1962; Curti, 1935; Dewey, 1916; National Society for the Study of Education, 1955). This pool was used as a source to construct a Q sort (Kerlinger, 1956a, 1958). The data from Q studies were used in part to construct summated-rating and other types of scales to measure attitudes toward education (Kerlinger 1961; Kerlinger & Kaya, 1959) The criteria used for selection of items were much the same in all studies. They were discussed earlier and are discussed again later.

The method used to help select items for the educational attitude scales from the data obtained with the Q sorts is effective though not well-known. Using the persons factors obtained in the Q studies, factor arrays were calculated for each factor. The procedure was suggested by Stephenson (1953) and consists essentially in using those individuals who have high factor loadings on a factor and obtaining the sum of the weighted Q values over these individuals for each item of the Q sort. Those items with high factor sums are considered likely candidates for inclusion in attitude scales. What the method amounts to is calculating factor arrays, which are essentially Q sorts expressing the essence of the persons factors, and using the items high on the arrays for conventional scales.[5] Two of the later educational attitude scales, ES-VI and ES-VII, can be found in Appendix B.

After a scale had been constructed with the aid of the factor arrays, its items were used and analyzed in the usual way. Scale items constructed without the aid of Q sorts and Q factor arrays had much the same genesis as the Q items. For both social attitude statement and referent scales references on liberalism and conservatism, political theory, and social philosophy (Burke, 1955; Hartz, 1955; Huntington, 1957; Kirk, 1960; McClosky, 1958; Orton, 1945; Rossiter, 1962; Viereck, 1962; Watkins, 1957) were studied for suggestions for items and for referents. Existing attitude scales were also studied for item ideas. After the publication of three attitude scale anthologies in the late 1960s (Robinson, Rusk, & Head, 1968; Robinson & Shaver, 1969; Shaw & Wright, 1967), suggestions for items were also gotten from them. Other sources of both statements and referents were newspaper articles, especially editorials, magazine articles, political speeches, and certain propaganda materials,

---

[5]On factor arrays, see Stephenson (1953, pp. 176–179). The method is highly useful but little known. Recently, Bem and Funder (1978) used a similar method they called "template matching," which lacked the Stephenson factor analytic basis and ignored the ipsative nature of item values. Further methodological details of Q methodology are given below.

as well as personal knowledge of the social and educational issues involved.

Items were categorized, when possible, as liberal *(L)* or conservative *(C)*, and equal number of *L* and *C* items were included in scales for balance and item-analytic purposes. In educational attitude scales, the categories were progressive *(P)* and traditional *(T)*. In calculating item-total correlations, appropriate totals have to be used, as mentioned earlier. If the criterial referents theory is approximately correct, then one cannot use the total of all items; one must use the *L* and *C* (or *P* and *T*) totals. This appeared to be good policy because the correlations of items with *L* and *C* totals, *L* items with *L* totals and *C* items with *C* totals, were usually substantial. The reliabilities of the separate scales were also satisfactory.

It was realized at an early stage that the *L* and *C* categorizations and calculating item-total correlations with *L* and *C* totals could bias results in favor of the theory. For example, if a supposed *C* item did not correlate substantially with the *C* total it might be eliminated. But it might be one of the items whose presence in a factor analysis could help to upset the theory. Eliminating it removes the possibility, in other words, of disconfirming the theory. I concede the grave danger of such an item selection procedure. But some item selection procedure is of course always necessary. I have guarded against the danger by including all items in factor analyses, except for those items that are obviously poor: they correlated close to zero with all other items, for instance. If an item correlated negatively and consistently with other items it was not eliminated. Most items used have correlated either with the *L* or the *C* totals. They sometimes have correlated with both, depending on sample characteristics and the items themselves. If items do not correlate with other items, providing there is a wide variety of items, then it is doubtful that they are measuring social attitudes, though they may be measuring them poorly. Some examples of "poor" referent items from past research are: *rationality, character, Soviet Union* (except in Spain), *modern society, civilization, culture, social classes, the past.*

TYPES OF MEASUREMENT INSTRUMENTS

Most of the research testing the theory has used standard instruments that have been similar in format though differing in numbers of and kinds of items (from 30 to 80 items). The two major instruments have been summated-rating scales (Likert scales) and *Q* sorts, though other kinds of instruments have occasionally been used (pair comparisons and other forced-choice items).

Summated-Rating Scales

The summated-rating scales used in most of the studies were 7-point scales obtained by asking subjects to express varying degrees of approval-disapproval, from approve (or agree) very strongly through disapprove (or disagree) very strongly. Examples of both statement and referent scales, with their instructions, are given in Appendix B. The decision to use summated-rating scales was based almost exclusively on two considerations. First, summated-rating scales provide data suitable for factor analysis of items. Other types of scales almost all use some form of forced-choice items: rank-order tetrads or pentads, choices among tetrads or pentads, and so on. The forced-choice feature in items introduces spurious negative correlation among items, and the assumption of independence of responses to items is systematically violated.

The second consideration came from research designed in part to study the comparative characteristics of different scale types (Kerlinger 1961). The results of the research showed that forced-choice scales did indeed produce negative correlations among items and the summated-rating scales did not. In another earlier study (Kerlinger & Kaya, 1959), in which a summated-rating scale and a forced-choice scale were used, many more substantial negative correlations were found among the items of the forced-choice scale as a function of the forced-choice feature than among the items of the summated-rating scale. Subsequent experience with summated-rating scales, moreover, has shown them to be reliable and factorially valid.

A major argument against the use of summated-rating scales is that their items are subject to response set (Bass, 1956; Couch & Keniston, 1960; Cronbach, 1946, 1950; Crowne & Marlowe, 1964; Edwards, 1958; Edwards & Walsh, 1964; Guilford, 1954). If such items are used, it is said that some sort of "corrective" procedure has to be followed. The most common procedure appears to be "reversed items." The idea is that response set, for example, the tendency to agree with all positively worded items no matter what their content, can be counteracted by having half the items in a scale phrased negatively. The negative items can be virtually direct "reversals" of the positively worded items, or they can express ideas different from but logically the opposite of those of the positive items.

For example, Bass (1956) used reversed F items to avoid acquiescence response set in the F Scale (Adorno, Frenkel-Brunswik, Levinson, & Sanford, 1950). An original F Scale item and its Bass reversal are:

People can be divided into two distinct classes, the weak and the strong. (F)

People cannot be divided into two distinct classes, the weak and the strong. (Reversed F)

This pair of items was deliberately chosen because it is so poor: the second item (the reversal) is psychologically not the opposite of the first item. People talk and think like the first item, but hardly like the second.[6]

The evidence on the strengths and weaknesses of using reversed items is mixed. In this book the whole idea of item reversal is rejected on psychological and attitude theoretical grounds. It is possible that some items can be successfully reversed. The basic condition is that a reversed item has to have the same psychological meaning to respondents but in the opposite direction. Accomplishing this is not easy. The reversed item can too often have a different psychological meaning from the original item. The original F Scale item given above is a strong item: it expresses a sentiment felt by many people, and it expresses it well. The reversed item, however, is not as likely to be said. The original item, in other words, measures authoritarianism, as intended, but the reversal probably does not measure anti-authoritarianism, or whatever the opposite of authoritarianism is. In any case, the use of reversed items is psychologically and psychometrically questionable and is inconsistent with the theory of criterial referents (see Kerlinger, 1967a).

While conceding the possible influence of response set bias, I believe that such bias does not and has not seriously affected the factor analytic evidence to be described later. (See Rorer, 1965.) If it indeed operates, it is a much less potent source of variance in the attitude measures used than the substantive attitudinal sources of variance. If response set is a potent source of variance, then it should, in factor analysis, emerge as a factor or factors. But it has not done so. Or it should somehow interfere with the emergence of clear substantive factors. It has again not done so. I have little doubt that the mean levels of items, particularly liberal and progressive items and especially referent items, some of which tend to be socially desirable, or socially undesirable, are affected. But this general upward (or downward) bias has evidently had little effect on the factors and factor structures to be reported. In any case, reversed items have not been used in any form, nor has reversed scoring been used. Seven-point summated rating scales were used for all items. Negative sentiments toward statements or referents could be expressed on such scales in which cases low scores would be assigned. But in no case were scale values reversed to indicate a conservative or a liberal position. Items, in other

---

[6]Later we examine the less naive and more widely practiced reversal of the *scoring* of items. The argument to be presented then also rejects this practice on theoretical and empirical grounds.

words, were always either liberal or conservative but not both. *Desegra-gation,* for example, is a liberal item, and high scores indicate approval or positive sentiment and low scores indicate disapproval or negative senti-ment. Even if there are strong negative sentiments of conservatives against desegregation or means taken to achieve it (e.g., busing), the items were not reversed and then conceived as conservative. Evidence that the scales used were not affected by common forms of response bias will be presented later in the book. (Results of studies of response set in relation to attitude statement and referent scales are reported in Appen-dix C.)

Q Methodology and *Q* Sorts

Because knowledge of *Q* methodology is not widespread, a brief descrip-tion of *Q* and its purpose in the context of the present chapter may be helpful. Scientifically, *Q* is probably most helpful for exploring mea-surement domains and for providing factor arrays or *Q* profiles that ex-press the essence of persons factors. In one recommended procedure, subjects are chosen for "known" characteristics—in Chapter 6 known educational progressives or traditionalists. These individuals—20 to 40 of them, say—sort a deck of cards, each one of which presumably expresses a domain of measurement, for instance, liberalism and conservatism, in-troversion and extraversion, social values, political figures, aesthetic ob-jects.

A *Q* sort ordinarily has 40 to 80 or more items. The items can express one or more factors, as just indicated. Subjects are asked to sort the cards into six, seven, or more piles, the numbers in the piles representing a quasi-normal distribution: from, say, two cards at each end of the distri-bution to 10 to 12 cards in the middle, with appropriate numbers in be-tween. One would then have a rank-order continuum from "Most Approve" to "Least Approve" (or other instruction), the items at the ends, with varying degrees of approval and disapproval between the ex-tremes. Here is the *Q* distribution of the 80-item educational attitudes *Q* sort used in QED-1 and QED-2, studies to be described in Chapter 6:

Approve									*Disapprove*	
Most									*Most*	
2	4	6	9	12	14	12	9	6	4	2
10	9	8	7	6	5	4	3	2	1	0

The numbers 0 through k (k = number of piles minus 1) are assigned to the pile items as sorted by each subject. In the *Q* distribution above, the numbers above the line are the numbers of items in each pile and the numbers below the line are the values assigned.

The Q values of each person are correlated with the Q values of every other person yielding an N by N correlation matrix, N being the number of subjects. This matrix is factor analyzed and each person has rotated factor loadings on each factor. The "nature" of the factors is judged by the known characteristics of the persons loaded on them as well as by the items high on the factor arrays (see below). Examples will be given in discussing the results of QED-1 and QED-2 in Chapter 6. One judges from such factor analytic (and other) results whether the "theory" or measurement variables built into the Q sort have empirical validity.

An important contribution of Stephenson is the structured Q sort. A structured Q sort has categories (of items) built into it, the categories being derived from a theoretical or measurement framework. Stephenson derived the idea of constructing and using structured Q sorts from analysis of variance, especially factorial analysis of variance, paradigms for the analysis of data. For example, an educational attitude Q sort (Kerlinger, 1956a) had 80 items with two categories, one of which, Permissive-Restrictive (the other category based on areas of educational activity, and discovered to have little importance), seemed to express a basic dichotomy in educational thinking and practice. Later, this categorization became Progressive-Traditional. In other words, the Q sort was structured into two kinds of items, permissive and restrictive, and analyses of individuals' sorts took statistical advantage of the categorization (with analysis of variance).

Another and perhaps better example was a social attitudes Q sort with two categories: Liberal-Conservative and Abstract-Specific (Kerlinger, 1972a). It followed Stephenson's principle of a structured Q sort modeled after a two-by-two factorial analysis of variance. In this case there would be two main effects, Liberal-Conservative and Abstract-Specific, and an interaction effect of the two main variables. The structures of both Q sorts and the actual analysis of variance data obtained with them will be further explained in Chapters 6 and 7.

An important final step is to calculate factor arrays (Stephenson, 1953, pp. 176–179). This is a sort of regression averaging procedure, which amounts to calculating weighted averages for all the Q items using the Q values of the persons with the highest factor loadings on each factor. One uses these averages to create "new" Q sorts that presumably are clear expressions of the factors. One has, in other words, highly useful and powerful descriptions of persons factors which are, in effect, "pure" expressions of the factors. These factor arrays or factor Q sorts can be advantageously used in other research or practical situations. One can correlate the Q sorts of new subjects, for example, with the Q arrays to categorize the new subjects. The reader will find extended discussions of *Q* methodology in Stephenson (1953) and in Kerlinger (1973, Ch. 34).

SUBJECTS, SAMPLES, AND ADMINISTRATION OF INSTRUMENTS

Most subjects used in the studies have been graduate students of education, especially in the larger samples. Other subjects in the United States have included undergraduates and people outside the university. In the European study to be reported later, undergraduates and a random sample of the citizens of The Netherlands were used. The reasons for using graduate students of education predominantly were as follows. (1) Their large numbers and widespread availability made it possible to obtain the large samples required for factor analysis. (2) The original studies of attitude factor structure were of educational attitudes. (3) Graduate students of education tend to be older, more mature, and substantially in contact with the social issues involved. Finally, and most important, their resonses to educational attitude scales have been shown to yield factor structures similar to those yielded by people outside the university (Kerlinger, 1961), and their responses to social attitude scales have appeared to be consistent enough and heterogeneous enough to produce reliable factors. In short, samples of graduate students of education, many of whom were teachers and educational administrators, have been for the most part highly satisfactory respondents.

An important question arises: Have the samples of respondents used yielded results similar to those that would have been obtained from non-students? The answer appears to be Yes, but it is not possible to so state unambiguously because little research has been directed to the question. In the study of educational attitudes cited above, the answer was clearly Yes: the graduate students of education produced a factor structure substantially the same as that produced by a sample of people outside the university (clerks, nurses, and housewives). No direct evidence on the factor structures of social attitudes produced by graduate students of education and people outside the university is available, with one exception. The factor structures yielded by graduate students of education in the United States and that yielded by younger students of psychology in Spain and The Netherlands were similar enough to know that some factors were much alike, especially second-order factors (Kerlinger, Middendorp, & Amón, 1976). (Second-order factors are defined and explained in the next section of this chapter.) In addition, the social attitude factor structures obtained from the responses of a random sample of The Netherlands were compared to those obtained from American graduate students of education. One would hardly expect high congruence, especially because a random sample of a whole country is hardly a desirable sample for factor analysis purposes (Thurstone, 1947, p. xii). Nevertheless, there was sufficient factor congruence in structure and substance to warrant comparable assertions from the two samples.

Whenever possible the principle of replication was followed. That is, it was not considered satisfactory to administer Q sorts and scales to only one sample. At least two, and often three, samples were used in any one study. Although the results of the analyses of all samples will not be reported (for space reasons), replications that produced essentially the same results will be mentioned. In some cases where the results from two different samples were highly similar, the data of the samples were merged to form larger samples for greater factor analytic stability. In the latest studies, which were cross-cultural (Kerlinger, 1978; Kerlinger et al., 1976), replication took a general form. Since languages and cultures differ in social ideas and issues, it was necessary not so much to translate the instrument used as it was to "transform" it in the context of the languages and cultures.

In sum, the theory was tested using three Q sorts, five statement attitude scales, and three referents scales, including in all some 200 items, in five states of the United States, and three countries of Western Europe.[7] The breadth of attitude content, then, was considerable, and the subjects and their locales were varied.

FACTOR ANALYSIS

First-Order Factor Analysis

In the earlier Q studies, the centroid method of factor extraction (Thurstone, 1947, Ch. 8) and graphical rotations of factors were used. All subsequent factor analyses, except the survey analysis of covariance structures study reported in Chapter 10, used the principal factors method of factor extraction (Harman, 1976, Ch. 8), usually with squared multiple correlations, SMC's or R^2's (Guttman, 1956), but sometimes with highest r's, as communality estimates.[8]

---

[7] More attitude scales were actually used than indicated above because different types of scales were constructed and tried out. In this book, however, the results obtained with the scales used in published studies are emphasized.

[8] There were two situations in which R^2's were not possible to use. One was in Q methodology. The nature of Q is evidently such as to create a dependency in the R matrix, even when there are clearly two or more factors. The R^2's are then very high, preventing an adequate solution. The second situation was when a very large R matrix was analyzed. Computer time became prohibitive. Thus highest r's had to be used. With large R matrices, of course, it makes little difference what is put in the diagonal provided it is less than 1.

The number of factors to extract has of course always been a difficult problem. In the earlier studies, a crude criterion was used. If two or more factor loadings in any single unrotated factor were greater than .30 (absolute value), the factor was a candidate for inclusion. Fortunately, the faster computers and increasing availability of factor analysis programs of the 1960s and 1970s improved the situation. The method used in all later studies—except those reported in Chapter 10—was to extract a large number of factors with the principal factors method and then to use four criteria for the number of factors. (1) An eigenvalue of 1. or greater associated with a factor made it a candidate for inclusion. (2) Two or more factor loadings greater than .35 recommended consideration of a factor. (3) A relatively sharp break in the magnitudes of the eigenvalues indicated a possible stopping point of factor extraction.

The fourth criterion is really a "condition." It is usually not too difficult to decide approximately how many factors to rotate, for example, six, seven, eight, or nine. But it is often difficult to decide which of these is "correct." After the solutions have been rotated, it is possible to check a solution against the correlation matrix. One can, for instance, check the correlations behind a particular factor to determine whether the factor accurately reflects the correlations.

Suppose one has chosen nine factors, but one rotated factor seems peculiar. One notes the variable with substantial loadings and then, from the correlation matrix, copies down the intercorrelations among these variables. The rotated factor and the correlations should of course "agree": the correlations among the substantially loaded variables should also be substantial. If they are not, the factor—and perhaps that particular factor solution—must be treated with suspicion. The method is indirect, laborious, and tedious. But it seems to be the only way to be reasonably sure of a "correct" rotated factor solution. In any case, it was one of the methods often used to decide on the number of factors to have in a solution.[9]

Both orthogonal and oblique rotations were used, varimax (Kaiser, 1958) for the orthogonal and promax (Hendrickson & White, 1964) for the oblique. Although orthogonal rotations were preferred because of their greater simplicity and interpretability, oblique solutions are those reported and interpreted, especially in later studies. The reason is that it was necessary to estimate the correlations among the factors for second-order factor analysis, and to tie in the first- and second-order analyses and interpretations. Actually, the orthogonal and oblique solutions were in

---

[9]The first- and second-order factor analysis computer programs used facilitated the procedure because it was possible with them to instruct the computer to rotate 2, 3, 4, and so on factors up to a number of factors, k, all in one run. The subsequent study of the factors and comparison of solutions were obviously facilitated.

most cases quite similar. Moreover, the orthogonal solutions were used to find the range of solutions (mentioned above) in which the "correct" solution was probably embedded.

The goal of selecting the "right" number of factors and rotating the factors was simple structure (Thurstone, 1947, Ch. XIV). The rotations were analytic, of course: determined by the varimax and promax criteria. But the simple structure principle helped guide the final selection of solutions. Special care was taken with rotated negative factor loadings to be sure that they were consistent with the original correlations. These procedures are admittedly somewhat subjective, but they are better than total reliance on objective criteria that may or may not be adequate.[10]

Second-Order Factor Analysis

Discussions of higher-order factor analysis are rare. The idea is not new: Thurstone (1947, Ch. XVIII) discussed it in considerable detail many years ago. But it has not been used much, perhaps because its scientific and theoretical usefulness has not been appreciated, or perhaps because of its somewhat recondite nature.[11] Since some readers may not be familiar with second-order factor analysis, and since it is a vital part of this book's methodology, its rationale is briefly discussed.

The rather simple ideas of second-order factor analysis are expressed succinctly in Figure 4.2. Suppose we have eight tests which have been administered to a number of individuals. The tests, indicated in Figure 4.2 as arabic numerals in boxes, have been intercorrelated and four first-order factors, F_1, F_2, F_3, and F_4, extracted and obliquely rotated. Tests 1 and 2 are on Factor 1, tests 3 and 4 are on Factor 2, and so on. Obliqueness of factors of course means correlations among the factors. It is these correlations that are factor analyzed. It should be obvious why such analysis is called second-order factor analysis. When the correlations among the four first-order factors were themselves factor analyzed they yielded two second-order factors, denoted in Figure 4.2 as G_1 and G_2.

This is the basic paradigm of most of the factor analytic research to be reported in this book. Replace "Tests" with "Attitude Scales" or "Attitude Items" and the model is the same. This dual mode of analysis, given certain conditions, is a powerful one for identifying underlying dimen-

[10] For example, the well-known criterion for numbers of factors being eigenvalues 1 or greater is, strictly speaking, applicable to principal components extraction of factors (or components), which of course uses 1's in the diagonal of the correlation matrix rather than communality estimates. Moreover, solutions whose number of factors are determined by this criterion can and do have too many factors or even too few factors. (See Coan, 1964; Humphreys, 1964; Overall, 1964; Peterson, 1965.)

[11] For an excellent research use of second-order factor analysis for an important theoretical end—studying the nature of human intelligence—see Cattell (1963).

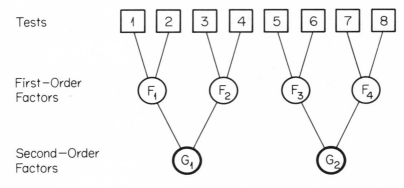

FIG. 4.2

sions or factors behind the responses of many people to attitude instruments and items. One can find the multiple first-order factors that underlie
social attitudes in the usual factor analytic way, a valuable scientific
undertaking in its own right. In the process one can learn a good deal
about both the first-order structure and the content of social attitudes.
One can, moreover, go to the deeper level of second-order dimensions or
factors. At the first order one can expect considerable diversity from
sample to sample—of both items and persons. At the second-order, one
can expect much more commonality.

Factor Analysis as a Research Method

It has been said that factor analysis is an exploratory method: researchers
explore a domain to find what variables go with what variables, what are
the factors behind tests, scales, items. Then, perhaps, they can use the
factors as variables in other research. Factors as variables should be
potent aids in explaining human behavior, more potent than the elements
from which they are derived because, properly handled, they can perhaps
account for more variance in dependent variables than the elements from
which they come. Although there is no doubt of the value of factor analysis as an exploratory method, it can also be a powerful hypothesis-testing
method (Fruchter, 1966; Mulaik, 1972, Ch. 15), as we show in the chapters that lie ahead.

We will, then, use factor analysis in two ways. First, we will try to
discover the structure and the nature of the domain of social attitudes. We
will try to identify both the first- and second-order factors that lie behind
the responses people make to attitude items and scales. In doing so, we
will also attempt to identify those factors that reliably appear in different
samples. Do Economic Conservatism, Religiosity, and Social Welfare,
for example, appear in both European and American samples? Do the

same or similar second-order factors appear in different samples and with different instruments? Part of the methodology is geared to answering such questions.

The second approach and use of factor analysis is model and hypothesis-testing. Simply put, we seek to test the implications of the criterial referents theory of attitudes by predicting the general structure and nature of both first- and second-order factors. This is done in two ways. The first is the usual extraction and rotation of factors, identification of the substance of the factors, and ascertaining whether the factors agree with the theoretical predictions. This is the method used most in the book. The second approach is newer, only having become available in the last five to ten years: the analysis of covariance structures (Jöreskog, 1978; Mulaik, 1972). We turn now to this powerful, flexible, and more objective new method.

ANALYSIS OF COVARIANCE STRUCTURES

Scientific theories imply models, and these models are structural in the sense that relations among observed and unobserved concepts or variables are specified. We should be clear what we mean by "model." The word is sometimes used to mean "theory." A model is not a theory (Brodbeck, 1968), which is a systematic attempt to explain a natural phenomenon by specifying the relations among the variables related to the phenomenon, together with pertinent definitions, assumptions, axioms, and hypotheses (Kerlinger, 1979). A theory attempts to spell out not only what is but why it is as it is. A model, on the other hand, is a "copy," plan, or scheme of the theory, or of some of its implications, in a different form or transformation. Equation 4.1, below, provides a mathematical model of some of the implications of the criterial referents theory. It is a formalization of the theory. There is an isomorphism between a theory, or part of a theory, and a model of the theory. In science, it is the models of theories that provide the framework for empirical testing. Matrix equation 4.1 (see later) gives a clear framework for testing the criterial referents theory. One subjects data to factor analysis, forces the resulting factors in the mold of the model, so to speak, and then tests the fit of a covariance (correlation) matrix produced from the modeled solution for its correspondence with the data covariance matrix. In any case, models are useful devices that enable us to express aspects of a theory succinctly, with implications for empirical testing of the theory. Models should not be mistaken for theories, however.[12]

---

[12]The term "model" is sticky. The above statement would probably not satisfy Brodbeck (1968) who has deeply analyzed the relation between theories and models and shown the complexity of the theory-model relation.

TABLE 4.3
Target Matrix Expressing the Predicted Factor Loading
Pattern of the Data of Table 4.1

| Variables | Factors[a] | |
(Items)	I	II
civil rights	1	0
socialized medicine	1	0
free enterprise	0	1
private property	0	1

[a] 1: significant factor loading; 0: near-zero loading.

In Chapter 3, Thurstone's "theory" of intelligence was briefly described: seven "primary" factors were postulated to underlie the responses of children to a large variety of mental tests and items. This is a model like that of matrix equation 4.1, below; it specifies the relations among many test stimuli: their variety and complexity can be more parsimoniously and effectively described by the seven factors Thurstone found. That such models of intelligence as Thurstone's are not usually termed "theories" does not alter their theoretical nature. They *are* explanations of the relations among variables, both observed and unobserved.

Early in this chapter—see Tables 4.1 and 4.2 and Figure 4.1—a simple fictitious attitude example was given. The correlations among four attitude items (Table 4.1) were analyzed into two factors (Table 4.2 and Figure 4.1). The "model" of this example, implied by the criterial referents theory, can be expressed in different ways. One way is to construct a so-called target matrix like the matrix of Table 4.2 indicating by 1's and 0's where the predicted factor loadings will be. Such a target matrix for that problem is given in Table 4.3. Note that the high and low factor loadings of Table 4.2 agree with the 1's which indicate predicted substantial factor loadings, and the 0's which indicate predicted near-zero loadings, of Table 4.3. The data of Table 4.2 agree with the "model" of Table 4.3.

There are other ways to express models. One can set up a hypothetical graph that looks like Figure 4.1, which is a graphic expression of the "data" of Table 4.2, a "model," if you will. This is not the usual way to do so, however. A better way is to set up the implications of the theory in the manner of Figure 4.3, which is like the diagram of Figure 4.2, above. y_1, y_2, y_3, and y_4 are the four items or "variables" of Tables 4.1 and 4.2: $y_1 = civil\ rights$, $y_2 = socialized\ medicine$, $y_3 = free\ enterprise$, and $y_4 = private\ property$. F_1 and F_2 are the two unobserved or latent variables or factors underlying the y's, and the a's represent "significant" or substantial factor loadings. The e's indicate errors or residuals. The variance of measured variables almost always includes error. Good models

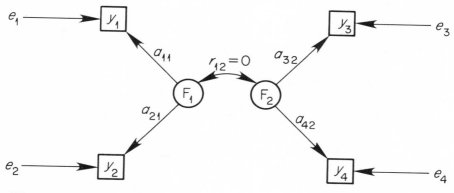

FIG. 4.3

include such errors for reasons to be discussed in the later chapter on analysis of covariance structures. The single-headed arrows indicate presumed influences, for example, the arrow from F_1 to y_1, labeled a_{11}, the factor loading in the upper left of Table 4.2, indicates that the factor F_1 "influences" y_1, and the amount of influence is a_{11}. The model of Figure 4.3 also specifies that the correlation between the two factors is zero, as the theory dictates (liberalism and conservatism are "relatively orthogonal"). The double-headed arrow indicates the correlation between two variables or, as in this case, factors.) This may of course be unrealistic, but it is nevertheless a model and its specified relations, its covariance structure, can be tested for agreement with observed data.

Still another way to express a model, as mentioned earlier, is through matrix equations. The complete model of Figure 4.3 is expressed in the following matrix equation:[13]

$$\begin{pmatrix} y_1 \\ y_2 \\ y_3 \\ y_4 \end{pmatrix} = \begin{pmatrix} a_{11} & 0 \\ a_{21} & 0 \\ 0 & a_{32} \\ 0 & a_{42} \end{pmatrix} \begin{pmatrix} F_1 \\ F_2 \end{pmatrix} + \begin{pmatrix} e_1 \\ e_2 \\ e_3 \\ e_4 \end{pmatrix} \qquad (4.1)$$

Sets of equations like 4.1 can be used to test the criterial referents theory, as will be explained in more detail in Chapter 10. In outline, the procedure amounts to estimating the a and e values (r_{12} can either be set at 0, following the theory explicitly, or its value can be calculated) using the correlation matrix, **R**, as the input data and following the model of equation 4.1. The computer program that accomplishes this (called LISREL)

---

[13] The reader unfamiliar with matrix algebra can omit this discussion without serious loss. Elementary treatments of matrix algebra can be found in many books, for instance, Harman (1976, Ch. 3), and Tatsuoka (1971, Ch. 2). The above equation can be easily read as four separate equations: $y_1 = a_{11}F_1 + e_1$, $y_2 = a_{21}F_1 + e_2$, $y_3 = a_{32}F_2 + e_3$, and $y_4 = a_{42}F_2 + e_4$.

then uses the estimated values to produce a matrix, $\mathbf{R}^*$, under the conditions specified in the model. If the model fits—and the LISREL system provides statistical tests of the adequacy of fit—the values in the matrix $\mathbf{R}^*$ are close to those of the original input matrix, $\mathbf{R}$. If the model does not fit—$\mathbf{R}$ and $\mathbf{R}^*$ are not alike—then the model is rejected, or, in other words, there is something wrong with the model, the theory, or both.

The system is more complex than this, but we leave further details to a later chapter. As expressed above, it is actually a sophisticated and powerful factor analytic method using advanced ideas of multivariate analysis and scientific hypothesis-testing of a structural kind. It does the same things that an experienced researcher would do to test structural hypotheses, as outlined earlier, but it does so more thoroughly, rigorously, and objectively. It should be clear that the two approaches are really the same; they are different in details of conception and analysis. The analysis of covariance structures will be used in Chapter 10 not only to test models like that expressed in equation 4.1, which is in effect a duality hypothesis, but also to test alternative bipolarity hypotheses.

SOME DIFFICULTIES

Some or perhaps all of the above discussion may have given the impression of a tight, neat, and orderly methodological framework for doing research and testing theory. Such an impression would be incorrect. The harmony is not simple: there are a number of augmented fourths and major sevenths. There are ragged edges and irritating obscurities. There are technical, semantic, and philosophical difficulties. So, while factor analysis and analysis of covariance structures are potent tools of the behavioral scientist, they often do not provide clear and unambiguous results. We conclude this chapter by briefly examining some of the most important difficulties.

Factor Reification and Naming Factors

One of the dangers of a method that in effect sorts or classifies things is that we may believe that the classifications and categories produced by the method are God-given. This is especially so in psychology and psychological research where we may find that certain traits cluster together, form factors, and we believe that the trait clusters are part of natural law. And once we have named the trait cluster the danger sharply increases because it seems that naming things, especially things that can't be seen, has a compelling force to make us believe that the named thing really exists and has the character the name we give it suggests. The named thing may "exist" and it may have the character its name suggests. Then, again, it may not "exist" and, even if it does, it may not be what its name suggests.

"Reification" expresses part of the problem. To "reify" means to endow an abstract concept, name, or category with virtual material existence. "Introversion-Extraversion," an abstract term expressing certain human tendencies to behave in certain ways, is endowed with a sort of life of its own apart from its creators, an almost magical power to explain human behavior. It is possible, in other words, to believe that "Introversion-Extraversion" is almost a "thing," an "entity" that directs much of people's lives and behaviors. The expression, "No wonder he did that; he's an introvert," shows the tendency.

One of the major difficulties with the theory and research discussed in this book is how to label and talk about the clusters or factors of attitudes yielded by factor analysis. Names like "Economic Conservatism," "Religiosity," "Civil Rights," and "Sexual Freedom" are used because they seem to express the apparent nature of the clusters of items yielded by factor analysis. For example, in a large American sample the referents *faith in God, religion, church, Christian,* and *teaching spiritual values* appeared as a factor. Since all the referents expressed religious ideas the factor was named "Religiosity." Is there really such an entity? When the same or similar items form a factor in the United States, Spain, and The Netherlands, does this give "Religiosity" greater weight, greater significance?

Another less easily interpreted factor that has appeared is "Sexual Freedom." Its referents in Spain were *evolution theory, equality of women, women's liberation, birth control, divorce, coeducation, freedom.* In a random sample of The Netherlands, this factor had the referents *sexual freedom, homosexuals, free abortion,* and *pornography.* In a student sample of The Netherlands, its referents were: *childless couples, homosexuals, birth control,* and, to a lesser extent, *liberalized abortion laws.* It is apparent that there is some underlying unity of attitude responses. But what is it? How should it be named? Is it indeed "Sexual Freedom"?

An even greater problem is the nature and structure of the second-order factors and their names. As we will see again and again, liberal factors, such as "Sexual Freedom" and "Social Welfare," are positively correlated and usually appear together on one second-order factor. Similarly, conservative factors like "Religiosity" and "Economic Conservatism" (*profits, money, business, capitalism,* and the like) appear together on a second-order factor. The two second-order factors have accordingly been named "Liberalism" and "Conservatism."

There seems to be little doubt, then, about the data facts: first- and second-order factors consistently appear in different samples, although often with differences. What does this mean? It means only that subjects consistently tend to agree and disagree similarly with the items of a factor. If one subject approves of *corporate industry* and another subject disapproves of it, then the first subject will be likely also to approve of *private property,* and the second subject will be likely to disapprove of *private property.* The responses of the subjects to the items of the same factor, in other words, will on the whole tend to be similar. Some will say that this does not justify naming the factor "Economic Conservatism" or anything else. Such naming can easily lead to reification, to supposing the factors have a reality they do not possess. The danger, they may continue, is even greater with second-order factors and their putative names. They are abstractions of abstractions. To call them, for example, "liberalism" and "conservatism" is, then, highly questionable. Besides, liberalism and conservatism are old-fashioned terms that have little correspondence to the complex multiplicity of modern economic, political, and social life.

This position does not lack validity. But it's too restrictive. An important part of science is categorizing things and naming the categories. After all, we have to name variables. And, besides, theories must be couched in variable names. Nevertheless, we have to be very careful not to give our factor names, especially the second-order names of liberalism and conservatism, any surplus meaning that can lead us astray.

Technical Problems

Factor analysis has several technical problems, a few of which bear on the results and conclusions of our study. There are unfortunately no clear-cut and completely satisfactory answers to any of them. Indeed, some of the answers can even be matters of taste! The most important of these problems in the present context are the number of factors to extract, the kind of rotation of the factors to be used, the "significance" level of factor loadings, and, in item factor analysis, which we use generously, the low reliability of single items and thus relatively low correlations among items. Another quite different problem is the "delicacy" of second-order factor solutions.

The most difficult of these problems is the number of factors to extract and rotate. To my knowledge there is no really satisfactory way to know how many factors to extract, except in the simplest cases.[14] If not enough

---

[14] A promising development, the parallel analysis technique, has been worked out by Montanelli and Humphreys (1976) based on an earlier approach to the problem by Humphreys and Ilgen (1969). A second correlation matrix with the same number of variables and observations is calculated from normally distributed random numbers. Both matrices are factor analyzed with the principal factors method. The eigenvalues obtained from the data correlation matrix are then compared to those obtained from the random number generated matrix by plotting them on the same plot, with number of eigenvalues on the abscissa and size of eigenvalues on the ordinate. The point at which the two curves cross determines the number of factors to use and rotate. The idea, of course, is to use the random numbers

factors are extracted, important factors can be missed and one or more of the factors extracted and rotated may be muddied by variables that really "belong" to other factors. If too many factors are extracted, the variance can be so spread that some factors may be "splintered." In both cases the factors can be difficult to interpret. The methods used in the studies reported were discussed earlier and need not be repeated here. On the whole, they seemed to have worked well.

What kind of rotations should be used? It depends, of course, on the purpose of a factor analysis. In the present studies both orthogonal and oblique rotations were used, though my usual preference is for orthogonal rotations because interpretation from study to study is facilitated. The main purpose, however, is to test the theory—which requires second-order analysis. Therefore oblique rotations are always used with first-order factors in order to obtain the correlations among the factors (as explained earlier). Second-order factors were rotated orthogonally (except in the analysis of covariance structures analyses discussed in Chapter 10) because the theory predicts near-zero correlations between the liberal and conservative second-order factors. Fortunately, the rotation problem was a minor one since orthogonal and oblique rotations for the most part yielded the same factors.

The significance level of factor loadings has troubled researchers for decades. There appears to be no clear statistical solution with the usual factor analytic methods. With orthogonal solutions, therefore, a criterion of $\geq.35$ was adopted. Since oblique solutions in general produce lower factor loadings, a criterion of $\geq.25$ (sometimes $\geq.30$, depending on the general level of the correlations) was used. The problem is actually only serious when assessing the significance of negative loadings.

There is little that can be done about the two remaining problems: low correlations among items and the delicacy of second-order factor solutions. As indicated earlier, items that did not correlate with other items were eliminated or changed, and, naturally, items that correlated substantially with other items were retained. (In some cases, items that did not correlate with other items in a sample were reintroduced in a later sample in the hope that they would correlate with new items that were introduced.) In any case, constant efforts were made to include sets of items as heterogeneous as possible, under the restriction that all items had to reflect social attitudes as defined. Despite average low item intercorrelations, there were sufficient substantial correlations and heterogeneity of correlation patterns to ensure fairly clear definition of factors.[15]

---

eigenvalue curve as a random baseline against which to assess the data matrix eigenvalues. An ingenious idea that seems to work.

[15]The principle is similar to that in estimating reliability. A test or scale can have high reliability even though its items have low correlations with each other, and, taken singly, are relatively unreliable. Cronbach (1951), in a classic article in which he defined the alpha

Second-order factor analytic solutions are obviously tricky because we are, so to speak, dealing with abstractions of abstractions. The first-order factors are rotated obliquely and the correlations among the factors are estimated from the cosines of the angles among the factor vectors. Most of our first-order analyses are of the correlations among single items. Obviously such correlations are not always too stable, especially when compared to the correlations among whole tests or scales. Given the generally low level of correlations among items and their less than optimum stability, and given that second-order analysis is based on the correlations among the factors produced by the items, it is surprising that the second-order solutions to be reported later are as good as they are. The reason is, evidently, that the underlying first- and second-order attitude factor structures are strong.

What Factors Are and Are Not

Since factor analysis is the central method used to test the criterial referents theory, it is especially important to know what one is talking about when one says, for example, "This factor reflects social welfare ideas and is basically liberal," or "The name of this second-order factor is 'General Conservatism.'"

A factor is a construct, a hypothetical entity, a latent unobserved variable that is assumed to underlie the elements that are its parts. More mundanely put, a factor is a cluster of variables, tests, scales, or items that are substantially related to each other. Factors express the variance that is common to their elements. The name given to a factor is an attempt to express what is common to the elements that make up the factor. But it is only a name. And it may be right or wrong—or more likely, neither right nor wrong.

For example, people tend to respond similarly to the referents *business, money, profits, private enterprise, capitalism,* and *real estate.* This produces positive correlations among these items, which, upon factor analysis, produce a factor. The factor was named "Economic Conservatism." "Economic" is more or less obvious. But why "Conservatism"? Does approval of these items mean conservatism? One answer is that conservative individuals, judged in other ways, tend to approve the items. A second answer is that these items also correlate positively with other "known" conservative items, like *discipline, law and order,* and *competition.* Still another answer is that business people tend to be conservative,

---

reliability coefficient, showed that if there is a strong factor running through the items the variance of this factor will be picked up, as it were, and add up to high reliability. The Spearman-Brown formula encapsulates the same idea. The attitude items of the present study perform similarly, but separately for *L* items and for *C* items.

at least in economic matters. The label "Economic Conservatism," in any case, seems reasonable. The same factor in much the same form has been found with different samples. Nevertheless, it is quite possible that the "real" factor is not "Economic Conservatism" but something else. Suppose, for example, that next year it was found that the following items were also on the factor: *patriotism, law and order, military training,* and *church.* Is the factor still "Economic Conservatism"? Have two factors been collapsed into one? These are plausible possibilities.

Does a factor have "reality" above and beyond the correlations that produce it? Some observers would say No, and, in a sense, they are right. In a broader scientific sense, however, there is more to the problem. The simplest possible answer to "explain" a matrix of correlations is one factor. This is part of the fascination and power of the so-called "g" of intelligence, a general intelligence that runs through many ability tests and items. How much simpler it is to invoke g rather than Thurstone's group factors! But is it "correct"? Maybe both explanations are "correct." (This seems to be the case.) If g exists is it some sort of general ability that all of us have to varying degrees? If so, then there is a sort of reality behind or reflected by the test items, in the correlations, and, finally, in the g factor.

Similarly, "Liberalism" and "Conservatism" have been found at the second order. *Sets* of liberal attitude items, the L first-order factors, have been positively correlated, and *sets* of conservative items, the C first-order factors, have been positively correlated. Factor analysis of the correlations among the L and C sets have yielded two (sometimes three) relatively orthogonal second-order factors. They have been named "Liberalism" and "Conservatism" simply because their "elements," their constituents, have been L and C factors. In addition, however, the nature of the first-order factors has in general agreed with historical and philosophical descriptions and analyses (e.g., Smith, 1968; Rossiter, 1962) and with commonly accepted knowledge of liberalism and conservatism. This, then, is their reality.

The basic purpose of research methodology is to obtain answers to research questions. Appropriate methodology may obtain satisfactory answers; then, again, it may not. It is a long and often tenuous and difficult way from theory to empirical test. Even with the best methodology adequately used, slips occur. This is especially so in psychological research generally and attitude research specifically. The purpose of this chapter has been to give readers an overview of the research approaches used in the studies to be reported. They should then be in a better position to judge the adequacy and legitimacy of the answers and the interpretations of the answers of the book. We will perforce return to these problems later and especially at the end of the book.

5 The Measurement of Liberalism and Conservatism: A Review

Until now we have neglected the social scientific literature on liberalism and conservatism. We must add perspective by citing and discussing some of the empirical work on the nature, structure, and measurement of liberalism and conservatism. The literature on attitudes, however, is very large, and we can do little more than sample the work most pertinent to the theory and research of this book.[1]

Anthologies of Attitude Scales

The best sources of social scientific work on the measurement of attitudes are probably the attitude scale anthologies of Robinson, Rusk, and Head (1968), Robinson and Shaver (1969), and Shaw and Wright (1967). While many of the instruments reproduced and discussed are not really measures of attitudes, the books are a rich source of the work done to measure attitudes. Unfortunately, the sections of two of the books (Robinson et al., 1968; Shaw & Wright, 1967) devoted to liberalism and conservatism

---

[1] Psychologists reading this book may wonder at, even deplore, the lack of consideration of the tradition and literature on the structure of attitudes *within the individual* (e.g., Katz & Stotland, 1959; Krech & Crutchfield, 1948). The reason for the neglect is not lack of interest or denigration of value. It is precisely because the preoccupation of social psychological attitude theorists and researchers has been with the structure and organization of attitudes within the individual. Our major though not exclusive concern is the structure of attitudes over many individuals, as stated earlier. Moreover, our concern is also more static in that we have little direct interest in attitude change, which can be said to be the central preoccupation of most attitude theorists.

measures are marred by the bipolarity assumption. When both liberal and conservative items are used in a scale, for example, the instructions invariably direct the user to reverse the scores of either the liberal or the conservative items, thus forcing what may be two continua on to one. (See, for example, the instructions with my social attitudes scale: Robinson et al., 1968, p. 100; Shaw & Wright, 1967, p. 323. This scale was meant to yield two scores, one L and one C, for each subject.)

Even scales labeled "Conservatism" are handled similarly. For instance, one form of the well-known Political-Economic Conservatism (PEC) Scale (Form 78) used in *The Authoritarian Personality* (Adorno et al., 1950), reproduced in Robinson et al. (1968, p. 110), has 16 items, ten conservative and six liberal. The ten conservative items are scored normally and the six liberal items are reverse scored, yielding a single "conservative" score for each individual. Still, the authors of these anthologies have provided not only many valuable scales and items—one can use them without reverse scoring, for example—they have also provided good, often excellent, discussions of attitudes and attitude measurement and research, as well as critical evaluations of the scales reproduced.

Study of these volumes gives the justifiable impression that a vast amount of work has been devoted to attitude measurement, but that little of it has been theoretical or structural. Robinson et al. (1968) published 17 scales designed to measure liberalism-conservatism. The research behind only three of these was concerned with attitude structure. Four used factor analysis. Six used reverse scoring. In their chapter, "Political and Religious Attitudes," Shaw and Wright (1967, Ch. 8) included 18 scales (seven of these were religion scales). In three of the studies done on these scales there was concern for structure. Five used factor analysis. The purpose of most of the scales has been simply to measure social attitudes. There has been little preoccupation with attitude theory and attitude structure. We turn now to consideration of attitude work that was directed toward theory or the study of the structure of attitudes.

Structural and Factor Analytic Studies

Kerr. That social attitudes are multidimensional was asserted years ago by Kerr (1946, 1952). His liberalism-conservatism scale was constructed to measure political, economic, religious, aesthetic, and social areas of attitudes. Kerr claimed that there was no general liberalism-conservatism factor, and that the areas of social attitudes should be measured separately. The importance of his work, then, is that it assumed multidimensionality of attitude and provided for the measurement of separate attitude areas. Factor analysis was evidently not used; the categories seemed to have been a priori.

Ferguson. Two of the most influential sets of factor analytic studies are those of Eysenck and Ferguson, both of whom proposed what can be called general systems of attitude organization and structure.[2] Ferguson (1939, 1973), in an analysis of Thurstone equal-appearing interval scales, identified what he called "primary" social factors: Religionism, Humanitarianism, and Nationalism, and each of these factors was evidently bipolar. Ferguson replicated the study in the 1970s, using the same scales—ten Thurstone-type scales developed by Thurstone and others— administered to 1471 students. Virtually the same factors were found. The correlations between the 1939 and 1973 factor loadings were high. Many of the loadings were negative, indicating bipolarity of attitudes.

The studies are important because they are structural, the second is a replication of the first after many years, they are based on what seems to be good measurement, and, especially for our purpose, the results appear to be genuinely bipolar. Their weakness—and this need not necessarily be viewed as a weakness—is that the ten Thurstone scales cover only a small part of the range of social attitudes. One can hardly talk about the structure of social attitudes when only ten scales, or ten variables, are the basis of study.[3] Nevertheless, although the structure yielded by the study cannot be accepted as depicting the fundamental structure of attitudes, the bipolarity finding is highly important because it appears to be genuine bipolarity, that is, bipolarity not due to an artifact of measurement or analysis but actually reflecting "true" attitudinal states. If so, it should be a good clue to the conditions that produce bipolarity.

Eysenck. Evaluation of Eysenck's structural attitude studies is difficult, as is assessment of the adequacy of his structural claims, because it is not always possible to know just what was done. Since the purpose here is not to survey the literature or to criticize the methodology of research and the interpretation of data, but rather to mention attempts to study attitude structure that are pertinent to the study and measurement of liberalism and conservatism, systematic analysis of the research of others will not be done. Nevertheless, methodological points must sometimes be mentioned. Because Eysenck, for example, earlier

---

[2] There have of course been a number of other factor analytic studies; for example, earlier studies of Eysenck (1944, 1947), Comrey (1966), Sanai (1950a, 1950b, 1951), and Stagner (1936). The purpose here, however, is not to summarize the literature but to characterize what appear to have been the most influential studies. Moreover, it is difficult to assess the studies done, including those of Eysenck and Ferguson, because details of scoring, factor extraction, and rotation are not always given—or clear when they are given.

[3] The scales were: Belief in the reality of God and attitudes toward evolution, birth control, war, capital punishment, treatment of criminals, communism, censorship, law, and patriotism. Two forms of each of these were included in the analysis, a total of 20 scales.

drew structural conclusions on the basis of interpretation of unrotated factors (Eysenck, 1944), the conclusions must be questioned and the methodological reasons for the questions must be given. When Wilson (1973) bases conclusions about conservatism on a possibly defective measurement instrument (see Pedhazur, 1978), the conclusions must be questioned and, again, the methodological reasons for the questions given. As far as possible, however, such methodological criticism will be avoided. It can distract us from our purpose.

The structure that Eysenck has postulated over the years is a dualistic one. Two orthogonal factors, "Radicalism-Conservatism" and "Toughmindedness-Tendermindedness," provide the framework for the attitude items used. The idea is compelling and almost convincing. It is relatively simple and yields neat interpretations. The trouble is that evidence from my studies indicates that with attitude items all scored in the same manner (no reverse scoring) and appropriate factor analysis a radicalism-conservatism factor does not appear. We skip Eysenck's earlier studies (e.g., Eysenck, 1944) since they used unrotated factor matrices.

A recent study done by Hewitt, Eysenck, and Eaves (1977) seems to be valued by Eysenck since he included it in one of his books (Eysenck & Wilson, 1978). Its methodology is satisfactory until one examines the factor analysis of the correlations among the 60 items of an attitude scale. An iterated principal components analysis clearly yielded a substantial number of factors, some eight or ten.[4] But the authors rotated only the first two factors, and then interpreted the results as Radicalism-Conservatism and Toughmindedness-Tendermindedness.

In another study, Eysenck (1971) factor analyzed the correlations among 28 social attitude items. (I was able to categorize all the items as liberal *(L)* or conservative *(C)*. There were 13 *L* items and 15 *C* items.) Principal components analysis was used with oblique rotations. Eight factors were rotated and their descriptions make good sense (they were not reported in detail, unfortunately). The author says that the intercorrelations of the eight factors were factored. He reports the loadings of the 28 items on two presumed second-order factors. But nothing is said about how this was done. Ordinarily in a factor analysis of an eight-by-eight correlation matrix yielding two second-order factors, one would report the unrotated and rotated loadings of the two factors. Presumably some other method was used (perhaps factor scores?). In any case, the two

---

[4]Many experts will dispute the use of principal components analysis (analysis of the correlation matrix with 1's in the diagonal instead of communality estimates) because all the variance, including unique and error variance, instead of common factor variance, is extracted. A consequence is that there are too many factors. In the above study, for instance, fifteen factors had eigenvalues greater than 1.

reported factors conform to Eysenck's theoretical structure of Radicalism-Conservatism and Toughmindedness-Tendermindedness. The structure reported is bipolar.

The final Eysenck study to be reported will lead us gracefully to Wilson's work since in this study (Eysenck, 1976) a Wilson-type scale of 68 attitude referents was used. The sample was large, $N = 1442$, and presumably representative. Principal components analysis and oblique rotations were again used. Thirteen factors were included and their intercorrelations calculated. Two second-order factors were obtained, but again, loadings of all 68 items were reported without details on how they were calculated. The reported results (Table 1 of the report) are hard to understand. First, most of the loadings of both factors have minus signs (only two substantial loadings on each factor are positive). Second and more important, a plot of the two factors shows that the plotted points cluster rather near the zero point somewhat as loadings calculated from random numbers would. At the least, the plot of the two factors is hardly a structure strong enough to support the Radicalism-Conservatism and Toughmindedness-Tendermindedness interpretation. (Note that the plot of the previously reported study [Eysenck, 1971] is clearer and stronger.)

In sum, methodological ambiguities in Eysenck's structural studies are such that the interpretation of the data as supporting the Radicalism-Conservatism and Toughmindedness-Tendermindedness structure is questionable. The hypothesis may be correct, but on the basis of the evidence presented in the studies one can hardly say that it is.[5]

Wilson.   Recently I had a computer search made of the attitude literature concentrating heavily on structural studies.[6] One of the most-cited names was Wilson and one of the most-cited scales was Wilson's Conservatism Scale (Wilson, 1973; Wilson & Patterson, 1968). We include brief consideration of Wilson's work because of its wide influence and because he postulates a "general" factor of conservatism (Wilson, 1973, p. 73). Wilson's Conservatism or C Scale has 50 referent items: *death penalty, evolution theory, beatniks, chastity,* and so on. The idea of using referents is a good one.

---

[5]Birenbaum and Zak (1982) recently compared the factor analytic results of Eysenck and Kerlinger and concluded that the results of studies of both researchers published in 1976 supported the criterial referents theory and did not support Eysenck's theory. The results of their own study of educational attitudes done in Israel and reported in the same article also supported the duality hypothesis. They also studied, through canonical correlation analysis, the relations between educational attitudes and personality measures. Their important conclusion was that Kerlinger's and Eysenck's "theories" are complementary rather than contradictory. "Kerlinger explains the structure, whereas Eysenck provides the motivational background of the underlying process" (p. 512).

[6]I am grateful to my former colleague at the University of Amsterdam, Dr. Harrie Vorst, for his help in having the search made.

Actually, we are interested only in Wilson's structural assertion: the claimed general factor of Conservatism. In one study (Wilson, 1973, Ch. 5), the C Scale was administered to 200 male subjects. The items were intercorrelated and analyzed with principal components analysis. Wilson reports four of these factors (pp. 57–58 and pp. 75–76) in unrotated form and says that Factor I "is clearly the general *(conservatism)* factor" (p. 73). He bases this conclusion on a large break between the first latent root or eigenvalue and the second root or eigenvalue. He compares the "strength" of this first factor with the well-established general intelligence factor, and says that the item-total correlations are nearly all positive and almost identical to the loadings of the first principal component (p. 58). (This is because the item-total correlations and the first factor loadings reflect the same thing: the variance that each item shares with the other items.)

The trouble, as Pedhazur (1978) has pointed out in his review of the C Scale, is not only the principal components method but the fact that the first principal component always appropriates the largest variance, often considerably more than the second and subsequent components. This does not mean that it is a general factor. A rotation of the four factors Wilson reports would undoubtedly shift a good deal of the first component variance to other factors. In a study done specifically to test Wilson's claim of a general attitude factor, Robertson and Cochrane (1973), administered Wilson's C Scale to 329 students at Edinburgh University, intercorrelated the items, extracted four factors with the principal components method, and rotated all four factors, including the first. There was no general factor. The variance of the first factor was spread over the factors. The above criticism, supported by the results of Robertson and Cochrane's study, nullifies Wilson's structural argument and claim.

Although our interest is mainly in structural studies and hypotheses involving liberalism and conservatism, one or two other features of Wilson's work need to be mentioned. These are the scoring system and the general item scheme or format. The scoring is based on the notion that all the items measure conservatism. Although it does not seem possible to categorize a number of the items clearly as either conservative or liberal—*nudist camps, jazz, pyjama parties, modern art, striptease shows, horoscopes,* for example—and although some of the items are clearly liberal—*birth control, legalized abortion, colored immigration, coeducation, socialism, disarmament, mixed marriage, divorce*—all are scored as though they measure conservatism. This is accomplished, in effect, by scoring the odd-numbered items positively and the even-numbered items negatively. The results obtained with such a system are suspect since all the items are forced into the conservative mold, whether they are or are not conservative.

In addition, the mechanics of the scoring system and the scale format are somewhat peculiar. Subjects respond "Yes," "No," or "Uncertain" ("?"). A "Yes" to an odd-numbered item and a "No" to an even-numbered item are scored 2; "?" responses are scored 1. Wilson says that this is a 3-point Likert scale: liberal response = 0, ambiguous response = 1, and conservative response = 2. All items are thus forced on the procrustean bed of presumed conservatism. It is assumed, for example, that a "Yes" response to *birth control* indicates low conservatism, and a "No" response to the same item indicates high conservatism. If liberalism exists, in other words, it has no chance of emerging. A minimum requirement to allow correlations that reflect the actual relations among the items to emerge, and thus factors and factor loadings that reflect the relations, is a free response format, such as Likert, in which all items are responded to in the same way. If both liberal and conservative factors exist, they should emerge. Similarly, if bipolarity exists, it too will emerge. In sum, the methodological deficiencies disqualify Wilson's structural notion of a general attitude factor from serious consideration.

Comrey and Newmeyer.   In one of the more methodologically sophisticated studies of social attitudes, Comrey and Newmeyer (1965) found bipolar first-order factors and a single bipolar second-order factor, which they called Radicalism-Conservatism. Thirty social attitude variables were selected and four items were written for each variable. The 120 items were intercorrelated and factor analyzed for item analysis purposes. From this analysis the authors selected 25 variables for the main factor analysis. Each of the 25 variables was the sum of two or more homogeneous items. Factor analysis yielded nine factors which were rotated obliquely. The correlations among the nine factors, when factor analyzed, produced one bipolar second-order factor, as mentioned above. Three of the nine first-order factors were bipolar.

The methodology of this study seems to have been good. The items were well-written, the analytic procedures probably sound, and the first-order and second-order factor analytic procedures appear to have been well-conceived and well-executed. Possible weaknesses of the study were the initial factor analysis of the 120 items with only 212 subjects, certain details of scoring, and the possible extraction of too many factors (nine factors from 25 variables). The correlations among the factors reported (their Table 1, p. 366) also do not seem to be consistent with the reported factors. For example, a very large r of $-.71$ was reported between factors III and IV. But factor III is Punitive Attitudes and factor IV is Nationalism; both are conservative factors and should correlate positively. The inconsistencies may be due to scoring or to the sometimes predominant negative factor loadings reported, a confusing practice.

Despite the possible deficiencies, this study seems to be the best that has been done to study liberalism and conservatism. Thus, it cannot be ignored. Its findings of three bipolar first-order factors (among nine factors) and a single bipolar second-order factor are the only data so far encountered that cannot be dismissed on grounds of methodological inadequacy. True, there are murky points in the reported study, and one would certainly want replication to support the weight of the finding of one bipolar second-order factor. The study is nevertheless impressive. I confess myself baffled: Comrey and Newmeyer's results are so different from my own. The resolution of the problem might be to replicate their study using both item factor analysis as well as their clustered variable analysis and being sure that the scoring of all items and cluster variable is the same.

There have been a number of other factor analytic studies of attitudes, some of them well-conceived and well-executed, but, to my knowledge, none of them has been theoretically inspired. That is, none has been specifically designed to test structural hypotheses. Nor have they been designed, with one or two notable exceptions (McClosky, 1958, for instance), to study liberalism and conservatism as "objects" of scientific interest.[7] This seems a strange and regrettable omission. There is a respectable, sometimes distinguished, general literature on liberalism and conservatism. Evidently social thinkers consider them important enough to devote books to them. Most social scientific research, however, has concentrated on their measurement, almost always guided by the bipolarity assumption, and on studying their correlates, or rather, the correlates of the presumed liberalism-conservatism continuum. For example, Sherman and Ross (1972), although they specifically say that liberalism-conservativism is not a single dimension, make no distinction between the two. In a large-scale national survey of faculty members in the natural sciences and engineering, Ladd and Lipset (1972) used only a 5-item scale and assumed that liberalism-conservatism is one continuum.

An influential body of thought even decries the validity and viability of

---

[7]It is of course possible that my literature searches and the computer search mentioned earlier have missed relevant studies.

the concepts of liberalism and conservatism. Converse (1964), for example, specifically decries the terms. He says, ". . . the yardstick that such an account takes for granted—the liberal-conservative continuum (sic)—is a rather elegant high-order abstraction, and such abstractions are not typical conceptual tools for the 'man in the street' " (p. 215). The data on which he bases this statement, however, were much too limited to bear the statement's heavy weight. Converse evidently made little attempt to cover a broad range of social questions. Even given the truth of the statement that liberalism and conservatism are abstractions that are not conceptual tools of the man-in-the-street, this has little to do with their scientific use. The man-in-the-street (also an abstraction, though not elegant) can well be conservative in his social beliefs and be quite unaware that he is a conservative. He may even deny being conservative or liberal. This makes little or no difference to the outcome of measuring his beliefs. Provided he gives honest answers—and most people respond honestly—his conservatism, whether the term is or is not used, has a high probability of being successfully measured.

The purpose of the above discussion, as stated earlier, has been to characterize the social scientific literature on liberalism and conservatism. The discussion has unfortunately been negative. I would like to cite and summarize technically competent structural research of relevance and worth. But such research is scarce. I think this may be because the social scientists who are interested in attitudes either share Converse's disdain for liberalism and conservatism or care only about attitude change or both. Despite the negative flavor of the discussion, let's summarize what appears to be the situation.

First, there is little or no recognition or admission that liberalism and conservatism may be separate dimensions. The assumption of bipolarity, that liberalism and conservatism are opposite poles of one or more dimensions of attitudes, is overwhelmingly accepted without question. Moreover, the assumption of the presumed polarity of attitudes is general: If many people believe something, then there must be many other people who oppose it. Attitudes, in short, are characterized by "versus." Some social scientists even deny the scientific legitimacy of the concepts of liberalism and conservatism.

Second, the methodology of many published studies is marred by improper or at least questionable factor analytic methodology, reverse scoring of items, inadequate item format, and other deficiencies. Inadequate methodology of course casts doubt on structural outcomes and conclusions.

Third, in contrast to the study of intelligence, whose structure has been well-explored with adequate measurement and factor analytic methodology (see Guilford, 1967), there has been relatively little systematic study of the structure of social attitudes, and, as has been indicated, that little has been methodologically marred. The paucity of such theory and research is surprising, especially when it has been said that attitude is a central concept of social psychology (Allport, 1935; Fleming, 1967; McGuire, 1969).[8]

---

[8]It should again be mentioned that there has been theory and research using what I have called the individual structural approach (see McGuire, 1969, pp. 153–157). This is the notion that attitudes in the individual have cognitive, affective, and behavioral components, or as Krech and Crutchfield (1948) long ago said, emotional, motivational, perceptual, and cognitive components.

6 Attitudes toward Education

Education is rich in potential conflict. Each year, each decade, virtually the same battles are fought over what children should learn and how they should learn. The conflict is probably unavoidable because educational thinking and practice go deep into beliefs. Indeed, we can say that education has its "ideologies," its sets of beliefs, so strong that many bitter battles have been fought over them and their implications. The existence of large numbers of private schools and religious schools testifies to the important differences of belief about appropriate education for children. Sometimes the differences are so acute they cannot be reconciled. The conflict then becomes severe, even violent.

Examples are not hard to find, and they sometimes show the relations between educational attitudes and other social attitudes. One of the most dramatic examples is the conflict of beliefs about desegregation, integrated schools, and school bussing. Another example with great potential for conflict is religious manifestations in public schools. But these are larger social as well as educational issues. Differences of beliefs and opinions also run through most thinking and ideas about teaching and learning. What are the goals and purposes of education? Should they be basically intellectual or personal and social? That is, is the main goal of teaching to build children's intellects or to help develop their personalities? Is subject matter paramount, or is it secondary to problem solving and to the development of character and citizenship? Should schools be democratic? What subjects are central in the curriculum? Should the lower schools be geared to preparation for later schools, or should they be educational ends in themselves? Are intellectual growth and scholarly learning the central preoccupations of the university, or should their basic purpose be to prepare their students for occupational and professional service and generally to help the society solve complex technical, social, and other problems?

The first four decades of the century saw the remarkable growth of the progressive education movement, inspired by the thinking of John Dewey (1902, 1916) and others (see Cremin, 1961). Most education in America and Europe until the twentieth century was traditional, so-called. Emphasis was on subject matter, especially "hard" subjects, moral development, discipline, and, for the select few, college and university preparation. Educational goals and purposes were externally imposed on teaching and learning. There was little thought of democracy in education. Under the strong influence of the progressive education movement, however, more and more emphasis was put on the needs and interests of the child, the development of personality, social learning, cooperation, problem solving, and democracy in education and the view of the school as an agent of social change (Beale, 1936; Brubacher, 1962; Cremin, 1961; Curti, 1935; Dupuis, 1966; Henry, 1942; National Society for the Study of Education, 1955). However they developed, during the first forty years of the century two broad general philosophies or sets of beliefs about education, usually called "progressivism" and "traditionalism," competed with each other for influence in the schools of America.

The ideas of these "ideologies," these set of beliefs, were the inspiration of the *Q* and *R* studies to be described in this chapter. We want to understand and explore the operational expression of these broad general views of education and their connections to attitudes. Specifically, we ask: What is the structure of attitudes toward education and what is the nature, the substance, of these attitudes? In trying to answer these questions we describe two *Q* studies done in the 1950s and another done a decade later and two *R* studies done during the same years.[1]

Before describing the actual research, it should be pointed out that there was little explicit theoretical purpose that drove the early investigations. It was more an attempt to grope for the nature and structure of educational attitudes. How do traditional and progressive beliefs manifest themselves empirically? Do people "known" to be progressive appear together on persons factors, and similarly for "known" traditionalists? Are there factors associated with areas of education: curriculum, disci-

---

[1] Although the distinction between *Q* and *R* methodologies and studies was mentioned earlier, it may be useful to make it again. A *Q* study is a factor analytic study that analyzes the correlations among individuals, the correlations being obtained through *Q* sorts. An *R* study is the usual factor analytic study of the correlations among tests, scales, or items. In *R* methodology variables (tests, items) are analyzed (correlated); in *Q* persons are analyzed (correlated).

pline, and instruction? If the correlations among items are factor analyzed what kinds of items appear together on what factors? In the very beginning it was even thought that progressive and traditional items would appear together on factors, with opposite signs. In other words, the early attempts were explorations of content, structure, and measurement.

Before the 1950s there had been efforts to measure educational attitudes, but they suffered—if "suffered" is the right word—from lack of theoretical direction and psychometric and analytic sophistication, not to mention the pervasive influence of the bipolarity assumption. The beginning of the research to be described was little better. Where it differed was in assumptions and methodology. It began with the conviction that factor analysis had to be used to discover the dimensions underlying educational attitudes, and the methods of obtaining attitudinal responses and analyzing these responses had to be such as not to prejudice the emergence of persons and attitude factors.

Q STUDIES[2]

Q Education 1 (QED-1)

The basic purpose of two of the three Q studies to be reported (Kerlinger, 1956a, 1958) was to measure attitudes toward education based on the sets of beliefs called "Progressivism" *(A)* and "Traditionalism" *(B)* using Q methodology (Stephenson, 1953), and to explore the structure of attitudes toward education of individuals. A major premise of this early work was that areas of attitudes can be profitably explored by using a methodology focused on the individual, by selecting a limited number of individuals with "known" attitudes, and by exploiting the structural and statistical possibilities of Q to see if the Q measurement agreed with the "known" attitude classifications. Descriptions of the Q sort and the studies may help to clarify what is meant.

The Q sort constructed to measure attitudes toward education, called QED, was a so-called structured sort of the factorial kind. That is, it was modeled after a 2×4 factorial analysis of variance model. One factor was Progressive-Traditional: each item was either Progressive or Traditional (earlier called Permissive and Restrictive). Thus there were 40 P items and 40 T items. The other factor was four areas of educational activity or thinking, e.g., Teaching-Subject Matter-Curriculum. There were 20 items in each of the four areas. Each item of the Q sort reflected a combination of the two factors. For example, "Knowledge and subject matter are not

---

[2] See Chapter 4 for a description of Q methodology.

so important as learning to solve problems" is a Progressive item in the Teaching-Subject Matter-Curriculum area. Since later analysis showed that the Areas factor was not important, it is dropped from further consideration. We are in effect left with a structured *Q* sort of one factor, Attitudes, divided into Progressive and Traditional, each with 40 items. Analysis of variance is used with each *Q* sort: the *F* ratio indicates the statistical significance of the difference between the means of a *S*'s placement of the *P* and *T* items. The values that are analyzed are the values 0 through 10 assigned to the 11 piles of the *Q* sort into which each *S* sorts the 80 items, 9 indicating "Approve Most" and 0 "Approve Least."

Twenty-five middle-Western subjects were selected on the basis of occupational roles and "known" attitudes toward education. The roles were simple: a subject was either a professor or not a professor. Eight education professors (EP) and ten liberal arts professors (LAP) whose educational beliefs were fairly well-known were chosen from two faculties of a large university. All eight EP's were known to be progressives; four LAP's were believed to be progressives, three were traditionalist, and three were unknown, but believed to be "mixed." Six subjects were people outside the university (OP's). Three were active Republicans, and the beliefs and affiliations of the other three were unknown. It was believed that the EP's would be highly progressive and would form a factor, and that the four LAP's believed to be progressive would also be on the same factor as the EP's, if with somewhat lower factor loadings. The three LAP's believed to be traditionalist should form another cluster and thus produce another factor on which the three Republicans might also appear. One of the unknowns among the OP's would probably not be loaded on any factor since she had said that she was not interested in education and knew little about it. Indeed, she was included for this reason. In addition, one university administrator was chosen as a marginal person: he was neither a professor nor an OP.

The results obtained with the *Q* sorts were intercorrelated and factor analyzed with the centroid method and oblique rotations (Thurstone, 1947). Each person's *Q* sort was also subjected to analysis of variance, as described above, It was predicted that the EP's and three of the LAP's known to be progressives would intercorrelate substantially and form a persons factor, that the OP's, or at least the three Republicans would form another factor and that the university administrator would have a modest or low loading on the same factor as the three Republicans. It was also predicted that the EP's and three of the LAP's would have progressive *Q*-sort means significantly greater than traditional means. (For example, the mean of the 40 progressive items for subject 1, an EP, would be significantly greater than the mean of the 40 traditional items.) The opposite prediction was made for the three Republican women: traditional means greater than progressive. The other subjects were expected not to have significant differences.

To lighten the factor analytic computations involved, seven subjects were dropped at random from the factor analysis: two EP's, four LAP's, and one OP.[3] The analyses of variance included a measure of the consistency of each individual, the intraclass correlation coefficient, r_a. This coefficient is an index of consistency because it reflects how homogeneous the scores are within each classification, progressive or traditional. That is, a high r_a indicates that the subject tends to place the items of one of the classifications, progressive or traditional, together at the high end of the Q sort. A zero r_a indicates that the subject makes no differentiation between the progressive and traditional categories: he virtually sorts the cards "at random." It was predicted that the EP's would have high r_a's, the LAP's substantial but lower r_a's, the three Republicans substantial r_a's, and the remaining subjects nonsignificant r_a's.

The results generally supported the predictions. All EP's had highly significant F ratios and substantial to high r_a's: an average of .56. Nine of the ten LAP's also had significant F ratios ($p < .001$), with one exception ($p < .01$) in the progressive direction. The r_a's, however, were lower than the EP r_a's: an average of .42. The tenth LAP had a significant F ratio in the traditional direction. The three Republicans had significant F ratios in the traditional direction, as predicted. Their r_a's were lower than those of the EP's and LAP's: an average of .27. Two other OP's had significant F's in the progressive direction, but their r_a's were low: average of .16 (.27 and .05). The remaining two subjects were the individual with little knowledge or interest in education and the university administrator. The F ratios of neither subject was significant, and their r_a's were .09 and .14. Evidently the Q sort accurately reflected the "known" attitudes of the subjects since the main predictions were supported.[4]

The factor analysis, too, confirmed the predictions—but rather roughly. Four factors were extracted and rotated. Six EP's were all substantially loaded on factor I, and the LAP whose means were in the traditional

---

[3]At the time the study was done (1954), all calculations were done on mechanical desk calculators! Electronic calculators had not yet appeared, and computers were not generally available in the university. To factor analyze an 18-by-18 correlation matrix took many, many hours; to do the full 25-by-25 matrix would have taken far more time. Nevertheless, in the second study to be reported below, the full persons correlation matrix was analyzed. (We have come a long way in twenty-five years!)

[4]Results obtained from analysis of variance of Q sorts must be considered only suggestive. Because of the ipsative nature of Q-sort data, conventional statistics are suspect. One cannot trust the probabilities associated with F ratios, for example, since the degrees of freedom of Q-sort data do not correspond to the degrees of freedom of the conventional significance tests.

direction was negatively loaded ($-.39$). Four of the six LAP's were loaded on factor III and not on factor I. (Factors I and III were positively correlated: about .40.) All the OP's and the university administrator were loaded on factor II. Factor I was clearly progressive, factor III was also progressive but different from factor I, and factor II was traditional. Factor IV did not seem possible to interpret. A good deal more analysis of the *Q*-sort data was done, including case studies, but the above description is sufficient for our purpose.

Q Education 2 (QED-2)

The second *Q* study need not be described in such detail since it was essentially a replication of the first study in the Eastern part of the United States. Its methodology was the same, except that only two factors emerged in the factor analysis and orthogonal rotation was used. The same *Q* sort was used. The researcher had greater knowledge of the attitudes of the subjects in the second study.

Twenty-five subjects were selected on the same bases as in QED-1. There were ten EP's, all of them well-known as progressive in their educational attitudes, eight LAP's, known to be both progressive and traditional, and seven OP's, of whom four were reputed to be traditional.

Two factors emerged from the factor analysis, which, when rotated orthogonally, presented a rather clear picture. The ten EP's and four of the LAP's were loaded on factor I, and the OP's known to be traditional were loaded on factor II, together with three LAP's, two of whom were believed to be traditional. Factor I, then, was associated with progressivism and factor II with traditionalism. In addition, factor I had three fairly substantial negative loadings, indicating some bipolarity.

A unique and valuable feature of *Q* methodology is that "factor arrays" can be calculated and the array values used to create "ideal" *Q* sorts (see Stephenson, 1953, p. 176). These are new *Q* sorts that presumably express the "essence" of the factors. A kind of regression equation is in effect constructed using as weights the values of the factor loadings of those individuals highly loaded on a factor and on no other factor. These weights are applied to the actual values that those individuals had on each item of the *Q* sort and then summed to form a total value for the item. After this is done for each item, the sums—80 in the case of the education *Q* sort—are rank ordered and forced into the *Q* distribution. The resulting *Q* sort, with its "factor-calculated" values for each item, then expresses the "pure" factor. This was done twice for the present study yielding a progressive *Q* sort or factor array and a traditional *Q* sort or factor array. To give the reader an idea of what these arrays are like, the highest six

TABLE 6.1
Items High on Progressivism and Traditionalism
Factor Arrays, QED-1

Progressivism Array

Education is not so much imparting knowledge as it is encouraging and prompting the child to use his potentialities for learning.
True discipline springs from interest, motivation, and involvement in live problems.
Education is growth toward the capacity for more growth.
The goals of education should be dictated by children's interests and needs, as well as by the larger demands of society.
Right from the very first grade, teachers must teach the child at his own level and not at the level of the grade he is in.
Children must have social experiences under intelligent guidance so that they can learn to live and work with other people.

Traditionalism Array

Schools of today are neglecting the three R's.
Children need and should have more supervision and discipline than they usually get.
One of the big difficulties with modern schools is that discipline is often sacrificed to the interests of children.
Discipline should be governed by long-range interests and well-established standards.
The true view of education is so arranging learning that the child gradually builds up a storehouse of knowledge that he can use in the future.
Schools should teach children dependence on higher moral values.

items from the progressive array and the highest six from the traditional array, both from QED-1, are given in Table 6.1.

The real importance of these studies is that they gave the first clues that there was more to educational attitudes than a bipolar continuum of progressivism versus traditionalism, that perhaps progressivism and traditionalism were two separate and distinct factors of educational attitudes. (The progressivism and traditionalism arrays correlated − .19 in the first study and − .11 in the second study.) There *was* evidence of bipolarity: the Q sorts of three of the subjects of QED-1 and of three of the subjects of QED-2 correlated negatively, though not substantially, with a number of other Q sorts. Nevertheless, the results were suggestive: maybe there are two major persons factors. If the research were extended to scale factors and item factors, perhaps similar factors would emerge. Let us now look briefly at the third Q study, done a decade later.

Q Education-3 (QED-3)

In a study directed toward the relation between attitudes toward education and perceptions of desirable traits of teachers (Kerlinger, 1966; Kerlinger & Pedhazur, 1968), both *Q* and *R* methodologies were used. In the *Q* study, the education *Q* sort described above, together with a teacher characteristics or traits *Q* sort, was administered to 36 judges (called "judges" because they were asked to assess the importance of the traits of the teacher traits *Q* sort). Three factors were extracted using the principal factors method (Harman, 1976, Ch. 8). Orthogonal varimax rotations (Kaiser, 1958) were used. (We omit consideration of the results of the traits *Q* sort.)

Among the 36 judges were 12 professors of education. With one exception—a professor well-known for his traditional attitudes—they loaded on the first factor. Among seven elementary school teachers, six also loaded on this factor, as did seven of ten secondary teachers. Knowledge of the attitudes of the judges who loaded on the first factor and study of the items they placed high led to the conclusion that factor I was progressivism. Four of the judges were parochial school nun teachers. They loaded together on factor II, together with one military officer—there were three in the sample—two secondary teachers, and one elementary teacher. The factor was called (by independent judges) "Traditional Teacher," or "Traditionalism." The three military officers who were judges loaded together on factor III, together with one secondary teacher and one elementary teacher. The outside judges and the writer could not agree on the name of factor III.

QED-3 produced similar persons factors to those of QED-1 and QED-2. Although the specific items of the arrays of the three studies differed, they had substantial commonality. For example, the correlations between the progressivism factors of QED-1 and QED-2 was .71, and that for traditionalism was .61. The *Q* sorts were also reliable. Reliability, however, is a somewhat different concept in *Q* methodology than it usually is, because it is tied to both the internal consistency and the stability of individuals rather than whole groups of individuals. It is also tied to the concept of "structure": if an individual's attitudes are well-structured—if he consistently puts progressive items or traditional items together in the *Q* piles—then he is internally consistent and internal consistency reliability is substantial to high. Individuals who have high internal consistency also have high repeat reliability. For example, in QED-2 the intraclass coefficients of correlation for two of the LAP's (see Kerlinger 1958, Table 7, p. 127) were .56 and .60, rather high values, and the repeat reliability coefficients were .74 and .72, also high. On the other hand, individuals who have low internal consistency can have either low or substantial repeat reliability. An OP of QED-1, for example, had an intraclass *r* of .25 and a repeat reliability of .39, both low, whereas an OP of QED-2 had an intraclass *r* of .15 and a repeat *r* of .66, quite discrepant values.

TABLE 6.2
Representative Q Results, QED-1 and QED-2

Persons[a]	F[b]	p	r_a	r_{12}	a	Category[c]	Type[d]
1	90.77	.001	.56	.88	.82	EP	P
2	71.64	.001	.52	.84	.79	LAP	P
3	25.01	.001	.25	.39	.63	OP	T
4	90.31	.001	.56	.74	.75	EP	P
5	20.95	.001	.25	.60	.53	LAP	T
6	1.	n.s.	0	.56	.38	OP	T (?)

[a] Persons 1-3: QED-1; Persons 4-6: QED-2.

[b] F: F ratio; p: probability; r_a: intraclass coefficient of correlation; r_{12}: repeat reliability coefficient; a: factor loading.

[c] Category: EP: education professors; LAP: liberal arts professors; OP: other persons.

[d] Type: P: progressive; T: traditional.

In sum, the reliability of the results was satisfactory. For those individuals familiar with and interested in education, both internal consistency and repeat reliabilities were substantial. For those individuals unfamiliar with and not interested in education, both kinds of reliability were low. These statements, however, are based on only four subjects of QED-1 and seven of QED-2. Further evidence is found in QED-3. Twenty-two of the 36 judges sorted the Q sort twice. The range of r's was .45 to .89; the average r, via z, was .73. Evidently repeat reliability is satisfactory.

To give the reader a capsule idea of the data discussed above, the statistics of six individuals of QED-1 and QED-2 are given in Table 6.2. (The complete data sets, including the correlation matrices, are given in the original articles.) Persons 1, 2, and 3 sorted QED-1, and persons 4, 5, and 6 sorted QED-2. Persons 1 and 4 were professors of education, both strongly progressive. Their statistics are all consistent: high F ratios, in the progressive direction, substantial intraclass correlations (r_a), high repeat reliability coefficients (r_{12}), and high factor loadings (a). Persons 2 and 5 are liberal arts professors, one of them a progressive and the other a traditionalist. Their statistics are consistent, except that No. 5 has a rather low intraclass correlation, .25, moderate repeat reliability, .60, and a fairly substantial factor loading, .53. Persons 3 and 6 are persons outside the university, both traditionalists, except that No. 6 is marginal. The only indication of his traditionalism is the rather low factor loading of .38. No. 3, however, is clearly traditional: his F ratio is statistically significant, and his factor loading supports this assertion. He is, however, neither internally too consistent, $r_a = .25$, nor too reliable, $r_{12} = .39$.

The main point of this discussion of the three Q studies may have been dimmed by the plethora of details. The data of Table 6.2 illustrate some of the points. Accepted as representative of the *Q* findings, these data simply say that the *Q* sort works satisfactorily: the statistics show that progressives and traditionalists in education can be distinguished. They give us a clue to the structure of educational attitudes, but only a small clue. Better evidence on structure is given by the factor loadings of the persons. Rather than report them—they are given in the published articles—we plot the loadings of the first two (of three) factors of QED-3, which is the clearest of the three plots. It is given in Figure 6.1. The plot of QED-2 is much like it, except that it is more fan-shaped—a shape evidently common in *Q* plots—and has one substantial negative point. The plot of QED-1's first two factors was similar.

Earlier, we said that these *Q* studies had given the first suggestion for a basic dual structure of educational attitudes. The duality can be seen in the circled clusters of persons points in Figure 6.1. A large proportion of the points cluster around axis I, and most of the remaining points cluster around axis II. This seemed to cast suspicion on the bipolarity notion of progressivism versus traditionalism, and to indicate that progressivism and traditionalism may be separate and distinct sets of attitudes. We are here of course reasoning from clusters of persons to attitude structure, a

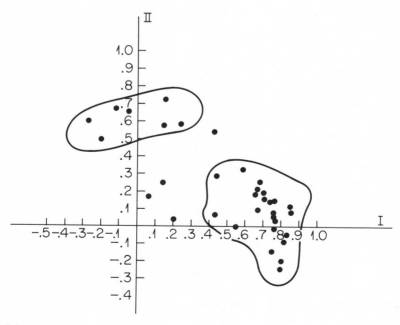

FIG. 6.1

possible precursor of reasoning from clusters of scales and items to attitude structure. The bridge between the two can be the Q factors arrays, as described earlier. From the persons who cluster together the items of the Q arrays can be found. The nature of the Q arrays, as judged from the items of the arrays, and the relations between the arrays can suggest hypotheses on the structure of educational attitudes. These hypotheses can then be tested using R methodology. This is the main significance of the evidence of the three Q studies and the structure shown in Figure 6.1.

R STUDIES

Education Scale I and II (ES-I and ES-II)

The results of the first two Q studies summarized above were used to construct scales to measure attitudes toward education. Factor arrays were calculated for the two main factors of QED-1 and the two factors of QED-2. Call these two factors P and T, progressivism and traditionalism. It is as though we had Q sorts that had been sorted by a "pure" educational progressive, array P, and a "pure" educational traditionalist, array T. Twelve statements at the high ends of the P and T arrays—all the statements in the top three piles of cards of the Q sorts—were taken as items for the scales to be constructed. This yielded 15 to 18 statements for each factor. Since this was deemed an insufficient number for reliable scales, more items were drawn from the next highest items of the P and T arrays until there was a total of 40 items, 20 A and 20 B.

The 40 statements were put into a 7-point summated-rating (Likert) scale and administered to about 200 subjects, approximately half graduate students of education and half various people outside the university. The purpose of this stage of the research was to find items that satisfied two criteria: high item-total correlations, P items with P total and T items with T total, and high P or T factor saturations. Some 12 to 15 items were wanted for each factor, but when both criteria were applied there were too few P items. Therefore compromises had to be made. The final scale included two or three items that did not satisfy both criteria. Twenty items, 10 P and 10 T, were finally incorporated into two attitude scales, the same items being used in both scales.

Education Scale I (ES-I) was a 7-point Likert-type scale in the same form as the 40-item scale. The order of the P and T items was randomized. Each individual had a P score and a T score. The instructions in effect asked subjects to indicate their degree of agreement or disagreement with each item.

A second instrument was also constructed, ES-II. This was a forced-choice scale of ten items, each "item" consisting of a tetrad of items. Each tetrad had two P and two T statements, one of which was a highly loaded P statement and one a highly loaded T statement. The other two statements in the tetrad were selected from those statements that had not had high values on the factor arrays. That is, there were two kinds of items in each tetrad: items high in factor saturation and items low in factor saturation. Subjects were asked to rank order the statements in each tetrad according to strength of agreement. It was reasoned that a person with a high degree of P-ness would place a 1 before the highly loaded P item, and that a person with a high degree of T-ness would put a 1 before the highly saturated T item. The other "buffer" items, the items with low P and T loadings, would not receive predictable ranks. Here is one of the tetrads ranked by a hypothetical T person, with each item identified as P, T, or buffer. (The values assigned for statistical purposes were the rank values, i.e., the rank 1 was assigned 4, the rank 2 was assigned 3, and so on.)

_4_   A good administrator discusses important matters of educational policy with his subordinates when he needs to. (Buffer)

_1_   Discipline should be governed by long-range interests and well-established standards. *(T)*

_2_   Teachers have a right to have unions to protect their rights and advance their interests. (Buffer)

_3_   Right from the very first grade, teachers must teach the child at his own level and not at the level of the grade he is in. *(P)*

The two scales were administered to a total of 598 persons: graduate students at a large Eastern university (136), graduate students of education at the same institution (157), and people outside the university (305) (Kerlinger & Kaya, 1959). The correlations among the items of ES-I and those among the items of ES-II were separately factor analyzed with the centroid method and the factors rotated orthogonally (graphic method). The essential results of both analyses are given in Table 6.3. The items have been rearranged so that the P (progressivism) and T (traditionalism) factor loadings are clear. In the ES-I analysis there were three factors, on the first of which the ten progressive items had significant ($\geq .35$) loadings, and on the second the ten traditional items had significant loadings. These loadings are given in the columns A and B. (The third factor loadings have been omitted. They were almost all small. This factor was used only to improve the rotations of the first two factors.) The factor analysis of the ES-II items—the rank values of the ten P and ten T items were used as scores—yielded one bipolar factor. The factor loadings are given in the column labeled "ES-II."

The method of selecting items using the Q approach was evidently successful. Curious readers may wish to plot the two factors. If they do

TABLE 6.3
Rotated Factor Loadings of the Items of ES-I and ES-II

Items	P Items A^a	B	ES-II	Items	T Items A	B	ES-II
1	.44	.01	-.42	3	-.38	.35	.52
2	.39	-.14	-.46	4	-.10	.38	.28
5	.42	-.13	-.54	6	-.05	.52	.51
7	.36	-.14	-.43	10	-.09	.50	.53
8	.45	.01	-.52	11	-.02	.58	.54
9	.51	-.05	-.48	12	-.31	.54	.60
15	.55	-.03	-.50	13	-.11	.48	.41
16	.37	-.09	-.35	14	-.01	.41	.42
17	.58	-.26	-.54	18	-.33	.52	.59
20	.35	-.03	-.31	19	-.10	.64	.56

^{a} A and B indicate the rotated factors; the loadings are those of ES-I. The column ES-II reports the factor loadings of the one bipolar factor obtained from the analysis. P items are progressive; T items are traditional.

so, they will see the clear dualistic almost orthogonal structure that was shown in Figure 6.1. The ES-II factor loadings form an interesting contrast. As expected, the P items have substantial negative loadings (or positive, if you wish) and the T have substantial positive loadings (or negative, if the P loadings are considered positive). We have here a nice demonstration of the effect of a technical artifact. The ipsative or forced-choice items have introduced spurious negative correlation and one bipolar factor. Other things assumed to be equal, interpretation of such a factor would be misleading. The "true" structure, in this case carefully built into the scale, is distorted.

Let us be clear about what the above study means. It is not direct evidence of the empirical validity of the duality hypothesis, though it suggests that the hypothesis *may* be correct. After all, only items high on the Q factor arrays in the positive direction were used to construct ES-I. Such usage was consistent with the belief that only items at the positive ends of arrays are criterial. But it is possible, of course, that items at the negative ends might be criterial, negatively, and that other items apparently not criterial to the subjects of QED-1 and QED-2 might be criterial to other subjects. The point is that the items were carefully and systematically selected, in effect, to produce the P and T factors—and they did. So what the study shows primarily is that it is possible to use a Q approach to attitude scale construction and thus create effective instruments.

More pertinent to the basic issue, it also shows that there is empirical substance to the P and T factors, and thus to progressivism and traditionalism, and it shows it in a methodologically interesting way since Q and R methodologies seem to produce similar results. Yet, because of the item selection procedure, it cannot be taken as confirming evidence of the validity of the theory. Zdep and Marco (1969) had a good point when they criticized these early studies for being item-bound. Nevertheless, the above study does show that the structure of educational attitudes may be dualistic.

FIRST- AND SECOND-ORDER FACTOR STRUCTURES OF ATTITUDES TOWARD EDUCATION

One of the major problems in studying the structure of attitudes and testing the duality hypothesis is that, given enough heterogeneous items, more than two, sometimes five or six, factors appear. The hypothesis predicts two "large" factors of social attitudes and of educational attitudes. The results just presented of two first-order factors were only possible because of the Q selection method used. That is, too few and insufficiently heterogeneous items were used. How can the problem be handled when four, five, six, or more factors emerge from the item intercorrelations? One solution is to talk about two *kinds* of factors, progressive and traditional. The theory predicts that first-order factors should have only items of one kind, progressive or traditional, but not both, on any one factor. While this prediction is legitimate and one we used in subsequent studies, it is incomplete: it does not direct itself specifically to the duality hypothesis.

In the late 1950s it was realized that second-order factor analysis was a solution to the problem. In the case of educational attitudes, the factor analysis of an item correlation matrix, given a substantial number of heterogeneous items, should yield several first-order factors, each of which should be either a progressive factor or a traditional factor. Oblique rotations of the first-order factors will yield the correlations among the first-order factors, which, when factored, should yield two second-order factors. These two factors should correspond to progressivism and traditionalism. That is, the progressive first-order factors should load on one of them and traditional first-order factors on the other. Subsequent experience with this mode of analysis showed it to be a good one: it was appropriate to the theory and to the data and accommodated both the first-order complexity of attitudes and their underlying simplicity at the second order. We now describe a study of the structure of attitudes toward education that used this general technique (Kerlinger, 1967b).

A 46-item scale, with 23 progressive items (called A items henceforth) and 23 traditional items (called B items) was constructed from a pool of about 100 items used in earlier research. Criteria of selection of items were: (1) factor loadings greater than .34 on one factor only; (2) item-total r's greater than .39, A items with A totals and B items with B totals; and (3) wide coverage of educational attitude content. Redundant items were deleted and some items were rewritten to improve wording. The reason for constructing the scale was to provide an instrument with adequate reliabilities of the A and B measures—the reliabilities of the ES-I measures were not always satisfactory—and to have a scale whose items covered a broad range of educational topics and content. The original goal was 50 items, but it was not possible to find 50 items that satisfied the criteria. Indeed, not all of the 46 items satisfied them. The 46 items were randomly inserted in a 7-point summated-rating (Likert) scale called Education Scale VI, or ES-VI. The instructions asked for expression of degrees of agreement or disagreement with the items, emphasizing honest response by stressing the wide variety of response possible. ES-VI is given in Appendix B.

ES-VI was administered to graduate students of education and teachers in New York ($N = 344$), North Carolina ($N = 404$), and Texas ($N = 556$) in 1964 and 1965.[5] The scale was usually administered during class time with a brief explanation of the purpose of the study. No extraneous motivation was used except an appeal to cooperate "for research purposes." Graduate students of education were used extensively in this and subsequent studies for reasons mentioned before: their data had yielded factor structures similar to those yielded by people outside the university, their beliefs about education and social issues, while predominantly liberal and progressive, were varied enough to ensure substantial variance, and they were available in large numbers.

The means, standard deviations, and alpha reliability estimates of the progressivism and traditionalism, A and B, subscales, r_{tt}, are given in Table 6.4. Odd-even and average-r estimates were also calculated. They were much the same as the alpha estimates: the largest difference was .032. The correlations between the A and B subscales are also given, r_{AB}.

The similarity of the statistics of the three samples is apparent. The differences are not large enough to warrant comment. The reliabilities of the A and B measures are satisfactory. The low negative correlations between the A and B subscales were as expected.

The correlations among the 46 items in each sample were calculated and factor analyzed with the principal factors method (Harman, 1976,

[5] I am grateful to Professors G. Kowitz and R. Sommerfeld who administered the scale in Texas and North Carolina. In addition, it was administered to graduate students of education in Canada ($N = 161$, by Professor T. Linton) and to a heterogeneous sample of professors and students in New York. The results were similar to those obtained with the three samples mentioned above.

TABLE 6.4
Means, Standard Deviations, Reliability, and Correlations
Between A and B Measures, ES-VI: NY, NC, and T Samples[a]

N		NY 344	NC 404	T 556
M :				
	A	5.51	5.51	5.24
	B	4.14	4.19	4.43
SD:				
	A	.70	.54	.67
	B	.85	.74	.74
r_{tt}:[b]				
	A	.85	.79	.83
	B	.86	.83	.82
r_{AB}:[c]				
		-.30	-.27	-.18

[a] NY: New York; NC: North Carolina; T: Texas; A: Progressivism, B: Traditionalism.

[b] r_{tt}: alpha reliability coefficient.

[c] r_{AB}: correlation between A and B subscales.

Ch. 8) and varimax orthogonal rotations (Kaiser, 1958). Four factors were extracted in each sample. The purpose of this analysis was to test factorial invariance. Only four factors were extracted and rotated because with increasing numbers of factors the agreement among factors of different samples tends to decrease (Peterson, 1965) because error and sample specificity have relatively greater influence. (More factors were extracted and rotated in the main analysis of the study described below.) The coefficient of congruence (Harman, 1976, p. 344) was used to compare factors.[6] Visual inspection of the rotated factors of the three samples indicated high similarity. The coefficients of congruence between the rotated factors of the three samples also indicated high similarity. The coefficients of congruence between the rotated factors of the three samples are given in Table 6.5. The coefficients for factors I, II, and III are all above .90; agreement is good. For factor IV the coefficients are lower though still substantial. It is apparent that the factors of the three samples are alike.

[6] The coefficient of congruence is a measure of association or congruence of factor vectors. It is similar to the coefficient of correlation but is not interpreted in quite the same way. The higher the coefficient of congruence the greater the congruence between the loadings of two factor vectors. Coefficients greater than .90 indicate very good congruence, between .80 and .90 good to fair congruence, and coefficients lower than, say, .75 or .70 poor congruence. These are only rough criteria, however (see Harman, 1976, pp. 344–345). My experience has indicated that the coefficients should be .85 and higher to indicate congruent factors.

TABLE 6.5
Coefficients of Congruence Between Rotated Factors of ES-VI
Orthogonal Four-Factor Solutions, Three Samples

	I	II	III	IV
NY - NC	.92	.94	.92	.80
NY - T	.97	.96	.91	.88
NC - T	.93	.95	.95	.75

The main analysis of the study was principal factors factor analysis and oblique promax rotations (Hendrickson & White, 1964), and second-order factor analysis in each sample of the correlations among eight obliquely rotated factors. Eight-factor solutions were chosen for all three samples because eight factors adequately defined the second-order factors, they yielded good simple structures in both the first- and second-order analyses, and they did not show excessive spread of factor loadings. (For a brief characterization of simple structure, see Appendix A.) Factor-by-factor comparisons showed good or fair agreement of the three samples. We limit discussion to the results obtained with the New York sample, $N = 344$.

The factor arrays of the eight first-order factors are given in Table 6.6. They are given in full because they suggest what the first-order factors of educational attitudes may be. There are four progressive factors, II, III, IV, and VII, and three traditional factors, I, V, and VI. Factor VIII had only two items and was therefore not named. It was clearly bipolar. We forego discussion of the factors. The interested reader can consult the original report. What is substantively important is the general nature of the factors. Factors I, V, and VI have only B items: they are traditional factors. Similarly, factors II, III, and VII have only A items: they are progressive factors. Factor IV has five A items and one B item negatively loaded. ($-.25$). These factors and loadings are in accord with the criterial referents theory. There is little bipolarity. (Later in the book we will deal with the nagging suspicion mentioned earlier that there might have been bipolarity had items opposite in meaning to the items of ES-VI been included in the scale.)

The correlations among the eight first-order factors are given in Table 6.7, and the unrotated and rotated factor matrices are given in Table 6.8. The first three eigenvalues were 1.64, .97, and .36, clearly indicating two second-order factors. Inspection of the correlation matrix shows that factor I appears to be bipolar; none of the other factors are. The bipolarity of factor I also shows up in the rotated second-order matrix (loading of $-.38$). The rotated matrix exhibits good simple structure. A plot of the two factors is much like the plot of Figure 6.1, except that there are of

I: Criticism of the Schools

One of the big difficulties with modern schools is that discipline is often sacrificed to the interests of children. (.53)

The movement to substitute "activities" for subjects in the curriculum of the modern school will operate against the best interests of American education. (.46)

The modern public school is sacrificing too much of our cultural heritage in its preoccupation with life-adjustment and group living. (.45)

Children need and should have more supervision and discipline than they usually get. (.42)

Many schools waste time and money on fads and frills: activity programs, driver education, swimming pools, social services, and the like. (.40)

What is needed in the modern classroom is a revival of the authority of the teacher. (.34)

The backbone of the school curriculum is subject matter; activities are useful mainly to facilitate the learning of subject matter. (.33)

Schools of today are neglecting the three R's. (.33)

The true view of education is so arranging learning that the child gradually builds up a storehouse of knowledge that he can use in the future. (.27)

Children need and should have more supervision and discipline than they usually get. (.26)

II. Experimentalism

In a democracy, teachers should help students understand not only the meaning of democracy but also the meaning of the ideologies of other political systems. (.58)

Subjects like communism and capitalism should be studied in the public schools. (.58)

Teachers should encourage pupils to study and criticize our own and other economic systems and practices. (.54)

Children should be taught that all problems should be subjected to critical and objective scrutiny, including religious, moral, economic, and social problems. (.45)

Learning is experimental; the child should be taught to test alternatives before accepting any of them. (.37)

Education is not so much imparting knowledge as it is encouraging and prompting the child to use his potentialities for learning. (.31)

III. Reconstructionism

Education and educational institutions must be sources of new social ideas. (.65)

Education and educational institutions must be sources of new social ideas; education must be a social program undergoing continual reconstruction. (.62)

The American public school should take an active part in stimulating social change. (.53)

The traditional moral standards of our culture should not just be accepted; they should be examined and tested in solving the present problems of students. (.32)

IV. Life Adjustment

Emotional development and social development are as important in the evaluation of pupil progress as academic achievement. (.57)

The healthy interaction of pupils one with another is just as important in school as the learning of subject matter. (.43)

The learning of proper attitudes is often more important than the learning of subject matter. (.41)

It is more important that the child learns how to approach and solve problems than it is for him to master the subject matter of the curriculum. (.37)

TABLE 6.6 *(continued)*

V. Learning as Storing Knowledge

Learning is essentially a process of increasing one's store of information about the various fields of knowledge. (.58)

Each subject and activity should be aimed at developing a particular part of the child's makeup; physical, intellectual, social, moral, or spiritual. (.45)

The true view of education is so arranging learning that the child gradually builds up a storehouse of knowledge that he can use in the future. (.42)

VI. Educational Conservatism

Teachers should keep in mind that pupils have to be made to work. (.50)

Schools should teach dependence on higher moral values. (.42)

One of the basic purposes of education is to conserve and transmit the values and standards of the society of which it is a part. (.40)

What is needed in the modern classroom is a revival of the authority of the teacher. (.39)

Since life is essentially a struggle, education should emphasize competition and the fair competitive spirit. (.34)

It is essential for learning and effective work that teachers outline in detail what is to be done and how to go about it. (.28)

One of the big difficulties with modern schools is that discipline is often sacrificed to the interests of the children. (.28)

Learning experiences organized around life experiences rather than around subjects is desirable in our schools. (.36)

The backbone of the school curriculum is subject matter; activities are useful mainly to facilitate the learning of subject matter. (-.25)

VII. Romantic Naturalism

We should fit the curriculum to the child and not the child to the curriculum. (.47)

The goals of education should be dictated by children's interests and needs, as well as by the larger demands of society. (.40)

Right from the very first grade, teachers must teach the child at his own level and not at the level of the grade he is in. (.40)

Teaching should be based on the present needs of the child. (.38)

True discipline springs from interest, motivation, and involvement in live problems. (.37)

Children should be allowed more freedom than they usually get in the execution of learning activities. (.34)

VIII. Unnamed

Teachers need to be guided in what they are to teach. No individual teacher can be permitted to do as he wishes, especially when it comes to teaching children. (.52)

Teachers should be free to teach what they think is right and proper. (-.56)

[a] Loadings $\geqslant$ .25 were considered significant. Factors I, V, and VI: Traditionalism; factors II, III, IV, and VII: Progressivism.

TABLE 6.7
Correlations Among First-Order Factors,
New York Sample, N = 344

Factor[a]	1	2	3	4	5	6	7	8
1	1.00	-.04	-.31	-.35	.38	.22	-.25	.26
2		1.00	.19	.40	.04	-.08	.30	-.08
3			1.00	.13	-.09	.06	.46	-.11
4				1.00	.00	-.10	.26	-.09
5					1.00	.27	.06	.36
6						1.00	.02	.28
7							1.00	-.14
8								1.00

[a] 2, 3, 4, 7: A factors; 1, 5, 6, 8: B factors.

TABLE 6.8
Unrotated and Rotated Second-Order Factor Matrices,
ES-VI, New York Sample, N = 344

Factors	Unrotated Matrix		Rotated Matrix[a]		Type
1	-.64	.17	-.38	.54	B
2	.35	.32	.47	.02	A
3	.46	.25	.52	-.11	A
4	.44	.22	.48	-.12	A
5	-.40	.58	.06	.70	B
6	-.27	.33	.00	.43	B
7	.53	.45	.70	.00	A
8	-.43	.30	-.13	.51	B

[a] Loadings $\geqslant$ .35 considered significant; they are italicized.

course fewer points. Factors II, III, IV, and VII cluster around the abscissa, and factors V, VI, and VIII cluster around the ordinate. (See Kerlinger, 1967b, for the plot.) Similar results were obtained with the Texas and North Carolina samples, especially at the second order. North Carolina agreed closely with New York. The Texas results, on the other hand, showed somewhat more bipolarity and certain differences in the first-order factors. The second-order results, however, clearly had the basic two-factor structure.

EDUCATIONAL ATTITUDES AND SOCIAL ATTITUDES

We have seen in this chapter that two orthogonal factors of educational attitudes, traditionalism and progressivism, emerged from the factor analysis of the correlations among a number of first-order factors (see

Table 6.8). We will see in subsequent chapters, similarly, that two second-order factors, conservatism and liberalism, emerge from the factor
analysis of social attitude first-order factors. An obvious question to ask
is: How are educational and general social attitudes related? In attempts
to answer this question, the correlations among the items of scales with
both social attitude (SA) and educational attitude (EA) items and administered to the same subjects have been factor analyzed. EA items have
behaved like SA items. For the most part EA traditionalism items have
appeared on conservative factors and EA progressivism items on liberal
factors. Sometimes the educational attitude items form their own factors;
sometimes they appear with social attitude items (see Kerlinger, 1972c).
We report here, however, stronger data on the relations between educational attitudes and social attitudes. These data, moreover, provide evidence that will be useful later.

Two social attitude summated-rating scales, one a statement (sentences
as items) scale and the other a referent scale (single words and short
phrases as items), and an educational attitudes (statement) summated-
rating scale were administered for another reason to five samples of
graduate students of education and people outside the university in New
York, North Carolina, and Texas (Kerlinger, 1972c). The social attitudes
statement scale had 26 items, 13 liberal (L) and 13 conservative (C) thus
producing two scores, L and C. The two measures are labeled SAL and
SAC. The social attitude referent scale had 50 items 24 of which could be
categorized as L items and 24 as C items. The two measures of this scale
are labeled REFL and REFC. The third scale, a statement scale, measured educational attitudes. It had 30 items, 15 progressive (P) and 15
traditional (T), which were taken from a longer scale of 46 items, Education Scale VI, or ES-VI, described earlier in this chapter. The P and T
measures are labeled ESA and ESB. (The three scales and their items are
given in Appendix B.)

The statistics of the four social attitude measures will be described in
Chapter 7. They were psychometrically satisfactory. The alpha reliabilities of SAL and SAC ranged from .72 to .86, those of REFL and
REFC from .83 to .90. We report in Table 6.9 the correlations among the
six measures of two of the samples, one from Texas, $N = 227$, and one
from North Carolina, $N = 206$. (We also report factor loadings in the
table. See below.) The correlations of the former sample are given above
the diagonal and those of the latter sample are given below the diagonal of
the R matrix of Table 6.9. For our purpose, the last two columns and the
last two rows of correlations of the R matrix are pertinent. These are the
correlations between the L and C measures of the social attitudes scales
and the P and T measures of the educational attitudes scale. The pertinent
correlations are italicized.

TABLE 6.9
Correlations Between Social and Educational Attitudes and Rotated
Factor Matrices, Texas, N = 227, and North Carolina,
N = 206

	REFL[a]	REFC	SAL	SAC	ESA	ESB	Texas[c] I	II	N.C. I	II
REFL	1.00	-.07	.53	-.37	.46[b]	-.16	.75	-.17	.73	-.23
REFC	-.15	1.00	-.15	.54	-.02	.55	.04	.68	-.15	.68
SAL	.43	-.23	1.00	-.18	.32	-.09	.64	.01	.57	.04
SAC	-.33	.54	.02	1.00	-.18	.65	-.24	.77	-.12	.71
ESA	.51	-.19	.18	-.15	1.00	-.09	.53	.07	.51	-.21
ESB	-.26	.50	.07	.51	-.23	1.00	-.01	.77	-.09	.68

[a] REFL and REFC: Referents Scale, L and C measures; SAL and SAC: Social Attitudes Scale, L and C; ESA and ESB: Educational Attitudes, progressive (A) and traditional (B).
[b] Italicized r's are those between the social and educational attitudes scale measures: L - A and C - B.
[c] Orthogonally rotated factors. Italicized loadings are those predicted to be positive and substantial.

It can be seen that, with one exception, the pertinent correlations between the $L - A$ and $C - B$ measures are positive and substantial. In the Texas sample (above diagonal), these are .46, .55, .32, and .65, and in the North Carolina sample (below diagonal) .51, .50, .18, and .51. The exceptions are the correlations between SAL and ESA in both samples: .32 and .18. These are lower than anticipated. The correlations in the other three samples are similar: all substantial and positive between the $L - A$ and the $C - B$ measures, except for the SAL − ESA correlations, which are lower. Evidently the social and educational attitude measures share substantial variance. The correlations are large enough to indicate that the educational attitude measures are in the same domain as the social attitude measures.

The rotated factors on the right of Table 6.9 show this more clearly. In both cases, factor I has substantial loadings on REFL, SAL, and ESA, and factor II has substantial loadings on REFC, SAC, and ESB. In addition, the cross-loadings—those of REFL, SAL, and ESA on factor II, for example—are all low. The rotated factors in the other three samples are similar. Progressivism and traditionalism appear to be "aspects" of liberalism and conservatism.

CONCLUSIONS

The results of the R and Q research reported in this chapter indicate that the structure of educational attitudes is basically dualistic. The evidence and the structure can be viewed in two stages, so to speak: the first order and the second order. Both orders show the dualistic character of the measured educational attitudes. In the R studies—factor analysis of item and scale correlations calculated over many individuals—the factors were generally in accord with the predictions. Progressive *(A)* items loaded together positively on first-order factors, and traditional *(B)* items loaded together positively on other first-order factors. There were few substantial negative loadings, indicating only weak bipolar effects. The correlations among the first-order factors (see Table 6.7), when factored, yielded two second-order factors, which also agreed with the predictions: *A* factors loaded positively and substantially on one factor and *B* factors positively and substantially on the other factor (see Table 6.8). Only one first-order factor had a substantial negative loading.

The results of the *Q* studies—studies in which persons' responses to attitude *Q* sorts are correlated and factor analyzed, that is, the correlations are between persons—were also dualistic. Individuals "known" to be traditional in their educational attitudes appeared on one persons factor, and individuals "known" to be progressive in their educational attitudes appeared on another factor (see Figure 6.1). And the two factors were relatively uncorrelated. Moreover, factor arrays—"new" *Q* sorts calculated from the results of the persons factor analyses, each *Q* sort or array expressing the "essence" of a factor—calculated in the *Q* studies clearly showed the traditional and progressive nature of the factors (see Table 6.1), as well as the near-orthogonality of the traditional and progressive arrays. (The correlation in one study was −.19; in a second study it was −.11.) In short, three *Q* studies yielded similar results that supported the duality hypothesis.

The results of the research discussed in this chapter, then—and other results to be reported later—support the criterial referents theory applied to educational attitudes. The most serious possible weakness of the research results and their interpretation, however, is the nature of the items used. While a fairly large pool of items (some 200) was used, it is possible that the inclusion of items that are logical opposites or negations of the items included would produce bipolarity. It is admitted, then, that the methods of item selection used may have precluded the possibility of legitimate or "true" bipolarity. There seems to be little doubt that progressivism and traditionalism are separate and distinct dimensions of educational attitudes and that they are, as predicted, relatively orthogonal to each other. But is it possible that the first-order factors that form the substructure of the second-order superstructure may be bipolar? Judging from the evidence of this chapter it appears that they are not. We must examine the question further at later points in the book, however.

If we assume that the findings reported in this chapter on educational attitudes and on the relations between educational attitudes and general social attitudes have empirical validity, then several important implications arise. First, individuals tend to be basically progressive or traditional but not both. Unless "radical" to the point of being extremely progressive or extremely traditional, individuals seem usually to be attitudinally centered in one or the other ideology. Perhaps this tendency is due to a cognitive economy or perhaps a need for simplifying the cognitive complexity of the belief world. A full-blown attitude theory, of course, would explain why this is so (if, indeed, it *is* so). Unfortunately, no such theory has been formulated. The present theory is really a set of structural hypotheses that state what exists, how it exists, but not why.

The second implication is that there appears to be empirical support for the dissertations of philosophers on the ideological background of educational thinking and practice (Brubacher, 1962; Dewey, 1902, 1916; Dupuis, 1966; Morris, 1961; National Society for the Study of Education, 1955). Philosophical idealism and realism may be the belief systems behind traditionalism, whereas pragmatism may be the belief system behind progressivism (Bell & Miller, 1979). Of course, the empirical situation is more complex than this. And there is virtually no research on the relations between philosophical positions and educational beliefs. In any case, these educational belief systems, on which there has been so much speculation but little research, emerge empirically as second-order factors of educational attitudes.

A third and, for this book, most important implication is closely related. First-order educational attitude factors, like social attitude factors, appear to be manifestations of two underlying second-order factors or latent variables. They seem to be what have been called by philosophers of education (and other scholars) traditionalism and progressivism. Moreover, they are evidently "aspects" of the general social attitude factors of liberalism and conservatism. This generalization is supported by the correlations between the L and C general attitude subscales and the P and T subscales and, somewhat more clearly, by the results of the factor analyses of the six measures of social attitudes and educational attitudes used to study the relations (see Table 6.9). In the next chapter we examine general social attitudes and their measurement and factor structure. In doing so, we also explore a new and promising method of measuring social attitudes.

7

Social Attitude Statement and Referent Scales

In this chapter and the next—indeed, throughout the book—we report research done with attitude scales that used two kinds of items: statements and referents. The conclusions of measurement are strengthened if what is measured is approached in more than one way and similar measurement results achieved. In the present case two entirely different kinds of items produced similar results and led to similar conclusions. The structural hypotheses stated earlier were also more firmly supported since similar results were obtained with both R and Q approaches. That is, the factor analytic results obtained with large numbers of people responding to a statement social attitudes scale and the results obtained from the factor analysis of correlations among persons' responses to a statement attitude Q sort both supported the basic structural hypotheses outlined earlier. In sum, two kinds of attitude items and two kinds of measurement instruments produced similar results and supported the hypotheses.

We will shortly defend the use of referents, single words and short expressions that stand for attitude cognitive objects, in attitude scales and Q sorts. The idea is so different from the traditional attitude statement in which each item is ordinarily a complete sentence or statement to which subjects respond in some approving or disapproving way, however, that more systematic explication seems desirable. In addition, the basic psychometric approach used in the research reported in this chapter and elsewhere in the book and described earlier (Chapter 3, Addendum) needs to be recalled and again characterized. This is the use of many attitude objects or referents rather than a single object or referent. We will first briefly review this approach and say how it differs from the usual approach and then discuss the use of referents as attitude items.

Recall that there are two general approaches to the measurement of social attitudes.[1] The more frequent approach is to have all items of an attitude scale aimed at one or a few attitude objects. Well-known scales with one attitude object are Thurstone's scales to measure attitudes toward the church (Thurstone & Chave, 1929), the Chinese (Thurstone, 1959, Ch. 25), the movies (Thurstone, 1959, Ch. 23), and crime (Thurstone, 1959, Ch. 7). An outstanding and extended example is Woodmansee and Cook's (1967) scale to measure attitudes toward blacks. Examples of scales to measure attitudes toward a few cognitive objects are: Free and Cantril's (1967) scale to assess attitudes toward government intervention, Messick's (1956) scale to measure attitudes toward capital punishment and war, and Ferguson's (1939, 1973) primary social attitude scales.

The second general approach assesses attitudes toward a number of attitude objects. Examples are Oliver and Butcher's (1962) attitudes toward education scales, Williams and Wright's (1955) liberalism-conservatism scale, and Hewitt et al.'s (1977) social attitudes scale. All the scales used in the research reported in this book (see Appendix B) used multiple attitude objects.

If one wishes to study the structure of social attitudes—defined in this book as the relations among social attitudinal cognitive objects, or, specifically, their factor analytic composition—one must perforce use many attitude objects. One can only study structure adequately by pursuing the relations among large numbers of attitude objects or referents because one needs to analyze the relations among them. Moreover, if one wishes to study and measure liberalism and conservatism, one similarly requires multiple attitude referents because, to capture the social attitudes of diverse groups and individuals, one requires sufficient representation of the attitude domain. This statement springs from the fact that many attitude objects have little or no relevance for many people but that some attitude objects should be relevant for most individuals or groups. Many conservative individuals, for example, may have little knowledge or interest in religion, but they may have knowledge and interest in issues expressive of economic conservatism. Both areas or factors should have

---

[1]When it is said that there are two approaches to the measurement of attitudes, it is not meant that these approaches are the only approaches. Indeed, there are many more. The general approaches we mean are focused on the numbers and representativeness of the referents or cognitive objects of attitudes, whereas analysis like Summers' focus more on techniques of attitude measurement: scaling, self-report, methods. (See Summers [1970] for descriptions of different approaches with original research studies illustrating the approaches.)

representative items if one is to tap such individuals' conservative attitudes. In any case, multiple attitude indicators are fundamental to social attitude measurement as conceived in this book.

In the research to be described, the early attitude scales were statement scales designed to measure general social attitudes and educational attitudes.[2] After the research done with statement scales, it was decided to measure social attitudes with referents. There were several reasons for this decision. First, the use of referents as attitude items is economical: many more items can be administered in less time. Second, the use of referents permits wide coverage of attitude content, though, to be sure, subtleties of attitude statements are lost. Third, the well-known ambiguity of the wording of attitude statement items can perhaps be avoided to some extent by using referents. This assumes, of course, that the referents themselves are not ambiguous. Critics can say that the use of attitude referents is context-bound. The meaning of referents like *abortion, sexual freedom, private property,* and *free enterprise,* it can be said, depends on the contexts in which they appear. True. But is it possible there is sufficient common response to referents alone so that commonality of meaning and interpretation can be assumed? Fortunately, this is an empirical matter. The statistics yielded by referent items should show whether there is such common response.

Fourth, factors yielded by factor analysis of referent items may be more readily interpretable than the factors yielded by statement items. There are usually more referent than statement items per factor simply as a function of the greater number of items in referent scales. The referent scales used had from 50 to 80 items compared to statement scales, which usually had considerably fewer items. Moreover, attitude referents, unaccompanied by verbiage, should point more directly to the nature of attitude factors. Referent factors are probably less subject to alternative interpretations than general statement items and thus probably less am-

---

[2]It may be wise to pause here to clarify concepts that have been defined earlier but that may still be unclear. Social attitudes are attitudes whose cognitive objects have wide societal relevance and thus meaning for most people of a society. We sometimes categorize them as "general" social attitudes to emphasize their large social relevance and their wide application to many areas of life: economic, political, ethnic, educational, and so on. So defined, most attitudes discussed in the social psychological literature are social attitudes. The difference is that we emphasize breadth of application and the fact that most social attitudes are believed to be related to the larger latent ideologies conservatism and liberalism: for the most part their referents can be validly categorized as liberal or conservative. Educational attitudes are conceived as a subset of general social attitudes. In other words, they *are* social attitudes but are limited to educational issues and beliefs. Their underlying latent variables, progressivism and traditionalism, are also conceived to be educational expressions of the more general liberalism and conservatism.

TABLE 7.1
The Factor of Religiosity as Expressed in Statements and in Referents

Statements[a]

Some sort of religious education should be given in public schools.
Our present difficulties are more due to moral than to economic causes.

If civilization is to survive, there must be a turning back to religion.

Referents[b]

faith in God
religion
church
Christian
teaching spiritual values

[a] From unpublished research to be reported later in this chapter.

[b] From Kerlinger et al. (1976).

biguous. In actual use in speech and writing referents are context-bound, but respondents seem to have had little difficulty in interpreting them in the scales used in the research to be reported. Referents are also more likely to yield clear factors, whereas statement scale factors are often muddied by the relative complexity of statements. To illustrate what is meant, consider the statement factor and the referent factor of "Religiosity" given in Table 7.1. These factors were obtained in two research studies to be summarized later in the chapter. It is clear that both sets of items express religious ideas, but the referents factor is simpler and even seems clearer. Not all referents factors are this simple and clear, as we will see. But even when they are more complex and difficult to interpret, they do not present as great interpretation problems as complex statement factors.

An important advantage of referent items, from the viewpoint of this book, is that unconscious bias in selecting and writing items is largely avoided. The possible bias involved in the wording of items is of course avoided. (Item reversal is also not possible.) And since many more referent than statement items can be used in a scale, possible selection bias is reduced. In other words, the suspicion mentioned in the last chapter, that the obtained dualistic results and lack of bipolarity may have been due to the method of item selection, is reduced by using large numbers of referents.

In item analysis, of course, one must be careful to eliminate only items that correlate with no other items. One must *not* eliminate items that correlate negatively with other items. If bipolarity is an important characteristic of attitudes, it must certainly appear in the correlations among the many referent items and in the factor analysis of the correlations, provided items with negative correlation potential are not screened out.

Whereas one cannot trust the bipolarity that appears with item reversals (Milholland, 1964, p. 317) as a true reflection of the nature of attitudes, one must pay careful attention if it appears with referents, provided the referents are legitimate expressions of social attitudes (items like *civil rights* and *private property*).

The final point to be made about referents is theoretically and psychologically important. Referents are categories, names. They are representations of social objects, and many of them are relatively abstract. They are close to conceptual cognitions. Therefore their use as items emphasizes the cognitive aspect of attitudes. Some may say that in so doing one neglects the emotional and motivational components of attitudes. This can be seen as an advantage, however.

What is essentially shared of attitudes, in the sense of what you share with me and with others, is mainly the cognitive aspect of attitudes. Emotions are shared, too, but they are diffuse and unspecific. Cognitions are activities of knowing (Neisser, 1976). The organizations or structures of attitudes are abstract schemata that delineate or represent the shared beliefs of individuals about the social world. And these organizations or structures are very likely made up in large part of attitude referents and their interrelations. As Rosch (1977) has pointed out, categories are coded in cognition in prototypes of the most characteristic members of the categories. I propose that the basic cognitive stuff of attitudes is beliefs about attitude referents. It is for this reason that it is the cognitive aspect of attitudes that is shared by people. The point here is that the cognitive aspect of attitudes, as epitomized in referents, is asserted to be the most important part as far as shared representations among individuals is concerned. One can say that social referents are the objects of social attitudes. We propose that an important part of the cognitive representation of the social world is attitude referents, which are organized or "classified" in people's mind in functionally effective ways.

SOCIAL ATTITUDE STATEMENT SCALES

Social Attitudes I (SA-I)

In the early 1960s, a 40-item social attitude statement scale, Social Attitudes I, or SA-I, was constructed to explore the factor structure of social attitudes, and to provide liberal and conservative measures to use in attitude research. It was a 7-point summated-rating scale with 20 presumably liberal *(L)* and 20 presumably conservative *(C)* items. Its reliability appeared to be adequate, but reliability data are not available because the original data were lost in a move of offices. Factor analytic data are available because the correlations among the 40 items were recovered and could be reanalyzed. We concentrate on the factors and the factor analyses. The scale items were inspired by a variety of sources: newspaper articles and editorials, magazine articles, historical, philosophical, sociological, and political science discussions of liberalism and conservatism, existing scales, and knowledge of attitude expressions.

Approximately 100 items were assembled or written. The best 40 items were chosen using the following criteria: representativeness of the social attitude domain (religious, economic, political, educational, and general social areas), nonredundancy, and apparent "appropriateness" (relevance, potency of expression, and aptness).

The scale was administered to 666 persons in New York: 210 graduate students of education, 251 undergraduate students of education, and 205 people outside the university (OP's)—housewives, nurses, organization members, and so forth. The responses to the 40 items were intercorrelated and factor analyzed using the principal factors method and orthogonal varimax and oblique promax rotations (Hendrickson & White, 1964). We concentrate on the oblique rotations because second-order factor analysis was used to test the duality hypothesis discussed in earlier chapters.

Ten factors were extracted and rotated in order to provide sufficient factors for second-order analysis. (A factor analysis using the usual criteria for numbers of factors to extract and rotate would have had only four to seven factors.) The correlations among the ten oblique factors were factor analyzed using the principal factors method. Two second-order factors were orthogonally rotated, although it is possible that three factors might have been rotated: the first three eigenvalues were 2.11, 1.22, and .54.[3] The unrotated and rotated second-order factors are given in Table 7.2. The rotated matrix exhibits a clean simple structure. The second-order structure of these data is undoubtedly dualistic; there is little bipolarity. The liberalism factors—numbers 1, 2, 8, and 10—are loaded on factor I, and the conservatism factors—numbers 3, 4, 5, 6, and 7—are loaded on factor II. One first-order factor, No. 9, has only a low loading .33. Second-order factor I is liberalism, and second-order factor II is conservatism.

---

[3] When this analysis was done, there had been little experience with the factor analysis of such item data. Consequently there were methodological weaknesses in the analysis. Three second-order factors should probably have been rotated, though the point is moot. I later rotated the third factor. The rotation actually improved the structure: three of the liberalism factor loadings became higher; other loadings were little affected. In other words, rotating the third factor improved the structure of factors I and II. I report only the two-factor rotation.

TABLE 7.2
Unrotated and Rotated Second-Order Factors, SA-I, N = 666

	Unrotated Factors		Rotated Factors[a]		Types
	I	II	I	II	
1	-.22	.30	.37	-.05	L
2	-.25	.55	.60	.05	L
3	.69	.18	-.17	.69	C
4	.50	.40	.11	.63	C
5	.63	.31	-.03	.70	C
6	.44	.03	-.19	.40	C
7	.55	.30	.00	.62	C
8	-.48	.49	.66	-.19	L
9	.36	.04	-.14	.33	C
10	-.45	.59	.73	-.11	L

[a] Rotated factor loadings considered significant ($\geqslant$.35) are italicized.

Social Attitudes II (SA-II)

The above study was exploratory. For this reason and because all the data were not available and the analysis was methodologically flawed, only the second-order factors were reported. We now report a subsequent study whose purpose was to construct a reliable and factorially valid social attitudes scale with fewer items (Kerlinger, 1970a.) This study profited from greater methodological sophistication, was done in three states of the United States, and its L and C subscales were correlated with other measures. Thus its results bear indirectly on the theory.

The best 26 items of SA-I, 13 liberal and 13 conservative, were selected for a second social attitudes scale, Social Attitudes II, or SA-II, on the basis of magnitude of factor loadings, item-total correlations, and heterogeneity of attitude content. Like SA-I, it was a 7-point summated-rating scale to whose items subjects expressed degrees of agreement and disagreement. The scale is given in Appendix B.

SA-II was administered to samples mainly of teachers and graduate students of education in New York, Texas, and North Carolina, one sample each in New York and Texas and three samples in North Carolina. One of the North Carolina samples ($N = 97$) consisted of people outside the university—housewives, clerks, and miscellaneous others. Another North Carolina sample of graduate students ($N = 64$) was said to be highly progressive in its educational attitudes. The means, standard deviations, alpha reliability coefficients, and correlations between the liberal and conservative subscales are given in Table 7.3.

The L and C means and standard deviations of New York, Texas, and the largest North Carolina samples are unremarkable: the L means are only a little higher than the C means. In the North Carolina OP ($N = 97$) sample the C mean is greater than the L mean, and in the highly progressive group ($N = 64$) the L mean is much greater than the C mean. Evidently the scale is sensitive to group differences. The internal consistency reliabilities of both L and C are satisfactory in the New York, Texas, and North Carolina OP samples, in the .80's, but those of the other North Carolina samples are somewhat lower. Repeat reliability estimates were obtained from the responses to the scale of a separate sample of 50 graduate education students. The second administration of the scale was done 3 months after the first administration. The repeat reliability coefficients were .85 for the L subscale and .84 for the C subscale. The two subscales appear to be reliable.

The correlations between the the L and C subscales are, with one exception, consistent with the theory and with the construction of the scale: -23, $-.09$, $.02$, and $-.12$. The exception is the highly progressive group ($N = 64$), whose L—C correlation is a substantial $-.64$, one of the highest negative correlations between L and C yet obtained.

For the factor analysis of the items of SA-II, the Texas ($N = 263$) and two of the North Carolina samples ($N = 206$ and $N = 97$) were combined (total $N = 530$). The 26 items were intercorrelated and factor analyzed with the principal factors method and oblique rotations. (Orthogonal rotations yielded similar though less clear results.) Four factors were ex-

TABLE 7.3
SA-II: Basic Statistics of New York, Texas, and
North Carolina Samples[a]

		N.Y.	Texas	N.C.		
N:		263	227	206	64	97
M:						
	L:	3.98	4.12	3.80	4.52	3.61
	C:	3.55	3.48	3.78	2.97	4.19
s:						
	L:	.92	.85	.82	.82	.97
	C:	.91	.92	.86	.76	.95
r_{tt}:[b]						
	L:	.81	.81	.77	.78	.86
	C:	.80	.82	.74	.74	.83
r_{LC}:		-.23	-.09	.02	-.64	-.12

[a] All samples, except N.C., $N = 97$, were graduate students of education; N.C., $N = 97$, consisted of people outside the university.

[b] r_{tt}: alpha reliability coefficients.

TABLE 7.4
SA-II: Oblique Factor Arrays, Four Factors, Texas and
North Carolina Sample, N = 530

Economic Liberalism - Socialism

To ensure adequate care of the sick, we need to change radically the present system of privately controlled medical care. (.54)

Our present economic system should be reformed so that profits are replaced by reimbursements for useful work. (.53)

The gradual social ownership of industry needs to be encouraged if we are ever to cure some of the ills of our society. (.52)

Unemployment insurance is an inalienable right of the working man. (.47)

Large fortunes should be taxed fairly heavily over and above income taxes. (.45)

Society should be quicker to throw out old ideas and traditions and to adopt new thinking and customs. (.42)

Public enterprises like railroads should not make profits; they are entitled to fares sufficient to enable them to pay only a fair interest on the actual cash capital they have invested. (.41)

Government Aid to Education

Federal Government aid for the construction of schools is long overdue, and should be instituted as a permanent policy. (.49)

Both public and private universities and colleges should get generous aid from both state and federal governments. (.42)

Funds for school construction should come from state and federal government loans at no interest or very low interest. (.40)

All individuals who are intellectually capable of benefiting from it should get college education, at public expense if necessary. (.39)

Government ownership and management of utilities leads to bureaucracy and inefficiency. (-.36)

Religiosity - Conventionalism

If civilization is to survive, there must be a turning back to religion. (.59)

Some sort of religious education should be given in public schools. (.58)

Individuals who are against churches and religions should not be allowed to teach in colleges. (.53)

There are too many professors in our colleges and universities who are radical in their social and political beliefs. (.46)

Inherited racial characteristics play more of a part in the achievement of individuals and groups than is generally known. (.42)

A first consideration in any society is the protection of property rights. (.30)

Economic Conservatism

Government laws and regulations should be such as first to ensure the prosperity of business since the prosperity of all depends on the prosperity of business. (.55)

The well-being of a nation depends mainly on its industry and business. (.55)

Individuals with the ability and foresight to earn and accumulate wealth should have the right to enjoy that wealth without government interference and regulations. (.51)

A first consideration in any society is the protection of property rights. (.36)

If the United States takes part in any sort of world organization, we should be sure that we lose none of our power and influence. (.35)

There should be no government interference with business and trade. (.33)

[a] The numbers in parentheses are oblique factor loadings. Loadings $\geqslant$ .30 were considered significant.

tracted and rotated, though even a two-factor solution yielded satisfactory results. (The first four eigenvalues were 4.03, 3.17, .87, and .54.) Four factors were extracted, however, to see if they would yield a sensible second-order structure. The correlations among the four factors were themselves factor analyzed in the usual second-order manner.

We want to study these factors for their own sake and for future comparisons with referent factors. Moreover, the factor structure of this scale has never been published, even though the scale itself has been published in two anthologies of scales (Robinson et al., 1968; Shaw & Wright, 1967). The essential results, therefore, are given in Tables 7.4 and 7.5. Table 7.4 contains the factor arrays of the four-factor oblique first-order solution, and Table 7.5 contains the correlations among the four oblique factors and the two-factor unrotated and rotated factor matrices yielded by the second-order factor analysis. As we will see later, the factor named Economic Liberalism–Socialism occurs again and again in different samples, though in somewhat different forms. It is of course a liberal factor. The factors, Religiosity–Conventionalism and Economic Conservatism also occur repeatedly, though the former appears as simply Religiosity. The factor, Government Aid to Education has not appeared in other samples, perhaps because appropriate items were not used. While three of the four factors are evidently important social attitude factors, we will see later that there are at least four or more other factors.

The correlations among the four first-order factors are given in Table 7.5. While the correlations are low, the structure is clear. It is shown more clearly by the orthogonally rotated second-order factors (given in the bottom half of the table with the unrotated factors). The structure is by now familiar: a conservative factor and a liberal factor with little bipolarity. Since the scale was constructed similarly to the educational attitudes scales described in Chapter 6, however, this is only weak support for the criterial referents theory. That is, SA-II's construction was perhaps biased because only items from the original 40-item SA-I were considered for inclusion in the scale.

The evidence obtained with these scales shows that the L and C subscales are reliable and that the first- and second-order factors are consistent with the criterial referents theory. L items loaded on L factors and C items loaded on C factors. L items did not in general load, positively or negatively, on C factors, nor did C items load on L factors. The four first-order factors were clearly interpretable, two being L factors and two C factors. The rotated second-order factor structure had two orthogonal factors, one L and one C. This evidence must be considered somewhat suspect, however, because the method of item selection may have been biased in favor of the theory. We therefore turn to a type of item (and scale) that perhaps lessens the bias.

TABLE 7.5

SA-II: Correlations Among Factors and Unrotated and Rotated
Second-Order Factors, Texas and North Carolina Sample, $N = 530$

	1	2	3	4	Type[a]
1	1.00	.33	.08	-.01	L
2		1.00	-.23	-.21	L
3			1.00	.39	C
4				1.00	C

	Unrotated Factors		Rotated Factors[b]		Type
1	-.19	.57	.08	.50	L
2	-.50	.34	-.30	.53	L
3	.58	.28	.64	-.01	C
4	.59	.19	.61	-.09	C

[a]L: liberal; C: conservative.

[b]Loadings $\geq .35$ were considered significant.   They are italicized.

SOCIAL ATTITUDE REFERENTS

From this point on, we emphasize the use of referents as items in attitude
measurement instruments. After it was realized that the data obtained
with statement scales, as described above and in Chapter 6, constituted
only weak support for the criterial referents theory, use of referents as
items, which had started in the mid-1960s, was reinforced. Could the
difficulties with statement scales described earlier perhaps be avoided, or
at least mitigated, by using referents as items? Inspired by early work in
directive-state theory (Allport, 1955) and Postman, Bruner, and McGinnies' (1948) use of value words as stimuli, I used single value words for
classroom demonstrations of value measurement. Another influence was
Hofman's (1964) doctoral thesis in which clustering of educational attitude concepts (referents) was studied. Hofman found a dual structure,
one factor consisting of progressive items and the other of traditional
items. The next influence was the work done in developing the criterial
referents theory (Kerlinger, 1967a). If referents were at the core of attitudes, why not use them as attitude items?

Referents I (REF-I)

The first referents scale developed was a 50-item instrument, with 24
presumed L items and 24 presumed C items, called Referents I, or REF-I.
(Two items of the scale were used for an extraneous purpose; they were
included in the item factor analyses.) The scale and the research done

with it (Kerlinger, 1972c) were described in Chapter 3. Therefore the main findings are only briefly recapitulated here. REF-I's L and C subscales were reliable: all alpha coefficients were in the .80's (see Table 3.1).

The six factors extracted from the 50-by-50 item correlation matrix (see Table 3.2), three L factors and three C factors, and the second-order factor analysis of the correlations among the six obliquely rotated factors upheld the expectations of the criterial referents theory. L items loaded on L factors and C items on C factors. With one exception *(racial purity)*, L items did not appear on C factors, and C items did not appear on L factors. The second-order factor analysis yielded two orthogonal factors on one of which L factors were loaded and on the other C factors (see Table 3.4). There was little evidence of bipolarity. The plot of these second-order factors, given in Figure 3.1, showed an almost classic orthogonal structure—as predicted by the theory.

The evidence from this study, done in three widely separated states, supports the theory. The possibility of biased item writing and selection mentioned earlier seems considerably lessened since the 50 items of REF-I were selected from a large pool of referent items using the criteria described in Chapters 3 and 4. While it is always possible that unconscious bias excluded items that might have produced bipolarity, it is considerably less likely that a scale of single words and short phrases chosen from a large pool of such items would be so biased. For one thing, wording bias is minimized. For another, the original compilation of the pool of items came from a wide variety of sources, and the criteria of selection, especially the criterion of representativeness of the social attitude domain, diminished the possibility of selection bias. As we will see, however, later research in different places, including two European countries, and with different referent scales did produce limited bipolarity.[4]

Referents IV (REF-IV)[5]

In an unpublished study of values and attitudes, a 76-item referents scale, Referents IV, or REF-IV, was constructed to study the factor structure of social attitude (and value) referents and to provide liberal and conservative measures for the study. To assure the strength of the L and C catego-

---

[4]Before leaving REF-I, it should be said that results highly similar to those summarized above and described in Chapter 3 were also found with a sample of graduate students of education in New York ($N = 263$). Indeed, the resemblance of the factors was marked.

[5]The numbers of the referents scales reported in this book are not consecutive because different kinds of scales were constructed and tested, but not used in research. REF-II, for example, was a 20-item "choices" scale ("Choose seven issues or ideas that are important to you") and REF-III was a 120-item paired-comparisons scale. They were constructed for teaching purposes.

ries, items high on the factor arrays of the factor analysis of REF-I were selected, for example, *religion, church, free enterprise,* and *private property* for *C,* and *civil rights, Supreme Court, children's interests,* and *Social Security* for *L.* In addition, the literature was again searched for more items.

REF-IV was also supposed to have both attitude and value items. Since the distinction between attitudes and values is not important for the present purpose, we only mention it and pass on. It was believed that the main difference between attitude referents and value referents was abstractness: the more abstract a referent, the more likely it was to be a value referent. *Civil rights* and *capitalism* are relatively abstract, especially when compared to *blacks* and *money.* The former are conceived to be value referents and the latter attitude referents. Since no empirical differences were found between the two kinds of referents—they were loaded similarly on the same factors, for example—we drop the distinction from further consideration.

As many of the 76 referents as possible were also categorized as liberal and conservative on the basis of knowledge of such sets of beliefs, previous research, and liberal and conservative literature (e.g., Rossiter, 1962, on conservatism, and Girvetz, 1963, on liberalism). It was possible to so categorize 54 referents, 27 *L* and 27 *C.* These items were used for psychometric analysis.

REF-IV and two statement values scales were administered to 237 graduate students of education in two large universities in New York City. The REF-IV means of 5.73 for *L* and 4.63 for *C* reflect the liberal predilection of the sample. The alpha reliabilities of .85 for *L* and .92 for *C* were highly satisfactory. The correlation between the *L* and *C* subscales was − .29, somewhat higher than expected but within the bounds of theoretical prediction. (Theoretical prediction was that r_{LC} not exceed − .30.) Item-total correlations, *L* items with *L* totals and *C* items with *C* totals, were mostly satisfactory ($\geq$.35) Evidently the *L* and *C* subscales measure liberalism and conservatism, as intended, and have satisfactory reliabilities.

Our principal interest in REF-IV is its first- and second-order factor structures. The intercorrelations among the 76 items of REF-IV were as usual calculated and the correlation matrix factor analyzed with the principal factors method, using R^2's as communality estimates and promax oblique rotations. It was believed that there would be 8 to 12 factors. All five solutions were run. The ten-factor solution was selected as the "best" because it was the most internally consistent and agreed the most with the original correlations. The ten referent factor arrays are given in Table 7.6.

Six of the factors are liberal, in the sense that the individual items of the factors can be identified as liberal referents—for example, *collective bargaining, trade unions, Social Security,* and *economic reform* of the factor Labor—and four are conservative—for example, *real estate, business, profits,* and so on of the factor Economic Conservatism. Names have been given to the factors to summarize their nature and to facilitate comparison with REF-I factors and factors of other scales. Two of the four *C* factors, Economic Conservatism and Religiosity, also appeared in the factor analysis of REF-I. The other two factors, Morality and Social Conservatism, did not appear with REF-I. The items of Morality were mostly not used in REF-I, and the same was true of the items of Social Conservatism.

Of the six *L* factors of REF-IV, three also appeared in the factor analy-

TABLE 7.6
REF-IV: Factor Arrays and Loadings of Item Factor Analysis,
Oblique Solution, N = 237

Conservatism Factors

Economic Conservatism

real estate (.66)
business (.60)
profits (.57)
private property (.49)
corporate industry (.48)
capitalism (.47)
money (.45)
free enterprise (.41)
national sovereignty (.33)
individual initiative (.30)
patriotism (.30)

world government (-.25)

Traditional Conservatism

Supreme Court (.45)
competition (.34)
authority (.36)
Americans (.35)
capitalism (.35)
money (.30)
social stability (.30)
law and order (.30).
private property (.29)
discipline (.27)
subject matter (.29)

free college education for all (-.32)
open admission to college (-.29)
women's liberation (-.29)
equality of women (-.27)
children's interests (-.26)

Religiosity

church (.64)
religion (.63)
religious education (.62)
Christian (.60)
Jews (.27)

liberalized abortion laws (-.32)

Morality

morality (.69)
moral standards (.63)
manners (.33)
subject matter (.31)

TABLE 7.6 *(continued)*

Liberalism Factors

Civil Rights

Negroes (.72)
racial integration (.59)
racial equality (.58)
blacks (.57)
civil rights (.49)
desegregation (.48)
poverty program (.44)
equality (.37)
federal housing projects (.31)

natural classes of men (-.29)

Social Liberalism

sexual freedom (.51
liberalized abortion laws (.45)
desegregation (.42)
racial integration (.40)
social change through education (.35)
equality of women (.27)
equality (.27)
freedom (.25)

objective tests (-.33)

Science

scientific theory (.67)
scientific research (.57)
human personality (.31)
women's liberation (.27)

Progressivism

children's interests (.61)
children's needs (.48)
child-centered curriculum (.44)
pupil personality (.43)
individual initiative (.42)
activity program in schools (.36)
social change through education (.36)
reason (.34)
character (.27)
social stability (.25)

Government Aid

socialized medicine (.49)
government ownership of utilities (.48)
government price controls (.35)
free college education for all (.32)
open admission to college (.32)
federal housing projects (.28)

character (-.26)

Labor

collective bargaining (.59)
trade unions (.57)
Social Security (.34)
economic reform (.26)

sis of REF-I: Civil Rights, Social Liberalism, and Progressivism. Progressivism, however, was called Child-Centered Education in the REF-I analysis. They appear to be essentially the same factor. Three L factors that did not appear at all with REF-I were Government Aid, Science, and Labor. The reason is simple: most of their items were not used in REF-I. To facilitate comparison of the two factor analyses, the names of the factors obtained with REF-I and REF-IV are juxtaposed in Table 7.7. (The names of the SA-II factors are also given in the table. We will refer to them later.) One can see clearly that five of the ten factors of REF-IV were virtually the same in REF-I. Educational Traditionalism of REF-I did not appear in the analysis of REF-IV no doubt because only two of its four items were used in REF-IV. The same is in general true of the *L* factors that appeared in the REF-IV analysis and not in the REF-I analysis. It is clear that the factor structures of the two sets of data are quite similar.

The REF-IV first-order analysis yielded more bipolarity than did the REF-I analysis: ten items loaded negatively, five of them on one factor, Social Conservatism. All ten negative loadings, however, were less than −.35 (in absolute value). Had the same criterion for "significance" of factor loadings in REF-IV been adopted as that of REF-I (≥.30)—≥.25 was used in REF-IV because oblique loadings are in general smaller than orthogonal loadings—there would have been far fewer "significant" negative loadings. In any case, the first-order factor analysis of REF-IV supports the criterial referents theory: *L* items loaded on *L* factors and *C* items on *C* factors. Cross-factor negative loadings were all low. Before leaving the first-order analysis, it is worthwhile to note that abstract and specific referents cannot be distinguished: both kinds of referents appear together on factors—for example, the specific referents *blacks* and *federal housing projects* appear with the abstract referents *racial equality* and *desegregation* on the factor Civil Rights.

The rotated factors of the second-order factor analysis of the correlations among the ten oblique factors are given in Table 7.8, together with the types of factors, *L* and *C,* and the names of the factors. The eigenvalues of the first three factors were 2.45, 1.65, and .38, indicating that there were two second-order factors. The factor loadings are as they "should be," with two exceptions: the loading of −.47 of factor 2 on second-order factor I, and the lack of a significant loading of factor 8. Otherwise, *C* factors load on second-order factor I, and *L* factors load on

TABLE 7.7
Comparison of Factors of REF-I, REF-IV, and SA-II

REF-I	REF-IV	SA-II
	Conservative Factors	
Religiosity	Religiosity	Religiosity
Economic Conservatism	Economic Conservatism	Economic Conservatism
Educational Traditionalism		
	Liberal Factors	
Civil Rights	Civil Rights	Economic Liberalism -
Child-Centered Education	Progressivism	Socialism
Social Liberalism	Social Liberalism	Government Aid to
	Social Liberalism -	Education
	Government Aid	
	Science	
	Labor	

TABLE 7.8
REF-IV: Rotated Second-Order Factors, Factor Types, and Names

| | Rotated Factors[a] | | h^2 | Type | Name |
	I	II			
1	.60	-.23	.41	C	Economic Conservatism
2.	.64	.02	.41	C	Religiosity
3	.73	.20	.57	C	Morality
4	.66	.27	.51	C	Traditional Conservatism
5	-.47	.41	.39	L	Civil Rights
6	.27	.52	.34	L	Progressivism
7	-.08	.48	.24	L	Social Liberalism
8	.26	-.04	.07	L	Social Liberalism: Government Aid
9	.11	.60	.37	L	Science
10	-.15	.68	.49	L	Labor

[a] Loadings ⩾.35 were considered significant. They are italicized.

second-order factor II.[6] The second-order results again support the criterial referents theory.

CORRELATIONS BETWEEN REFERENT AND STATEMENT SCALES

An important question that has not yet been answered is: How are the liberal and conservative subscales of the statement scales and the referent scales related? Fortunately, SA-II and REF-I were both administered to the five samples in North Carolina, Texas, and New York described earlier in the chapter. Two values scales, called Values-I, or VAL-I, and Values-II, or VAL-II, were also administered to the New York sample ($N = 237$) mentioned above. Since each of these scales had liberal and conservative subscales, we have further evidence of the "existence" of the latent variables liberalism and conservatism. We assume, of course, a certain validity of the statement scales, SA-II, VAL-I, and VAL-II. This is not unreasonable since the three statement scales are like many of the

---

[6] Earlier it was said that ⩾.35 was the criterion used for "significant" orthogonal factor loadings and ⩾.30 for oblique loadings. The former was used for all second-order factor loadings in all studies. But ⩾.30 and ⩾.25 were both used for first-order loadings. The reason was that in two or three of the studies the general levels of the correlation coefficients were low and the .30 criterion excluded items that seemed important as judged by the correlations among the items. In most cases, however, it has made little or no difference in the factor structures. Where it may make a difference is in judging whether an appreciable amount of bipolarity exists in a factor matrix. For example, in the factors reported in Table 7.6, a criterion of .30 would have excluded the last four negatively loaded referents of the factor Social Conservatism. In future cases of doubt, special care will be taken with negative loadings.

conventional attitude scales in past and current use (see Robinson & Shaver, 1969, for examples), except that the former assume the relatively orthogonal nature of the two dimensions.

SA-II and REF-I Correlations

We expect that the L subscales of REF-I and REF-IV will correlate positively and substantially with the L subscales of the statement subscales, and similarly for the C subscales of REF-I and REF-IV and the statement scales. We further expect low negative correlations between the L and C subscales of all the scales.

The expectations of positive substantial correlations betwen the L referent and statement scales and between the C referent and statement scales were justified. In the five samples in which both REF-I and SA-II were administered (see Table 7.3), the range of the L correlations was .43 to .58, with an average r, via the z transformation, of .51. The range of the C correlations was .54 to .66, with an average r of .59. On the other hand, the cross-correlations were higher than expected, especially the L-C cross-correlations between the two scales. The L-C cross-correlation between-scales range was $-.33$ to $-.53$, with an average of $-.40$. The L-C cross-correlations *within* the scales were within the limits of theoretical prediction: they were less than $-.30$ (in absolute value). That is, the higher negative correlations were those cross-correlations between the L and C subscales *between* the statement and referent subscales.

To illustrate typical correlations between the SA-II and REF-I L and C subscales, the correlations and cross-correlations within and between the scales of two samples, Texas, $N = 227$, and New York, $N = 263$, are given in Table 7.9, the Texas correlations above the diagonal and the New York correlations below the diagonal. The most important r's, those between the L subscales and between the C subscales, are italicized. It can be seen that three of the four are greater than .50. Evidently SA-II and REF-I, despite their differences in item type and response mode—the SA-II instructions asked for degrees of agreement and disagreement, whereas REF-I asked for degrees of positive and negative feelings—appear to be measuring liberalism and conservatism. Factor analysis of the subscales of these scales, together with the subscales of an educational attitudes scale, confirmed the L and C factors behind the six subscales. We take up these factor analyses in a later chapter.

The substantial negative cross-correlations of the L and C subscales *across* the statements and referents scales—for example, $-.37$ in the Texas sample and $-.40$ and $-.43$ in the New York sample—are not in line with expectation. These substantial negative r's between L and C dimensions across statement and referent scales—note that the L and C r's within scales are within theoretical expectation in Table 7.9: less than

TABLE 7.9
Correlations Between L and C Subscales of REF-I and SA-II,
Texas, N = 227, and New York, N = 263, Samples[a]

	SAL[b]	SAC	REFL	REFC
SAL	1.00	-.09	*.53*	-.15
SAC	-.23	1.00	-.37	*.54*
REFL	*.46*	-.40	1.00	-.07
REFC	-.43	*.66*	-.21	1.00

[a] Texas sample correlations are above the diagonal; New York sample correlations are below the diagonal. The correlations between the L subscales and between the C subscales are italicized.

[b] SAL: SA-II, L; SAC: SA-II, C; REFL: REF-I, L; REFC: REF-I, C.

$-.30$ (in absolute value)—also occur in the other three samples, though not consistently. Evidently they reflect some sort of artifact.[7] In sum, the L and C subscales of SA-II, the statements scale, and REF-I, the referents scale, are positively and substantially correlated.

SA-IV and Values Scales Correlations

The correlations between the L and C subscales of the two statement values scales, VAL-I and VAL-II, and the L and C subscales of REF-IV exhibit the same pattern as that reported for SA-II and REF-I. Before reporting the data, we need to describe briefly VAL-I and VAL-II. The unpublished study in which these scales were used was designed as an exploratory investigation of relations between attitudes and values. We need not give psychometric details of the values scales since we are only concerned with L and C correlations between the attitude and value scales. Each scale had 60 statement items, 40 of which could be categorized as L or C in VAL-I while 46 could be so categorized in VAL-II. The L and C alpha reliabilities were, for VAL-I, .80 and .80, and, for VAL-II, .79 and .82. The two scales were designed to be alternate forms.

The correlations between the L and C subscales of VAL-I and VAL-II and the L and C subscales of REF-IV (N = 237) are given in Table 7.10. We find here the same pattern of correlations that we found with SA-II and REF-I: substantial r's between the VAL-I and VAL-II L subscales and the REF-IV L subscale: .59 and .51, and even more substantial r's between the comparable C subscales: .70 and .66. Again, the statement

---

[7] I have been unable to find an adequate explanation of these substantial negative cross correlations. That they are artifacts seems clear since the within-scale $L - C$ correlations are within the usual bounds: $-.09$, $-.23$, $-.07$, and $-.21$ in Table 7.9, for instance. Colleagues to whom I have posed the problem have also been baffled.

scales and the referent scale are evidently tapping the same latent variables. The correlations between the L and C subscales of VAL-I and VAL-II themselves are .74 and .79. The r's between L and C *within* each of the scales are within theoretical expectation: $-.25$ for VAL-I, $-.28$ for VAL-II, and $-.29$ for REF-IV. But, again, the $L - C$ r's *between* the values scales and the referent scale are substantial and higher than expected: $-.43$, $-.42$, $-.49$, and $-.43$. The same conclusions arrived at earlier for SA-II and REF-I are applicable here except that the negative cross-correlations between the statements and referents scales are even higher than before.

STATEMENT AND REFERENT Q SORTS

At about the same time the study using REF-I and SA-II was done, a parallel Q study was undertaken (Kerlinger, 1972a). The purposes of the study were to test certain implications of the criterial referents theory in a Q methodological manner, to "parallel" the R study with a Q study, and to further investigate the virtues or lack of virtues of referents as attitude items. Q methodology was briefly described in Chapter 4, and educational attitudes Q studies were described in Chapter 6. We need only present the main features of the study.

Two Q sorts designed to measure social attitudes were used. One of these, called Social Attitudes Q Sort, or SAQ, was constructed for use in a doctoral study (Smith, 1963). It was a structured statement Q sort with 30 liberal and 30 conservative items. In addition to the L and C category, the items were also categorized as political-economic and general-social. The study itself, however, was not concerned with this latter dimension; so we omit its consideration. Two examples of items, the first liberal and the second conservative are:

TABLE 7.10
Correlations Among the L and C Subscales of VAL-I,
VAL-II, and REF-IV, $N = 237$

	VAL-I L	VAL-I C	VAL-II L	VAL-II C	REF-IV L	REF-IV C
VAL-I L	1.00	-.25	.74	-.28	.59[a]	-.43
VAL-I C		1.00	-.30	.79	-.49	.70
VAL-II L			1.00	-.28	.51	-.42
VAL-II C				1.00	-.43	.66
REF-IV L					1.00	-.29
REF-IV C						1.00

[a] The relevant correlations between the values subscales and the referents subscales are italicized. All correlations in the table are statistically significant at the .01 level.

The Constitution needs to be changed from time to time to meet the changing circumstances of our society.

If civilization is to survive, there must be a turning back to religion.

The items were written or selected using the pool of items mentioned earlier in the discussion of SA-I and SA-II.

The second Q sort, called Referents Q Sort, or REFQ, had 80 items, 40 liberal and 40 conservative. The items were referents like those used in REF-I: *civil rights, social reform, free enterprise, discipline,* and so on. (Many of them were the same.) REFQ was also a structured sort of the factorial kind. The first dimension was Attitude: half of the items were liberal and half conservative, as mentioned above. The second dimension was Abstractness-Specificity. But, again, we are not concerned with this second dimension: it was included in the sort for a purpose not pertinent to the present discussion. We have, then, two Q sorts both with a liberal-conservative dimension but with totally different kinds of items.

The two Q sorts were administered to 33 individuals in New York and California of "known" liberal and conservative attitudes—known by me or by others. Fifteen were purported liberals and 18 were conservatives. There were five business people, seven professors, ten graduate students of education, two nurses, seven housewives, one retired Navy captain, and a retired Army general. To estimate repeat reliability, eight of the 33 subjects sorted REFQ a second time at varying intervals, from one month to over a year. (The reliability of SAQ had been established by Smith, 1963.) The repeat reliability coefficients ranged from .66 to .91, with an average, via z, of .80. Evidently REFQ is a stable instrument.

The data were analyzed in two ways. First, the Q sorts of the 33 persons were separately intercorrelated and factor analyzed using the principal factors method and orthogonal varimax rotations. The highest r's in each column of the correlation matrices were used as communality estimates. The usual structural hypothesis of the criterial referents theory was thus tested, but using the predicted two-factor structure with persons factors rather than items or test factors. It was expected that the known liberals would be on one factor and the known conservatives on another factor. Bipolar factors were not expected.

Second, a "hit" procedure was used with the factor analytic results. If SAQ and REFQ, despite their marked item difference, measure the same thing or things, then we can expect the persons factor structures to be the same or similar. Two, three, and four factors were extracted and rotated from both sets of Q correlations. We expect the rotated factor loading

TABLE 7.11
Factor Analysis Predicted Success ("Hits"), SAQ and REFQ[a]

	SAQ		REFQ	
	L	C	L	C
Factor Analysis, Two Factors	15	16	14	16
Factor Analysis, Three Factors	15	18	14	18

[a] Entries in the table are numbers of predictive hits. Total numbers of L subjects: 15, C subjects: 18. L and C indicate liberal and conservative subjects.

patterns to be the same: known liberal individuals together on the same factor or factors, and similarly with conservative individual and factors. The factor analytic results of the two Q sorts fulfill the expectations. The numbers of factor analysis hits are given in Table 7.11 (A hit was recorded if the factor loadings of a person on the SAQ and REFQ factor vectors were both equal to or greater than .35.)

The results are encouraging. The most important information we seek must bear on the dualism hypothesis as to the basic feature of social attitude structure: Liberals should be loaded together on a factor, and conservatives, similarly, should be loaded together, but liberals and conservatives should appear on different factors. Few of the individuals (less than three or four, say) should have substantial negative loadings. The evidence is clear. The first and second data lines of Table 7.11 show high proportions of hits with both liberals and conservatives on both Q sorts. Using a criterion of loadings .35 or greater, all but one individual, a presumed liberal, were predicted accurately in the three-factor solutions. In the two-factor solutions, there were only five non-hits out of 66 predictions.

We need to know the pattern of the loadings of the individuals. The two-factor solutions of SAQ and REFQ were highly similar; the three-factor solutions were similar. The coefficients of congruence (Harman, 1976, p. 344) for the first and second factors of the two-factor solution were .94 and .95. For the three factors of the three-factor solution they were .95, .90, and .74. Only liberal individuals appeared on the first factor in the two solutions. In the three-factor solution, conservative individuals appeared on the second and third factors. Factor arrays, which are factor Q sorts calculated from the individuals loaded substantially on the factors (Stephenson, 1953, pp. 174–179), were also calculated for the solutions. The content of the items of these arrays corroborated the designations of the factors as liberal and conservative. There was, moreover, little bipolarity in any of the solutions. There were a number of smaller negative loadings, but not enough to make real differences in the final rotated factors.

Considered alone, the results of this Q study are modest. The limitations of Q methodology (Kerlinger, 1972b, 1973, pp. 595–597), of course, restrict the generality of the findings. Considered in conjunction with the studies reported earlier, however, the Q results are important. First, the criterial referents theory was supported using an entirely different approach and methodology. The orthogonal nature of liberalism and conservatism as latent variables underlying social attitudes was shown with persons factors. Second, the results obtained with the two Q sorts, one with statements and the other with referents, supported each other. Third, the seeming virtues of referents as attitude items were again demonstrated. They work and work well, and they yield results highly similar to results obtained with statement attitude items.

STATEMENT AND REFERENT SCALES

Before taking up the largest study of all that used a referents scale, we should ask and answer certain important questions about referents, referent scales, and the results obtained with referents as items. Are the statistics obtained with referent items comparable to the statistics obtained with statement items? How do the means and standard deviations compare? Are the reliabilities of referent scales higher or lower than those of statement scales? Are the factors obtained from factor analysis of referents the same or different from the factors obtained from factor analysis of statements? And perhaps most important, are the second-order factors obtained from factor analysis of the correlations among the first-order factors the same for different statement scales, for different referent scales, and for both statement and referent scales? We conclude this chapter with consideration of these questions and empirical answers to them.

Comparison of Statistics and Factors

The mean L and C scores of referent scales are about a scale unit higher than the means of statement scales. The standard deviations are about the same or a bit lower. Reliability coefficients are a little higher, while the correlations between the L and C subscales are virtually the same. These are only rough comparisons, however, because such statistics vary with samples and items, and the comparisons are based on different samples and different items. Nevertheless, it is safe to say that referent means are generally higher than statement means. Why? Perhaps the referents stimulate more socially desirable responses than the statements. We return to social desirability later in the book. In general, the referent scales generate similar statistics in different samples, they are substantially reliable, the correlations between the L subscales and between the C subscales are substantial, and the correlations between the L and C subscales are usually low negative.

A more difficult question is: How do the factors of statement scales and referent scales compare? We have already compared the factors of two referent scales, REF-I and REF-IV (see Table 7.7) and found substantial congruence. The names of the SA-II statement factors of Table 7.4 were also entered in Table 7.7 (third column). Two of the C factors, Religiosity and Economic Conservatism, agree quite well. Study of the factor arrays of the items of these factors in Tables 7.4 and 7.6 seems to indicate substantially the same underlying factors. For example, the SA-II statement items, "The well-being of a nation depends mainly on its industry and business" and "A first consideration in any society is the protection of property rights," are presumably expressed by the REF-I referent items *private property, real estate, capitalism,* and *free enterprise.*

The agreement of the L items is not as good. The referent factors of REF-I and REF-IV, Civil Rights and Child-Centered Education (or Progressivism), have no counterparts in the SA-II factors because SA-II had no items related to civil rights and no items directly related to child-centered education or progressivism. The two SA-II L factors, Economic Liberalism–Socialism and Government Aid to Education, had virtual counterparts in the referent factors Social Liberalism and Social Liberalism–Government Aid to Education. But there is little direct connection in the sense that statement items have direct referent counterparts. Rather, the ideas expressed are the same or similar. For example, the statement items of the SA-II factor, Government Aid to Education, and the REF-IV factor Social Liberalism–Government Aid express the idea of the government helping education and medicine, or of owning or financing public ventures. There is sufficient agreement between the referents and statements factor arrays to allow us to conclude that some of the same factors are tapped or measured by the different referent and statement items.

Latent Variables and Naming and Comparing Factors

Correctly categorizing or naming factors is a difficult business. Comparing factors and determining that two factors are the same underlying factor or latent variable is even more difficult. In some cases, as with the conservative Religiosity and Economic Conservatism factors just discussed, there is little problem since the same referents are parts of the factors being compared. But when there are no or few common referents, how is one to determine that the factors are the same? Categorizing, naming, and comparing factors has in the factor analytic literature been done more or less subjectively. The judge "feels" or "senses" what a factor is on the basis of knowledge and experience. To make the procedure more objective, of course, researchers can ask other experts to name and categorize the factors. It is still a loose procedure. Yet there seems to be no other way. Indeed, it is doubtful that science could continue as a viable procedure without conjecture as to the nature of latent variables and, of course, without empirical test of the results of such conjecture.

In recent years considerable scientific progress has been made in psychology in approaching such difficult problems. For instance, the idea of construct validity (Cronbach & Meehl, 1955) has been a large step forward. Part of the basic idea of analysis of covariance structures (Jöreskog, 1978) is the assessment of the influence of hypothesized latent variables on each other and on observed variables. And factor analytic research itself can be called the systematic pursuit of latent variables (Thurstone, 1947). One of the central purposes of this book is to try to determine the first- and second-order latent variables of social attitudes.

To this point, there has been substantial agreement between the results obtained with statement scales and referent scales. The ordinary statistics are similar and the reliabilities much the same for the L and C subscales. The factors obtained with both kinds of scales are similar, and the second-order factors have been virtually the same. There have been two relatively orthogonal second-order factors, and the L first-order factors have fallen on one second-order factor and the C first-order factors have fallen on the other second-order factor. Before allowing smug satisfaction to creep into the discussion, let it be hastily added that the picture is not that simple. As we will soon see, when we broaden our operation the nice clear picture becomes somewhat obscured. The main lines remain much the same, but the chiaroscuro becomes more complex.

8

The Structure of Social Attitude Referents: A Cross-Cultural Study[1]

Sooner or later in the development of measurement instruments one must ask the question: How general is this measure? Assuming that the instrument's validity has been established in the United States, one must wonder if it is also valid in France, England, and Germany. Attitudes are predispositions to respond to social objects or referents. So one would think that they are more heavily dependent on culture and environment than are ability and personality variables. If so, then the problem of generality is more acute. That is, it is less likely that one can legitimately use a social attitude scale in England if it was developed in the United States than one can use an intelligence test developed in the United States. The results of both measures are affected by the cultures in which they are used. But results obtained with attitude scales should be more affected since, by definition, social attitudes are intimately tied to social objects and referents.

A core question of the study to be reported in this chapter, then, is: Are social attitude factors approximately the same in different Western coun-

[1]The study or studies to be reported in this chapter could not have been done without the help and cooperation of many people. I wish to thank these people collectively. But I particularly want to thank Dr. C. Middendorp and Professor J. Amón for working with me on the research. In a sense they are really coauthors of this chapter as they were of one of the original reports. I am also grateful to Dr. G. J. Mellenbergh for reading and criticizing the original research report. Special thanks are also due Dr. G. Schild and the Netherlands Institute of Public Opinion for obtaining responses from a random sample of The Netherlands to the attitude referent scale used.

143

tries? We can expect "strong" first-order factors to emerge in different countries because most Western nations share similar political, economic, and general value systems. Christianity, for example, is the dominant religion of the Western world. Therefore, if a factor of religiosity has emerged in one country consistently, we would expect it to emerge similarly in other countries. Economic systems, while differing in many facets, share common values and beliefs. Most Western nations are fundamentally capitalist even though part of their social and economic systems may be socialist. One may also expect considerable political attitude divergence between the United States and Western European countries, however, because of the different political systems, parties, and traditions. The rather strong socialist orientations of some Western European countries, as contrasted to the lesser American socialist orientation, should produce concomitant attitude divergence. The results of the similarities and differences should be to produce some first-order factors that are highly similar and others that differ, sometimes substantially.

How much similarity and how much difference, what factors should be similar and what factors different, is not possible to say. Since the conservative factors Religiosity and Economic Conservatism have persistently appeared in American samples, and since they reflect themes probably common to Western society, one might suppose they may also appear in European samples. What liberal factors should be common to the United States and Western European countries? Since social welfare is a central issue in all countries there should be a social welfare factor. There may also be some sort of equality factor and perhaps factors associated with women's rights and with the "newer" emphasis on human warmth and affection.

The cross-cultural similarities of attitudinal second-order factors should be more pronounced. The simplest expectation is that, no matter what the similarities and differences among the first-order factors, there will be two second-order factors, one associated with liberal first-order factors and the other with conservative first-order factors. It is predicted, then, that this dual structure will emerge in all samples. There may be different numbers of first-order factors and they may differ in their content, but the structure underlying them will be the same: two orthogonal second-order factors, one liberal and one conservative.

When we ask questions about similarities among factors and factor structures, we really ask questions about latent variables and their relations. As indicated in the last chapter, such questions are scientifically important. One of the central preoccupations of science, in fact, is the relations among latent variables. While we perforce have to work with observed variables, our underlying scientific concern has ultimately to be latent variables and their relations.[2] In educational research, for instance, when we talk about the relations between teaching methods, ability, and achievement, we are talking, in part at least, of latent variables and their relations. When political scientists talk about the influence of political and social beliefs on voting behavior, they are talking about the influence of latent variables on important choice behaviors.

In Chapter 3, a simplified partly mathematical model of attitudes and attitude theory was given. (See Figure 3.3.) To help us understand the present discussion and a later more complex and technical chapter (Chapter 10), we now expand the model idea of Chapter 3. Although the symbolism differs from that of Chapter 10—where we will use the symbolism of analysis of covariance structures—the fundamental ideas are the same. We illustrate an educational research problem because it is fairly familiar. Suppose an educational researcher wishes to test the relative efficacies of two teaching methods. He also wishes to assess the effects of certain abilities or aptitudes on reading and arithmetic achievement. The situation is depicted in Figure 8.1. x_1, x_2, and x_3 are Verbal, Quantitative, and Spatial tests; y_1 and y_2 are Reading and Arithmetic achievement measures. x_4 stands for Method, the teaching methods used. X is *Ability-Aptitude*; Y is *Achievement*. Both X and Y are unobserved or latent variables. The arrows indicate "influences," which are labeled with a_i, for example, a_1 is the influence of Y on y_1. G_1 indicates the influence of the latent variable X on the latent variable Y, or the influence of *Ability-Aptitude* on *Achievement*. G_2 indicates the influence of x_4, Method, on Y, *Achievement*.

The latent variables are assumed to influence the observed variables. Thus the direction of the arrows labeled a. X, however, the independent latent variable, also influences Y, another latent variable. x_4 influences Y directly because we assume no latent variable for this experimental manipulation (note the arrow labeled G_2). While all the influences are important, the most important ones are G_1 and G_2, the latter because it stands for the influence of the experimental manipulation and the former because it stands for the presumed influence of the *Ability-Aptitude* latent variable on the *Achievement* latent variable. In scientific research, it is these influences of latent variables on each other that is often of central interest. Thus the most important influences to assess are G_1, the in-

---

[2]There are scientists who deny this. What can be called extreme empiricism espouses only working with—manipulating and measuring—observed variables. Skinner (1963), for instance, insists on this view. He even decries theory. I believe that most contemporary scientific psychologists would espouse views that stress the importance of both observed and unobserved or latent variables. Hebb (1949), Allport (1955), Guilford (1956, 1959), and Festinger (1957) are examples.

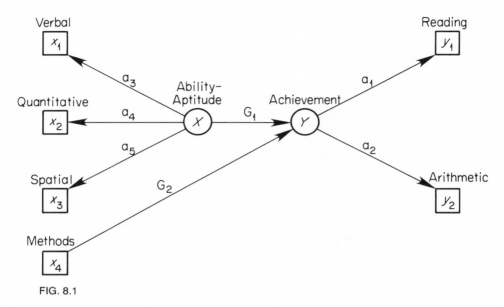

FIG. 8.1

fluence of the latent variable X, on Y, and G_2, the influence of x_4, the experimental variable, *Methods,* on Y, *Achievement.*

Later, in Chapter 10, we formalize these ideas and use them with attitudes to test the alternative duality and bipolarity hypotheses. In that chapter we are more precise about the models and the latent variables we use. It should then become clear that one of the major purposes of this book is to specify the nature of the latent variables or second-order factors, liberalism and conservatism, as well as to describe the first-order factors or latent variables of measured attitudes. One of the chief purposes of this chapter is to investigate the generality of the first- and second-order factors—in effect, latent variables at different levels—found in earlier research. After this rather long digression on latent variables, we turn to the cross-cultural research itself. One more word before doing so, however.

When the study to be described was first undertaken, it was seriously doubted that the expectations mentioned earlier would be upheld. The multi-party political systems of West-European countries in contrast to the American two-party system, the strongly socialist nature of public policy of some European countries, and the varying emphases on human and minority rights all might act to produce quite different factors than those found in America. Most important, is it possible that the dualistic L and C second-order structure found in American samples is bipolar or multifactorial in Europe? If, for example, second-order structures found in Europe are found to be consistently bipolar, then it is obvious that the criterial referents theory must be abandoned.

METHOD[3]

Measurement Instrument

A single attitude-value 7-point summated-rating referents scale, Referents VI, or REF-VI, was used in each of three countries: The Netherlands, Spain, and the United States. The original scale, in English, had 78 items selected from a large pool of referents constructed with the help of theoretical accounts of liberalism and conservatism (e.g., Orton, 1945; Hartz, 1955; McClosky, 1958; Kirk, 1960; Rossiter, 1962), selected from existing attitude and value scales (Shaw & Wright, 1967; Robinson et al., 1968; Robinson & Shaver, 1969), and from the author's own attitude scales and Q sorts. The criteria of selection of items were representativeness and wide coverage of the attitude domain and marker items from previous research, that is, items of known psychometric properties. The scale was a direct descendant of the referent scales in the research described earlier and thus had the benefit of American factor and item analytic information.

REF-VI was "transformed" for use in The Netherlands and Spain by translation when items expressed virtually the same idea in the different languages, by insertion of important Spanish and Dutch social concepts that were not on the American scale, and by omission of concepts not used in The Netherlands and Spain. In The Netherlands, the item selection and writing was influenced by the scales used in the doctoral thesis of one of the researchers who did the original research (Middendorp, 1976). We use the word "transformed" because direct translation, especially of attitude and value statements and words, seems inappropriate in cross-cultural work. The Spanish version of 78 items was closer to the original than the Dutch version: 59 items were virtually the same. The Dutch version had 86 items of which 45 were the same as or similar to the American items. The original scale of 86 items, however, was reduced to 72 items after preliminary analysis showed that 14 of the items had unsatisfactory psychometric properties: zero or near-zero correlations with other items, questionable as attitude referents (e.g., social harmony, the future, civilization), small variances.

Samples and Administration of Scales

In the United States, REF-VI was administered to 135 students of education in Virginia and 365 graduate students of education in two universities

---

[3]The description of the cross-cultural study that follows leans heavily on the published reports of the study (Kerlinger, 1978, 1980a, 1980b; Kerlinger et al., 1976).

in New York City. Preliminary factor analyses of the two samples yielded similar factor structures and factors. The two samples were therefore combined to form a sample of 500.

In Spain the scale was administered to 427 graduate evening students of psychology at a large urban university. They were grade school teachers, workers in private and state business in middle and lower status jobs, and students older than the average Spanish student.

There were two samples in The Netherlands, one a random sample of the country ($N = 685$, henceforth called Netherlands I), and the other psychology students and students of other social sciences at a large urban university ($N = 270$, henceforth Netherlands II). The larger sample was a random sample based on households, with random choice of household members, except that only persons 18 or over were used. The system of sampling was that developed and used by the Netherlands Institute of Public Opinion (NIPO) for its weekly surveys.

Analysis

It was, as usual, possible to categorize many of the items of the three instruments as liberal or conservative to assess reliability and to make general comparisons. The means, standard deviations, alpha reliability coefficients, and the correlations between the liberalism (L) and conservatism (C) subscales are given in Table 8.1. It is clear that the L and C subscales are reliable: with one exception, Spain's L, the coefficients are in the middle .80's and low .90's. The correlations between the L and C subscales will be discussed later. The means reflect the general conservatism and liberalism of the different samples. For example, in the Dutch random sample, there is little difference between the L and C means, but in the Dutch student sample the difference is very large, 2.71. These differences reflect the "known" difference between Dutch students and the general population.

The four sets of item intercorrelations were factor analyzed using the principal factors method (Harman, 1976) with R^2's in the diagonals as communality estimates. Numbers of factors in the solutions were decided on the basis of number and magnitude of loadings on obliquely rotated factors (generally three or more loadings $\geqslant .30$), magnitude of eigenvalues (1.00 or greater as a loose guide), and, most important, congruence of final rotated solutions with the original correlations. (In each case all solutions of 8, 9, 10, 11, and 12 factors were rotated and compared.) In the chosen "best solutions," there were 11 factors in the U.S. data, 12 in the Spanish data, 8 in the Netherlands I, and 11 in the Netherlands II data. The factors were rotated obliquely using the promax method (Hendrickson & White,

TABLE 8.1
Referents Scale VI (REF-VI): Means, Standard Deviations,
Reliabilities, and Correlations Between *L* and *C* Subscales,
United States, Spain, and Netherlands Samples

		U.S.		Spain[a]	Netherlands	
N:		365	135	470	685	270
$\bar{X}$:						
	L	5.65	5.65	5.91	5.45	6.12
	C	5.03	5.78	4.08	5.44	3.41
s:						
	L	.54	.58	.44	.63	.43
	C	.76	.64	.96	.74	.91
r_{tt}[b]:						
	L	.85[c]	.85	.74	.83	.83
	C	.92[c]	.90	.92	.88	.92
r_{LC}:		-.12	.37	-.26	.05	-.35

[a] Each *L* and *C* subscale had 30 items with the exception of the Spanish scale which had 28 *L* and 28 *C* items.

[b] Alpha reliability coefficients.

[c] Odd-even reliability corrected with the Spearman-Brown formula. (The computer output with the alpha coefficients was lost in an overseas move.)

1964). The correlations among the obliquely rotated factors were themselves factor analyzed using the procedure described earlier.

RESULTS

Recall that we expect a number of factors, and that *L* items will be loaded on *L* factors, and *C* items on *C* factors. *L* items will not appear on *C* factors, and *C* items will not appear on *L* factors. This implies, of course, no bipolar factors. The correlations among the first-order factors should be as follows: positive among *L* factors, positive among *C* factors, and low negative or zero between *L* and *C* factors. The factor analysis of these correlations should yield two relatively orthogonal second-order factors, one of which will be identified as a liberal factor and the other a conservative factor.

The first-order factor analytic results are complex. But there is little doubt of large common social themes in the four sets of data. We first present descriptive statistical data on all four samples. Then we present the American and Spanish first- and second-order factors in some detail so that the reader can see the cross-cultural similarities and differences in factors in the fine, so to speak. We then summarize the results from the Dutch samples. In doing so, we contrast the results obtained from a leftist student sample and the relatively conservative random sample of the population of The Netherlands. Finally, we try to ascertain the factor similarities, if any, in all four samples.

The American Data

In the American analysis ($N = 500$), eleven factors were obliquely rotated to simple structure, as indicated earlier. The referent factor arrays are given in Table 8.2. There are seven C factors and four L factors. Six of the 11 factors we have met before either in the REF-I analysis, the REF-IV analysis, or in both: the C factors of Religiosity, Economic Conservatism, Traditional Conservatism, and Morality, and the L factors of Equality and Civil Rights and Social Welfare. But we have relatively "new" factors, even though hints of them appeared earlier. These are the C factors of Science, Teaching, and Individualism, and the L factors of Human Warmth and Feeling and Equality of Women. We will see that they appear in other samples, though in somewhat different form.

If readers will take the trouble to look back at the factor arrays of REF-I and REF-IV in Chapter 7, they will see the similarity of the REF-VI factors Religiosity, Economic Conservatism, Traditional Conservatism, Morality, Civil Rights and Equality, and Science to the REF-I and REF-IV factors. There are of course differences as one must expect with different scales and different samples. Nevertheless, the factor resemblances are often marked. We note again that L items load on L factors and similarly for C items and factors. There is little bipolarity: only two items, *sex freedom* on Morality ($-.32$) and *rationality* on Individualism ($-.28$), are negatively loaded.

The second-order factor analytic results are also similar to those of the earlier studies, except for the number of second-order factors. The rotated second-order factor matrix is given in Table 8.3, together with the L and C designations of the factors and the factor names. The most important difference between this analysis and earlier analyses is that here we have three second-order factors, instead of two. Recall that the theory specifies two second-order factors, one L and one C. The reason three factors were rotated is that two of the four second-order analyses of the study seemed to require three factors because rotating two factors resulted in the "loss" of one or two first-order factors. For example, in the Spanish data, rotation of three factors made it possible to "recover" one more first-order factor in the second-order solution.

Second-order factor I is conservative: the first-order loadings greater than .35 are those of Religiosity, Economic Conservatism, Traditional Conservatism, Morality, Science, Teaching, and Individualism. Factor II

TABLE 8.2
REF-VI: Factor Arrays and Loadings of Item Factor Analysis,
Oblique Solution, United States, N = 500

Conservative Factors

Religiosity

faith in God (.66)[a]
religion (.65)
church (.63)
Christian (.55)
teaching spiritual calues (.43)

Economic Conservatism

profits (.62)
money (.50)
business (.48)
corporate industry (.44)
real estate (.43)
capitalism (.43)
private property (.35)
free enterprise (.31)
competition (.26)

Science

scientific theory (.63)
scientists (.60)
scientific research (.60)
reason (.27)
international cooperation (.25)

Teaching

professors (.60)
teachers (.57)
children's needs (.27)

Traditional Conservatism

discipline (.50)
duty (.45)
authority (.44)
military training (.39)
competition (.36)
manners (.35)
work (.25)
corporate industry (.29)
business (.27)
law and order (.27)

Morality

morality (.59)
moral standards (.56)
America (.25)

sex freedom (-.32)

Individualism

individual initiative (.51)
individual effort (.44)
privacy (.33)
cultural heritage (.26)

rationality (-.28)

Liberal Factors

Civil Rights and Equality

racial equality (.64)
civil rights (.50)
equality (.46)
freedom (.25)

Social Liberalism

labor unions (.49)
socialized medicine (.44)
government price controls (.39)
collective bargaining (.38)
social planning (.37)
social welfare (.37)
government ownership of utilities (.36)
economic reform (.34)
world government (.27)

Human Warmth and Feeling

love (.59)
human warmth (.50)
feeling (.37)
children's interests (.30)

Women's Equality

equality of women (.60)
women's liberation (.58)
birth control (.31)

[a] Parenthesized numbers are factor loadings.

TABLE 8.3

REF-VI: Rotated Second-Order Factors, United States
Sample N = 500

	I	II	II	h²	Type[a]	Name
1	.67[b]	.15	-.26	.54	C	Religiosity
2	.61	-.16	.13	.42	C	Economic Conservatism
3	.47	.13	-.13	.25	C	Traditional Conservatism
4	.72	-.22	-.15	.59	C	Morality
5	-.01	.61	.09	.38	L	Equality and Civil Rights
6	.47	.18	.27	.33	C	Science
7	.12	.73	.27	.62	L	Human Warmth and Feeling
8	.42	.43	.07	.36	C	Teaching
9	-.08	.46	.55	.53	L	Social Liberalism
10	-.13	-.13	.64	.44	L	Equality of Women
11	.50	.15	.37	.41	C	Individualism

[a] L: liberalism; C: conservatism.
[b] Loadings $\geqslant$ .35 were considered significant. They are italicized.

is liberal: Equality and Civil Rights, Human Warmth and Feeling, Teaching (see below), and Social Liberalism. The third factor is also a liberal factor: Social Liberalism (also on factor II) and Equality of Women, with a loading of .37 of the conservative Individualism (reminiscent of classic liberalism?). This third factor seems to be what Cattell (1952) long ago called a complementary factor: it complements factor II, the liberal second-order factor. It is a little strange that Science and Teaching are loaded on factor I, the C second-order factor. Are they conservative ideas? Teaching is loaded on both the L and the C factors. The explanation, perhaps, is that its two main items were *professors* and *teachers*, and liberals and conservatives share similar beliefs about teachers, producing enough positive correlation among the items to put the factor on both second-order factors. (This did not happen in the Spanish data, however. Called Teachers, it there fell on only a C second-order factor.)

Except for the third second-order factor, the first- and second-order factor analytic results support the theory. There are two distinct second-order factors, one L and one C, and a third complementary factor, an L factor. Virtually no bipolarity appeared in the second-order factors, and there were only two items, *sex freedom* and *rationality*, with negative loadings in the first-order factors, and both were low, $-.32$ and $-.28$. Otherwise, L items loaded on L factors, and C items on C factors. But this sample was American. Will the same clear picture emerge in the European samples? Let us look first at the Spanish results.

The Spanish Data

Twelve first-order factors were extracted from the correlations among the 78 Spanish items. The twelve factor arrays, six L and six C, are given in

Table 8.4. Again, the same or similar "strong" factors that appeared in the American data also appeared in these data. The conservative factors were Religiosity, Economic Conservatism, Teachers, and two factors associated with Traditional Conservatism. The liberal factors were Feeling and Affection, Equality of Women, Government Controls, and Children's Interests. The degree of content agreement of the "strong" factors is surprising. Three of the Spanish conservative factors are quite similar to those of the American sample. Religiosity and Economic Conservatism were much the same. Traditional Conservatism, too, was highly similar. Spain's Nationalism and Traditional Conservatism was like Traditional Conservatism except for its nationalistic emphasis. The remaining two conservative factors, Teachers and Foreign Influence, were unlike the American factors. The latter is interesting: it has both *America* and *Soviet Union* with substantial loadings!

The parallels between the Spanish and American liberal factors, were not as clear as those of the conservative factors except for Feeling and Affection and Equality of Women, which appeared in both samples. There were, of course, family resemblances, for example, the Spanish factor Children's Interests with its two heavily loaded items, *children's interests* and *children's needs* (the third item, *privacy,* has a loading of only .26), resembles the earlier Progressivism of REF-IV and Child-Centered Education of REF-I. But there is insufficient evidence to say it is the same factor. The conclusion is that qualitative study shows that the Spanish conservative first-order factors are highly similar to the American conservative first-order factors, but the Spanish liberal factors, while showing somewhat more than family resemblances, are different enough to make statements about direct similarities difficult. We return to these similarities and differences shortly.

The second-order factor analysis of the correlations among the twelve Spanish first-order factors provides a clearer picture of the latent variables (factors) underlying the social attitude referents. The results are given in Table 8.5. Factor I is conservative and bipolar. Its first-order factors are Religiosity, Economic Conservatism, Nationalism and Traditional Conservatism, and Relaxation of Restrictions (whose main items were *liberalization of censorship, strip tease, sexual freedom,* and *divorce*). Relaxation of Restrictions, however, is a liberal first-order factor and is loaded very substantially and negatively ($-.68$) on this C second-order factor. The factor is therefore bipolar, to some extent at least.

Second-order factor II is liberal: its first-order factors are Feeling and Affection, Equality of Women, Workers' Rights (a bipolar first-order factor), and Children's Interests. Factor III is again a complementary conservative second-order factor: its three first-order factors are Traditional Conservatism, Teachers, and Foreign Influence. (Had only two second-

Conservative Factors

Religiosity

faith in God (.61)
religion (.60)
Church involvement in sociopolitical
   problems (.38)
church (.32)
teaching of spiritual values (.31)
family (.25)

liberalized abortion laws (-.26)

Economic Conservatism

money (.52)
profits (.50)
real estate (.43)
private property (.42)
corporate industry (.40)
business (.38)
free enterprise (.34)
capitalism (.27)
free enterprise (.34)
manners (.34)
business (.33)
authority (.31)
competition (.31)
collective bargaining (.29)
corporate industry (.28)

Foreign Influence

America (.57)
Soviet Union (.46)
Jews (.38)
United Nations (.38)

Nationalism and Traditional Conservatism

patriotism (.53)
military training (.39)
national sovereignty (.39)
law and order (.32)
authority (.31)
tradition (.29)
moral standards (.27)
monarchy (.26)
competition (.26)
discipline (.26)

Traditional Conservatism

social welfare (.41)
individual effort (.41)
individual initiative (.38)
discipline (.37)
law and order (.36)

Teachers

teachers (.52)
professors (.49)
economic reform (.36)
objective tests (.32)
psychological testing (.30)
human personality (.26)

loyalty (-.27)

Liberal Factors

Relaxations of Restrictions

liberalization of censorship (in shows)
   (.53)
strip tease (.44)
sexual freedom (.43)
divorce (.30)
sex education (.27)
abstract art (.26)

Feeling and Affection

affection (.61)
feeling (.50)
love (.41)

Equality of Women

evolution theory (.47)
equality of women (.43)
women's liberation (.40)
birth control (.39)
divorce (.31)
coeducation (.26)
freedom (.25)

Government Controls

government price controls (.64)
government ownership of utilities (.57)
international cooperation (.39)
world government (.35)
discipline (.25)

TABLE 8.4 *(continued)*

Workers' Rights	*Children's Interests*
workers unions (.46)	children's interests (.66)
right to strike (.40)	children's needs (.52)
freedom (.32)	privacy (.26)
separation of church and state (.29)	
scientific research (.29)	
jazz (.26)	
socialized medicine (.25)	
capital punishment (-.37)	
capitalism (-.32)	

[a] *L*: liberalism; *C*: conservatism.

[b] Loadings ⩾ .35 were considered significant.

order factors been rotated, Foreign Influence would have been "lost." See earlier discussion of the rationale for rotating three factors.)

Do these data from Spain support the criterial referents theory? We have to be very careful. In general, the answer is Yes, but . . . Look at the factor arrays of Table 8.4. First, *C* referents appear together positively on *C* factors, and *L* referents appear together positively on *L* factors. Few "cross loadings" appear: *C* referents on *L* factors and *L* referents on *C* factors. *Capital punishment* and *capitalism, C* referents, are loaded − .37 and − .32 on Workers' Rights, a liberal factor. *Liberalized abortion laws,* an *L* referent, is loaded − .26 on Religiosity, a *C* second-order factor. *Loyalty,* a *C* referent, is loaded − .27 on Teachers, a *C* factor. This last

TABLE 8.5
REF-VI: Rotated Second-Order Factors, Spanish
Sample, *N* = 427

	I	II	III	h²	Type[a]	Name
1	*.61*[b]	.26	*.39*	.59	*C*	Religiosity
2	*.43*	-.17	.12	.23	*C*	Economic Conservatism
3	*.64*	.06	.26	.49	*C*	Nationalism and Traditional Conservatism
4	*-.68*	.02	.08	.47	*L* (-*C*)	Relaxation of Restrictions
5	.23	.15	*.41*	.24	*C*	Traditional Conservatism
6	.16	*.56*	.17	.37	*L*	Feeling and Affection
7	-.17	*.59*	.00	.38	*L*	Equality of Women
8	− .18	.08	*.60*	.39	*C*	Teachers
9	-.32	*.56*	-.09	.42	*L* (-*C*)	Workers' Rights
10	-.04	-.15	*.51*	.29	*C*	Foreign Influence
11	.20	.22	.11	.10	*L*	Government Controls
12	.14	*.62*	-.09	.41	*L*	Children's Interests

[a] *L*: liberalism; *C*: conservatism.

[b] Loadings ⩾ .35 were considered significant. They are italicized.

result is anomalous: a *C* referent loaded negatively on a *C* factor. The pattern of loadings, then, supports the theory: there is some bipolarity, but it is certainly not substantial (except for the large negative loading of Relaxation of Restrictions in the second-order analysis).

These obliquely rotated factor arrays (Table 8.3) are somewhat misleading, however. In the Chapter 4 discussion of methodology, it was said that in all cases the first-order factors were rotated orthogonally, even though they are not reported. The main reason for rotating orthogonally, it was said, was to find the "correct" number of factors to rotate. In most cases the orthogonal and oblique rotations "agreed": they both yielded similar solutions. This was not always true, however. The Spanish rotations are a case in point.

Whereas eleven factors were rotated obliquely based on the criteria outlined in Chapter 4, it was found through study of the different orthogonal solutions—especially by checking back to the 78-by-78 correlation matrix—that a nine-factor solution was "best." In this solution it was found that one factor, Religiosity, was strongly bipolar. (Another difference was that the items of Economic Conservatism and Traditional Conservatism appeared together on one factor. But this does not alter the results pertinent to the theory.) In addition to the Religiosity items given in Table 8.4, the following items also appeared positively loaded: *obligatory Mass on Sundays, moral standards, eternal hell.* These items are consistent with the Religiosity designation of the factor. More important for the criterial referents theory, three liberal referents were negatively loaded and the loadings were substantial: *liberalized abortion laws* (−.56), *divorce* (−.51), and *strip tease* (−.49). And these loadings were all consistent with the original correlations. The factor is definitely bipolar; it should probably be called Religiosity versus Sexual Freedom. There were no other negative loadings in the orthogonally rotated factors.

The second-order factor analytic results support the theory, with the exception of the high negative loading of Relaxation of Restrictions on factor I, a liberal second-order factor. There are no appreciable negative loadings and the structure is consistent with the theory, if one accepts the third second-order factor as a complementary factor.[4] Still, the substantial negative loadings of the orthogonal rotation and the three second-order

---

[4]A complementary factor, mentioned earlier but not defined, is like another factor in the same set of factors but has an aspect that keeps it apart. Without this aspect (or aspects) its items would be part of the other factor. The first-order factor, Foreign Influence, is evidently such a special aspect. On a two-factor rotation of the second-order factor matrix this factor does not appear at all. On a three-factor rotation, however, it does appear. Moreover, it splits off from other conservative factors forming a complementary factor, which, in the two-factor rotation, are parts of factor I, Conservatism.

factors are not consistent with the theory. We attempt to reconcile these inconsistencies later in the book.

The Netherlands Data: Netherlands II (N-II)

The results obtained in The Netherlands are perhaps the most interesting, complex, and difficult obtained anywhere—for three reasons. First, we have two quite different samples, one of them a sample of students from the Social Sciences Faculty of the University of Amsterdam, an institution generally believed in The Netherlands to be leftist, even radical. (The data support this belief, though one could hardly categorize the whole university as leftist. This sample certainly seemed to be, though there was considerable variability.) The other sample is interesting because it was a random sample of the country. Thurstone (1947, pp. 324–325) long ago said that for the discovery of an underlying factor domain representative samples should *not* be used. That he was probably right is shown by the first-order factor analytic results with this random sample. My colleagues and I, however, could not resist the opportunity to have a sample of a whole country.[5]

Second, the referents used in The Netherlands REF-VI instrument differed a good deal from the REF-VI scales used in the U.S. and Spain. There were 59 (of 78) items in the Spanish scale that were virtually the same as in the American original, but the Dutch version had only 45 items (of 72) that could be called the same or nearly the same. The reasons for these differences are not relevant here. But we must bear in mind that there is greater opportunity for factors to be different and less opportunity for factor congruence.

The third point of interest about the Dutch sample and data is that doing the study in The Netherlands is perhaps a difficult test of the theory. An anecdote will illustrate what is meant. Some years ago I was explaining the criterial referents theory to a colleague. He expressed skepticism, and particularly asked me if I thought the theory, especially the duality or two second-order factors part of it, would hold in Western European countries. He cited France and its many political parties, and thought that with such diversity of views there would be no neat two orthogonal factors as in the United States with its two major political parties. The Netherlands, too, has many political parties, well over thirty. If my colleague was right,

---

[5]The original sample consisted of 805 individuals drawn by a random sample of households, with a random choice of household members over 18 years of age. The sample was reduced to 685 because the responses of 120 persons were in one way or another inadequate. (See footnote 6).

then the two second-order factors, liberalism and conservatism, should not emerge from the Dutch data.

We first examine the Dutch student results (N-II) because the factors and factor arrays were more like those of the other two samples than were the factors and arrays of the Dutch random sample (N-I). In doing this we must remember that a number of referents used in the United States and Spain were not on the Dutch scale—for example, *civil rights, children's needs, religious education,* and *real estate*—and a number used on the Dutch scale were not used in the United States and Spain. Some of the referents are unique to The Netherlands and have special meanings that are not even translatable. *Medezeggenschap* and *inspraak,* for instance, are new words that mean participating in decisions; they have no English equivalents (that I know of). Other referents used were not used in the other scales: *democratization, profit sharing, aristocracy, Royal Family, employers, workers, maximum income.* Despite these considerable differences, will factors similar to those of Spain and the United States emerge? Above all, will the two main second-order factors, liberalism and conservatism, emerge?

Eleven factors of the student sample were rotated obliquely: four were conservative, six were liberal, and one was a bipolar two-item factor. The names of the conservative factors and some of the high-loaded items on them are:

Economic Conservatism: *competition, achievement, profits, free enterprise*
Religiosity: *religion, Christian, church*
Traditional Conservatism: *authority* (prestige), *law and order, police, discipline*
Morality: *good manners, morality, love of country, discipline* (also had *divorce* negatively loaded: $-.43$)

The names and highly loaded items of the liberal factors are:

Egalitarianism and Democracy: *workers, equality, "having a say," democratization, social equality* (also *aristocracy:* $-.49$)
Affection and Freedom of Expression: *affection, freedom of expression, freedom of private living* (privacy), *human warmth*
Militant Social Action: *action groups, demonstrations, equal opportunity, emancipation of women*
Income Equalization: *profit-sharing, maximum income, progressive taxation, income leveling*
Government Care: *government care, national health care, social legislation, government aid to education*

Sexual Freedom: *childless couples, homosexuals, birth control, emancipation of women*

The remaining unnamed factor had two items, one positively loaded and one negatively loaded: *conscription* and *conscientious objection*. There were three referents that had negative loadings (see above). As will be seen later, however, this is deceptive: there was a good deal of bipolarity in these student data.

It should be immediately obvious that five or six of these factors have appeared in earlier analyses: all four of the *C* factors and one, perhaps two, of the *L* factors. Again we see the stability of the *C* factors and the lability of the *L* factors. We also see the same kinds of factors as in the American and Spanish samples: *L* items together on factors, and similarly with *C* items and factors. In addition, we have new *L* factors generated by the referents that spring from the special, almost unique, conditions of Dutch society, especially student society; Egalitarianism and Democracy, Militant Social Action, and Income Equalization. Would these three factors have appeared in the American and Spanish samples if the items had been used? We of course do not know.

Now, the second-order factors of the student sample. The three-factor rotated factor matrix is given in Table 8.6 with, as usual, the factor types and names. With one exception, the large negative loading of $-.54$ of Traditional Conservatism on the third factor, this matrix is well-behaved. It conforms to the theoretical expectation of a major *L* and a major *C* factor, with a complementary factor, this time a bipolar *L* factor. Second-order factor I consists of Economic Conservatism, Religiosity, and Morality, while factor II consists of Egalitarianism and Democratization, Affection and Freedom, Militant Social Action, and Government Care. Factor III, the complementary factor, has Income Equalization, Sexual Freedom, and, negatively, Traditional Conservatism. Evidently the factor matrix supports the theory except for the substantial negative loading of $-.54$ on factor III. More bipolarity than appears in Table 8.6 was expected with this sample. As we have argued and will argue later, one of the prime conditions for bipolarity is a radical sample—of the right or the left. And this sample was leftist. But not much bipolarity has yet appeared in the data presented here. Actually, there was more bipolarity in this sample of Dutch students than appears here. We examine it toward the end of the chapter.

The Netherlands Data: Netherlands I (N-I)

The results of the analysis of the data of the Dutch random sample, Netherlands I, or N-I ($N = 685$), are in some respects different from the

TABLE 8.6

REF-VI: Rotated Second-Order Factors, Netherlands II

Sample, N = 270

	I	II	III	h²	Type[a]	Name
1	.53[b]	-.07	-.08	.29	C	Economic Conservatism
2	.64	-.01	-.22	.45	C	Religiosity
3	.30	.05	−.54	.39	C	Traditional Conservatism
4	.08	.43	.35	.31	L	Egalitarianism and Democratization
5	.07	.52	-.11	.29	L	Affection and Freedom of Expression
6	-.32	.41	.17	.30	L	Militant Social Action
7	-.07	.08	.57	.34	L	Income Equalization
8	.02	.62	.21	.42	L	Government Care
9	-.17	.32	.37	.26	L	Sexual Freedom
10	.16	-.29	.01	.11	C	Unnamed
11	.52	-.01	-.07	.28	C	Morality

[a] L: liberalism; C: conservatism.

[b] Loadings $\geqslant$ .35 were considered significant. They are italicized.

results of the other three samples. There were fewer first-order factors, separate factors of other samples merged in this sample, and there was a general lack of clear-cut definition of factors. This was probably due to what can be called inadequate responses to the referents instrument and greater random error. The general educational and intelligence level of a random sample is probably considerably lower than that of a student sample. This may mean that some of the referent items may not have been understood and may not have been responded to adequately. There are also probably more "idiosyncratic" responses. Of the 805 subjects drawn in the sample, 120 gave inadequate responses of one kind or another and had to be eliminated from the sample.[6]

Eight factors were extracted and rotated in the first-order factor analysis of the 72-by-72 item correlation matrix. The same criteria used in other studies for the "correct" number of factors to rotate were used: number and magnitude of loadings on obliquely rotated factors (generally, three or

---

[6]The criteria used for elimination of cases were five or more missing responses in any one scale and obviously deviant responding of one kind or another. (There were very few cases eliminated in the other three samples.) It can of course be argued that deletion of about 18% of the cases destroys the random nature of the sample. It is true that the loss of a substantial part of a random sample damages its randomness. But there appears to have been no alternative in this case. Estimating missing cases with a computer program, for example, is hardly an adequate solution. Nor is it appropriate to treat deviant responses as though they were "normal" responses. About all that can be done with the present sample, then, is to recognize that the loss is serious, and to make proper reservations when making statements about the representativeness of the sample. In what follows I will assume that the sample is fairly representative, though recognizing that it may not be so.

more loadings ≥.30), magnitude of eigenvalues (1.00 or greater as a loose guide), and, most important, congruence of final rotated solutions with the original correlations. The eight factors were rotated obliquely using the promax method. (They were also rotated orthogonally along with 9-, 10-, 11-, and 12-factor orthogonal solutions to help determine the "correct" number of factors to rotate.) To my knowledge, this is the only factor analysis of attitude responses of a "random" sample of a country that has been reported. As such, it is important. The factor arrays are reported in Table 8.7.

How are these first-order factors different from earlier first-order factors? First, there are fewer factors. While greater numbers of factors were rotated, the solutions were inadequate mostly in the sense that their results did not "agree" too well with the original correlations. Second, and closely related to the first explanation, factors that were separate and distinct factors in other samples merged in this sample. For example, the two factors in N-II, the student sample, Economic Conservatism and Traditional Conservatism (see Table 8.6, first-order factors 1 and 3), merged and became one factor, Economic and Social Conservatism in N-I. Third, the factor arrays are muddy. While they could be identified and named (with one exception), some of the factors contained different kinds of items. Economic and Social Conservatism is an example. Religiosity is another: it included items that were not religious, like *Royal Family* and *love of country*. The liberal factors were even more muddied. One of them (Unnamed) even contained both *L* and *C* items, both loaded positively, something that has happened only rarely in other samples. (Moreover, this factor appeared in the second-order analysis as a conservative factor when most of its items were liberal!)

Despite the factor merging and array muddiness, we still obtain recognizable factors, and some of these are clearly like those found in earlier samples. Religiosity has the three referents, *religion, church,* and *Christian,* with high loadings, as in other samples. Economic and Social Conservatism, as mentioned above, combines two previously separate factors. Sexual Freedom is quite clear: most of its items refer to various aspects of freedom in sexual matters. While further parallels can be found, it must be said that the remaining factors are not clear. Nevertheless, we will shortly try to list the factor similarities of all four samples, including the N-I sample factors.

The three orthogonally rotated second-order factors, with the types of factors and the factor names, are given in Table 8.8. Again we have three second-order factors. Had only two factors been rotated, then the loadings on Sexual Freedom and Socialism would have been lost—and this despite the eigenvalues of 1.28, .91, and .33, which seem to indicate only two factors. The third second-order factor is again liberal. It is a factor evidently complementary to factor II, the "main" L factor. There is only one negative loading and that moderate, $-.37$. Except for the third factor, the second-order structure supports the theory, even though the first-order factors were not clear.

COMPARISON OF THE FACTORS OF THE FOUR SAMPLES

Despite the difficulty and risk involved in comparing factors from different attitude instruments, in different languages, and with different num-

TABLE 8.7
REF-VI: Factor Arrays, Oblique Rotations, Netherlands I,
$N = 685$

Conservative Factors

Religiosity	*Economic and Social Conservatism*
religion (.69)	profits (.56)
church (.67)	achievement (.51)
Christian (.64)	industry-trade (.44)
Royal Family (.34)	authority (.41)
love of country (.35)	employers (.40)
film censorship (.28)	obedience of children (.40)
tradition (.28)	law and order (.39)
	money (.39)
free abortion (-.26)	existing economic relationships (.38)
	strong punishment for criminals (.38)
	multinationals (.38)
	competition (.37)
	private property (.34)
	good manners (.32)
	free enterprise (.28)
	respect for elders (.26)
	private enterprise (.26)

Liberal Factors

Sexual Freedom	*Social Freedom and Privacy*
sexual freedom (.61)	freedom in private living (.51)
homosexuals (.57)	morality (.46)
free abortion (.50)	freedom of expression (.46)
pornography (.42)	freedom (.43)
childless couples (.39)	human warmth (.40)
divorce (.38)	good manners (.38)
birth control (.37)	equal opportunity (.38)
demonstrations (.36)	social harmony (.33)
emancipation of women (.31)	private property (.31)
conscientious objection (.30)	achievement (.28)
equality (.26)	workers (.27)
authority (-.28)	

TABLE 8.7 *(continued)*

Social and Economic Equality	*Socialism*

Social and Economic Equality

income leveling (.48)
equality (.44)
social equality (.40)
higher minimum wage (.40)
"having a say" (.32)
participation - have a voice in (.26)

capitalism (-.43)
aristocracy (-.30)

Unnamed[a]

government aid to education (.51)
affection (.45)
social legislation (.36)
love (.35)
democratization (.36)
police (.33)
family (.33)
national health care (.31)
government price controls (.26)
discipline (.25)
social planning (.25)
government care (.25)

Socialism

social harmony (.43)
economic reform (.41
progressive taxation (.39)
social equality (.35)
social change (.33)
government ownership of utilities (.33)
government care (.32)
income leveling (.30)
public utilities (.28)
government price controls (.28)
industry-trade (.27)
democratization (.25)
social legislation (.25)

Militant Social Action

action groups (.54)
demonstrations (.43)
profit-sharing (.35)
participation - have a voice in (.33)
militant labor unions (.33)
social planning (.26)
government price controls (.26)

[a] Although this factor has mostly liberal items, it appeared on a conservative second-order factor. (See Table 8.8)

TABLE 8.8
REF-VI: Rotated Second-Order Factors, Netherlands I
Sample, N = 685

	I	II	III	h²	Type	Name
1	*.59*	*-.37*	-.06	.49	C	Religiosity
2	*.66*	-.10	-.08	.45	C	Economic and Social Conservatism
3	-.17	.06	*.40*	.19	L	Sexual Freedom
4	.27	*.37*	.13	.23	L	Privacy and Social Freedom
5	-.04	*.63*	.00	.40	L	Social and Economic Equality
6	.10	.07	*.44*	.21	L	Socialism
7	-.08	*.41*	.11	.18	L	Militant Social Action
8	*.57*	.22	.05	.37	C	Unnamed

[a] L: liberalism; C: conservatism.

[b] Loadings ⩾ .35 were considered significant. They are italicized.

bers of items and factors, we now attempt such a comparison. To do so, we lay out the factor names of those factors that were common to two or more samples, with the main referents associated with the names in Tables 8.9 and 8.10, the former for the stable conservative factors and the latter for the more labile liberal factors. The three highest loaded referents of each factor of the United States sample are used as a sort of standard and are given in the first columns of the tables under "U.S." If the same referents also had substantial loadings on another sample, the word "same" appears, but, in addition, other referents with substantial loadings on that factor are appended. Thus the reader can perhaps get greater insight into the substance of the first-order factors. Because of space limitations and the complexity of the data, only the items that loaded highest on the factors are given in the tables. If a factor did not appear in a sample, the space under the sample name and across from the factor name is left blank. If a factor resembles the standard factor but has a different name, then the different name also appears. For example, Sexual Freedom is clearly that in the Spanish and Dutch samples, but in the American sample the factor was dominated by women's equality items. Thus the

TABLE 8.9
Factor Names and Representative Items,
Four Samples, Conservatism

Factor	U.S.	Spain	Netherlands-I	Netherlands-II
"Religiosity"	*Faith in God* *religion* *church*	*same[a]* *and Church* *involvement* *teaching spirit-* *ual values*	same, and *Christian* *Royal Family*	same
"Economic Conservatism"	*profits* *money* *business*	*same,* *and* *private property* *real estate* *corporate* *industry*	same and *achievement* *industry-trade* *authority*	same, and *competition* *free enterprise*
"Traditional Conservatism"	*discipline* *duty* *authority*	*social welfare* *individual* *effort*	(merged with Economic Conservatism)	same
"Morality"	*morality* *moral standards*			*good manners* *(divorce:* *negative)*

[a] "Same" means that the same items given in the U.S. column also appeared in this country. Exceptions are minor and mainly linguistic and cultural.
Blank spaces mean that factors either did not appear or merged with another factor.

TABLE 8.10
Factor Names and Representative Items,
Four Samples, Liberalism[a]

Factor	U.S.	Spain	Netherlands-I	Netherlands-II
"Sexual Freedom"	("Women's Equality") *equality of women women's liberation birth control*	same, and *evolution theory divorce*	*sexual freedom homosexuals free abortion*	same as N-I, and *childless couples emancipation of women*
"Feeling and Affection"	*love human warmth affection*	same, and *feeling*	(merged on another factor)	same, and *freedom of expression freedom of private living*
"Social and Economic Equality"	*racial equality civil rights equality*		*income leveling social equality higher minimum wage*	*workers "having a say" democratization*
"Socialism' or Social Welfare"	*labor unions socialized medicine government price controls*	("Workers Rights vs. Capitalism": *workers' unions right to strike capitalism (-)*	*social harmony economic reform progressive taxation*	("Income Equalization" *profit-sharing maximum income progressive taxation)*
"Militant Social Action"			*action groups demonstrations profit sharing*	same as N-I, and *equal opportunity emancipation of women*

[a] See footnote, Table 8.9.

name Women's Equality is inserted. Other minor details of the tables should be obvious.

Three *C* factors appeared in the three countries: Religiosity, Economic Conservatism, and Traditional Conservatism (the last two factors merged in Netherlands I). Three *L* factors also appeared: Sexual Freedom (Women's Equality in the U.S.), Feeling and Affection (merged with another factor in Netherlands I), and Socialism or Social Welfare (which took different forms in the three countries but was nevertheless conceptually similar). One other factor, Social and Economic Equality, appeared in the U.S. and The Netherlands but not in Spain. Still another factor,

Militant Social Action, appeared only in the two Netherlands samples, but understandably: its items were only on the Dutch instrument.

There is of course room for disputing the above comparisons and factor names, especially those of the liberal factors. The three conservative factors seem solid: they appear in rather similar forms in the three countries, except for the merging of two of them in the Dutch random sample. The liberal factors, as already pointed out, are less stable. With appropriate items and samples, however, I believe they would appear in other Western European samples. The reader should recall that other factors not in these tables appeared in the different samples. For instance, Income Equalization appeared in Netherlands II but in no other sample. Foreign Influence appeared in Spain but in no other sample. Whether these are potential common factors or factors unique to their samples is not known.

CONCLUSIONS

The question asked earlier—Are social attitude factors approximately the same in different Western countries?—can be given somewhat more than a tentative answer. On the basis of the data of this study done in the United States, Spain, and The Netherlands, it appears that the conservative factors Religiosity, Economic Conservatism, and Traditional Conservativism appear in comparable form in the three countries. They seem to be stable factors. Two or three liberal factors—Sexual Freedom, Feeling and Affection, and Social Welfare or Socialism—also seem to appear in the three countries, but the evidence is now not so clear. In other words, stability seems to be characteristic of conservative factors and lability a characteristic of liberal factors. After the fact one can say that this is obvious: after all, that's what conservatism and liberalism mean!

There is little doubt that similar factors appear in different countries, and these factors are usually liberal or conservative but seldom both. This means that there is limited bipolarity, though there is no doubt that it occurs. In these samples there was relatively little bipolarity. It should be added here that a direct check on bipolarity was made in the four samples by counting the numbers of inter-item correlation coefficients that were $-.30$ or greater (in absolute value) in each sample. There were 10 such negative correlations in the American sample, 41 in the Spanish sample, 5 in Netherlands I (the random sample), and 36 in Netherlands II (the student sample). Considering the large number of correlations among the items, none of these numbers is high, except, perhaps, the 36 in the Dutch student sample and the 41 in the Spanish sample. In general, bipolarity appears to be a minor phenomenon—at least in these and earlier data.

The second-order factors are similar in the four samples and the three countries. The second-order rotated matrices have two main factors, one liberal and one conservative, and a third factor, considered to be complementary to one of the main factors. No regularity could be detected in these third factors. They were liberal complementary factors in three samples and conservative in one (Spain), for example. In general, then, the theory of criterial referents is supported by the data, but not unambiguously. We return to these factor data in Chapter 10, where we present reanalyses of the data of these and other studies in a hypothesis-testing multivariate framework.

9 Social Attitude Similarities and Differences in Four Western Countries[1]

The method of analyzing attitude data in this book has until now been mainly factor analysis, in large part a method for finding similarities among measures. There is a more direct way, however, to study similarities among different samples in their responses to attitude stimuli. We now examine the similarities and differences in attitudes among five samples—the four samples described earlier and a German sample—in their responses to individual social attitude referents and to groups of such referents. In short, the basic data of this chapter are the same as those of Chapter 8 except that another sample of German students provided additional data. The approach, analysis, and questions asked, however, are quite different.

METHOD

Recall that we had four samples of individuals who responded to Referents VI, or REF-VI: American education students ($N = 500$), Spanish students ($N = 427$), Dutch students ($N = 270$), and a random sample of Dutch adults ($N = 685$). For the present study a sample of German students was added to the earlier data. In West Germany, 130 students of

[1]The research reports on which this chapter is based are given in Kerlinger (1978, 1980b). I am grateful to Professor L. Eckensberger, University of the Saarlandes, for obtaining the German sample discussed below. Unfortunately, these data were received too late to include in the first research report (Kerlinger et al., 1976).

psychology responded to a 78-item German version of REF-VI, which closely paralleled the American version, 76 of the items being the same or quite similar. The alpha reliabilities for the L and C subscales were .85 and .93. The mean for L was 4.91 and that for C was 3.82. These means are in general lower than those of other samples. The correlation between the L and C subscales was $-.02$.

The basic approach to the data was through study of profiles, the profiles being the means of all the referents used in a sample. That is, the means of all the referent items were calculated over all individuals in a sample. For instance, over the 270 individuals in the Dutch student sample the mean of *family* was 1.22; the mean of *sexual freedom* was 2.46. Instead of the usual 7-point scale used earlier, with values from 1 through 7, a mean of 0 was used, yielding a scale from -3 to $+3$. The transformed scale was used because we wanted to highlight positive and negative tendencies of the different samples. The basic data, then, were the means of those referents that could be identified as liberal or conservative in each sample.

Two main forms of analysis were used: (1) comparison of factor cluster means and selected individual referent means, and (2) correlations of L referent profile means and C referent profile means between samples. The first analysis was based on the factor analyses reported earlier. The factors that appeared in two or more of the original analyses were those compared. Their names are given in Table 9.1. (They were also given in Tables 8.9 and 8.10.) In other words, we compare the referent factor means of the four samples on the factors presumably common to the countries. An example will clarify what was done. The factor Religiosity in the American sample had the referents *religion, faith in God, church, Christian,* and *teaching spiritual values.* The means of these referents were 1.00, 1.35, .53, 1.05, and .87; the means of these means was .96. This is the mean reported in Table 9.1 for Religiosity in the U.S. sample. The Spanish sample had four of these referents, and the mean of the four referents was .77, also reported in Table 9.1. The two Netherlands samples had only three Religiosity referents; the German sample had all five referents.

Because of the difficulty involved in comparing factors when some of the items used were different in the four countries, interpretation of the factors had to be relatively relaxed. In some cases, there was little problem: the factor of Religiosity was much the same in each sample, for instance. But other cases were more difficult. For example, the factors obtained in the Netherlands random sample differed from those of the other samples, perhaps due to the wide heterogeneity of the large random sample. In the other three samples, factors called Traditional Conservatism and Economic Conservatism appeared. In Netherlands-I these two factors appeared as one factor. The same "factor merging" happened to certain liberal factors. Feeling and Affection was a separate factor in the U.S., Spain, and Netherlands student samples, but in the Netherlands random sample its items appeared on other factors. In other words, while the general structure of the factors is apparent in all the samples, the details were sometimes obscured by first-order factor differences.

The means analysis had two aspects. First, the means of clusters of items on a factor and the differences among the five sample means were tested for significance with one-way analysis of variance.[2] The degree of association between sample membership and response to the factor items was estimated with the intraclass coefficient of correlation. The differences between all pairs of means were tested for significance with the Scheffé (1953) test. The .001 level of significance was used in both the analyses of variance and the Scheffé tests to make the tests conservative and to offset to some extent the large N's. In other words, a difference had to be substantial to be significant. The second means analysis was that just described but of the means of individual referents selected for their intrinsic interest and social importance. The purpose of both analyses, of course, was to compare the countries on what appear to be important factor clusters of referents and individual referents and thus, presumably, important attitudes and values.

A second and in some respects more important form of analysis to assess the *general* similarity between the referent profiles of the samples was the calculation of the correlations between all the L referents common to two samples and between all the C referents common to two samples. Items that were not clearly conservative or liberal—for example, *professors, objective tests, Jews, rationality, work*—were not used in the calculations. The U.S. and Spain samples, for instance, had 57 referents in common, 30 conservative and 27 liberal. Two correlations, one between the C referent profiles and one between the L referent profiles, were thus calculated between the mean values of the 30 conservative referents, the mean values having been calculated over all subjects in each sample, and similarly with the 27 liberal referents.

The correlation analysis summarized above entails methodological problems. First, the correlations are not the usual correlations between variables. Rather, they are between the sample profiles of referents. Their

---

[2] It has been pointed out to me (by G. J. Mellenbergh) that this analysis is strictly speaking not the most appropriate one. Because the clusters of referents within each of the samples were measured on the same subjects, the analysis should be multivariate profile analysis (see Morrison, 1967, pp. 186 ff.) rather than univariate analysis of variance. While the argument is valid, the multivariate analysis was not done because the original data from the American sample were no longer available. Moreover, because the N's are large, it is doubtful that the results of the two approaches would yield different conclusions.

TABLE 9.1
Means and Intraclass Correlations of Conservative and
Liberal Factor Clusters, Five Samples[a]

	U.S.	Spain	Neth-I	Neth-II	Germany	r_a[b]
Conservative Factors:						
Religiosity	.96	.77	1.16	-1.00	.09	.17
Economic Conservatism	1.01	-.23	1.22	-.38	-.41	.21
Traditional Conservatism	1.13	.27	1.49	-.65	-.30	.24
Mean C	1.03	.27	1.29	-.68	-.21	.21
Liberal Factors:						
Sexual Freedom	1.41	1.35	.13	1.93	.36	.17
Feeling and Affection	2.53	2.47	2.39	2.60	1.49	.31
Social and Economic Equality	2.46	2.50	1.46	2.21	1.45	.19
Socialism (Social Welfare)	.79	1.72	1.17	1.78	.25	.11
Mean L	1.80	2.01	1.29	2.13	.89	.20

[a] Tabled entries are means on a seven-point scale with a mean of zero.
[b] r_a: intraclass coefficient of correlation. Differences between the means of .50 are statistically significant at the .001 level by the Scheffé test and are also meaningful.

magnitude reflects the similarity in rank ordering of the means of the referents of two samples—and nothing more. Second, and more difficult, is whether to calculate the correlations over all the means, disregarding the distinction between conservative and liberal referents, or to calculate them as indicated above: within the conservative and within the liberal categories. (See later discussion.)

RESULTS

Factor Means

The means of the factor clusters, the means of the L and C means, and the intraclass coefficients of correlation are given in Table 9.1. All F ratios obtained from the analyses of variance of each set of five means were significant. The modest magnitude of the intraclass coefficients—they range from .11 to .31, with a mean of .20—and the statistical significance of the F ratios indicate that there are differences between the samples and that the sizes of the differences are, in general, moderate. In certain cases, however, they are relatively large.

In studying Table 9.1, first consider the means of the means in the rows labeled Mean C and Mean L. Note that Netherlands-I, the random sample of The Netherlands, has the highest C mean, 1.29, and Netherlands-II, the Dutch student sample, the lowest C mean, −.68. To assess the statistical significance of any particular difference, .50 can be used as a rough criterion. A difference of .50 or greater is statistically significant at the .001 level; it is also meaningful in the sense that it is large enough to indicate a substantial attitude difference between samples. The large difference of 1.97 between the two Dutch means, for example, is striking and far exceeds the criterion of .50. The Dutch random sample mean and the American student mean, on the other hand, are alike: 1.29 and 1.03; the difference is only .26, not significant. Most of the differences between the samples on C were significant. The rank order of the samples, from high to low, is: Netherlands-I, United States, Spain, Germany, Netherlands-II.

Consider the L mean differences (row labeled Mean L). The largest difference of 1.24 is between the Dutch and German student samples, with the former being higher than the latter. Perhaps more interesting, there are no significant differences between the American, Spanish, and Dutch student samples. Evidently there is substantial average agreement on liberal issues. The rank order on L, from high to low, is: Netherlands-II, Spain, United States, Netherlands-I, Germany. (There is no discernible relation between the C and L rank orders.) In sum, the American, Spanish, and Dutch students are rather strongly liberal and alike in their general level of liberalism. Netherlands-I and Germany, on the other hand, are significantly lower (1.29 and .89)—and they do not differ significantly from each other.

The mean profiles on C and L, while important, conceal the differences on the individual factors, which may be of greater interest. For example, the Netherlands random sample (Netherlands-I) has the highest mean on Religiosity (1.16), the Netherlands student sample has the lowest mean (-1.00), the U.S. and Spain means are close to the Netherlands-I mean (.96 and .77), and the Germany mean is in between (.09).[3]

Netherlands-I and the U.S. are alike on Economic Conservatism (1.22 and 1.01), and they differ considerably from the Spain, Netherlands-II, and Germany samples, which have negative means ($-.23$, $-.38$, $-.41$). A similar interpretation applies to Traditional Conservatism: Netherlands-I and the U.S. are the most conservative, Netherlands-II and Germany least conservative, and Spain is in between.

The American, Spanish, and Dutch student samples are positive toward Sexual Freedom, whereas the Dutch random sample and the German sample are not enthusiastic. The largest difference (1.80) between the two Dutch samples, taken at face value, indicates a wide value gap between the Dutch population and one group of university students on such issues

---

[3]In the published report (Kerlinger, 1978, p. 30), this mean of .09 was erroneously reported as .89.

as *women's liberation, birth control, divorce,* and *abortion* (see Table 9.3). The means on Feeling and Affection are, with the exception of Germany, very high. The differences among the U.S., Spain, and both Dutch samples are not significant, still using a difference of .50 as a criterion of statistical significance and meaningfulness. The lack of differences, however, may reflect the social desirability attached to concepts like *love, affection,* and *human warmth.* Germany, on the other hand, differs significantly from the other four samples: its mean is significantly lower than each of the other means.

The U.S., Spain, and Netherlands-II are very high on Social and Economic Equality. Netherlands-I and Germany are also relatively high, but significantly lower than the other samples. (Note, however, that the referents used in calculating these means were not common to all the samples. For example, the two Dutch samples responded to a number of referents that were not on the instruments used in the other countries.) If this evidence is representative of students in the four countries, perhaps a strong ethic of social egalitarianism is evolving.

The means on Socialism (Social Welfare) indicate that the Spanish and Dutch students are rather strongly socialistic, the Dutch random sample somewhat less so, but still substantially (1.17), while the American and German samples display less positive reactions. The difference between the two Dutch samples, while significant, is not as large as those of most of the other factors. This is probably not surprising in a country whose previous government and largest political party were socialist.

Individual Referent Means

The means of the five samples on individual conservative and liberal referents, chosen for their social importance and their centrality in large value systems, as judged by their repeated appearance on factors of different samples, are reported in Tables 9.2 and 9.3. All the analyses of variance again yielded highly significant *F* ratios.

If we rank order the conservative means of each row of Table 9.2 from high to low, we see a distinct pattern. The U.S. and Netherlands-I means are always ranks 1 and 2. They are the most conservative samples. They are strongly business-oriented, quite religious, and espouse private property, discipline, authority, law and order, and love of country (patriotism). The two lowest ranks of 4 and 5 are usually Netherlands-II and Germany. They are the least conservative. Spain usually has the middle rank with certain exceptions (e.g., *tradition,* rank 5, and *capitalism,* rank 4). The pattern is also shown by the means of the means reported at the bottom of the table.

The means of the liberal referents of Table 9.3 are more difficult to

TABLE 9.2
Means of Selected Individual Conservative Referents

	U.S.	Spain	Neth-I	Neth-II	Germ.	r_a
Profits	1.27	.18	1.55	-.27	-.84	.28
Corporate Industry	-.23	-.86	1.12	-.66	-1.36	.27
Free Enterprise	1.49	.17	1.71	.66	.00	.21
Capitalism	.39	-1.72	-.76	-1.74	-1.11	.23
Private Property	1.72	.21	2.11	.44	.42	.29
Competition	1.16	.06	1.09	-.99	-.19	.21
Religion	1.00	.71	1.28	-.84	-.14	.16
Church	.53	-.77	1.11	-1.26	-.79	.26
Discipline	1.65	.58	1.59	-.32	-.09	.25
Authority	.67	.02	1.58	-.73	-.92	.29
Military Training	-.44	-1.52	.63	-1.94	-1.51	.28
Law and Order	1.39	1.17	1.80	-.28	.28	.19
Tradition	.98	-1.31	.84	-.39	-.51	.29
Love of Country (Patriotism)	1.16	-.09	1.35	-1.20	-1.18	.32
Means:	.91	-.23	1.21	-.68	.57	

summarize. The students of the U.S., Spain, and The Netherlands are high on *sexual freedom* and *women's liberation,* with Netherlands-I and Germany low. All samples are relatively high and positive on *birth control.* The U.S. and Netherlands students are high on *abortion;* the other three samples are low. All samples are generally lower on *divorce;* Netherlands-I and Germany are lowest (and negative). All are high on *equality* and *freedom* (social desirability?). *Labor unions* are perceived very positively by the Spanish students and quite low by the Netherlands

TABLE 9.3
Means of Selected Individual Liberal Referents

	U.S.	Spain	Neth-I	Neth-II	Germ.	r_a
Sexual Freedom	1.59	1.39	.33	2.46	.12	.19
Women's Liberation	1.45	2.50	.82	1.98	.14	.23
Birth Control	2.15	1.31	1.48	2.33	.89	.10
Abortion	1.20	-.58	-.50	1.89	.06	.21
Divorce	-.02	.97	-.83	1.04	-.35	.19
Equality	2.49	2.47	1.64	2.52	1.21	.16
Freedom	2.76	2.77	2.55	2.80	1.72	.15
Government Price Controls	.52	1.53	.69	1.24	.05	.09
Labor Unions	.36	2.23	-.31	.47	.45	.30
Government Ownership of Utilities	.05	.59	2.23	2.50	.06	.39
Economic Reform	1.68	2.05	1.31	1.92	.25	.14
Social Change	1.99	2.28	.98	2.22	.49	.25
Government Care (Social Welfare)	.99	1.28	1.87	1.90	1.02	.09
Means:	1.32	1.60	.94	1.94	.47	

random sample. They are also low, though positive, in the U.S., Netherlands-II, and Germany samples. *Economic reform* and *social change* are generally favored by all samples but Germany. The means of the means (bottom) again show the overall pattern. Netherlands-II (students), Spain, and the U.S. are high in liberalism, whereas Netherlands-I (the random sample) and Germany are lower. All are positive, however. It is obvious that these predominantly student samples are liberal.

The individual referents obviously have considerable diversity. Nevertheless, the conservative individual referents yielded much the same pattern as the means of the means of the factor clusters: the U.S. and Netherlands-I are high and Netherlands-II and Germany low, with Spain in between. There is not the same agreement, however, between the patterns of means of the means of the liberal factor clusters and the means of the liberal individual referents. One can say that Netherlands-II is in general the highest and Germany the lowest. Further generalization does not seem possible. A tentative explanation for the difference between conservative and liberal referents is that the conservative referents reflect, virtually by definition, the ideas and practices that are stable and long-enduring in and across societies, but the liberal referents reflect the social ideas and practices that change more rapidly—and change in different ways and at different speeds in different countries. This speculation can of course only be made more than speculation by systematic research.

CORRELATIONS OF REFERENT PROFILES BETWEEN SAMPLES

The correlations between the conservative and liberal referent profiles of the five samples are given in Table 9.4. Recall that the means of the referents common to each pair of samples formed the set of ordered pairs that were correlated. Each sample has a profile of referent means that, taken at face value, represents the attitude "constellation" of that sample. The common N's varied from 17 to 36, the lower N's occurring between the Netherlands samples and the other samples.

The most important feature of these correlations is their generally substantial level: the average correlation among the C referents, via z transformation, is .75 and that among the L referents is .62 (r_{tav} in the table). All r's except that between the L referent means of Spain and Netherlands-II profiles, .27 (not significant), and the Spain and Netherlands-I profiles, .52 ($p < .05$), are significant at the .01 level. Evidently there is substantial agreement among the Dutch, Spanish, German, and American samples in their average rankings (ratings) of both conservative and liberal referents,

TABLE 9.4

Correlations Between Profiles of Means of Conservative
Referents (C) and Liberal Referents (L) Common to Samples[a]

C	Spain	Neth-I	Neth-II	Germany	r_{av}[b]
United States	.83	.76	.78	.62	.76
Spain		.78	.79	.68	.73
Neth-I			.81	.66	.76
Neth-II				.72	.78
Germany					.67
				r_{tav} =	.75

L	Spain	Neth-I	Neth-II	Germany	r_{av}
United States	.59	.58	.70	.75	.66
Spain		.52	.27	.67	.53
Neth-I			.68	.72	.63
Neth-II				.58	.58
Germany					.69
				r_{tav} =	.62

[a] Correlations are based on different N's: from 17 to 36.

[b] Average r's: the mean, via z transformation, of each sample designated on the left with the other samples. All r's except those between Spain and N-I and Spain and N-II, liberal profiles, are statistically significant at the .01 level. The r (.52) between Spain and N-I is significant at the .05 level, while the r (.27) between Spain and N-II is not significant. r_{tav}: average of the average r's.

but especially of conservative referents. There is little variation in the general level of the C referent correlations: the range is from .62 to .83. There is greater variation in the L referents: the range is from .27 to .75.

The general level of profile agreement between each sample and each other sample is shown by the mean r's in the last column of the table. It is clear that the agreement of conservative referents is uniformly high—the range is from .67 to .78—and that the mean of the means, .75, indicates the substantial general agreement. The level of profile agreement of the liberal referents is lower—the range is from .53 to .69—and the mean of the means, .62, reflects this lower level. Students of the four countries and the Netherlands random sample, despite often wide differences in mean responses to the referent factor clusters (Table 9.1) and to the individual referents (Tables 9.2 and 9.3), evidently share to a surprising extent similar rank orders of sentiments toward the referents *within* the conservative and *within* the liberal referents.[4]

[4] Note that the correlations of Table 9.4 were calculated separately for the C and for the L referents. At first blush, one might think one should correlate the referent profiles over *all* the referents, C and L. If the criterial referents theory is valid, however, this would be a

Referents Common to Different Samples

Another approach in the search for similarities is to find referents that have appeared in the rotated factors of all samples. This approach was used in Chapter 8, but we now wish to be more specific and detailed in our pursuit of similarities. We ask the question: What referents were common to the different samples? More specifically, what referents had substantial factor loadings on rotated factors that could be considered the same or similar in different samples? The answer to this question may have important theoretical and practical implications. If the answer is "successful" in the sense of describing those referents that appear in all or most samples in different languages, we may learn some of the substance of what is attitudinally common to the different countries and samples.

In Tables 9.5 and 9.6, the referents common to two or more of the four original samples' obliquely rotated factors are given. (The number of cases in the Germany data, $N = 130$, was too small to permit factor analysis of the large number of items.) The conservative factors and their common referents are given in Table 9.5, and the liberal factors and their common referents in Table 9.6. A number of the referents appeared in all four samples, for example, *religion, authority,* and *corporate industry* in Table 9.5. Other referents appeared in three or only two of the samples partly because the referents were not used in a sample or samples and partly because they had low loadings (<.30) in some samples. For instance, *faith in God* and *business* were not included in the REF-VI scale used in the two Netherlands samples, and *discipline* and *free enterprise* had loadings lower than .30 in Netherlands-I. Items somewhat different from the original English items but with substantially the same meaning (*authority* and *women's liberation* in the Dutch samples, for example) are also appropriately marked in the tables.

If we accept the rather loose method of item listing and categorization of Tables 9.5 and 9.6, we have a core of referents that tells us the nature of

---

mistake since two distinct and different attitude profiles would be thrown together. (If the bipolar hypothesis were correct, such a method of correlating the referents would be appropriate.) Indeed, calculating the r's over both kinds of referents can yield misleading results. A dramatic example is shown by the r's of the two Netherlands samples. The r's calculated separately for N-I (the random sample) and N-II (the student sample) are .81 for the C referents and .68 for the L referents (see Table 9.4). But the r calculated over both C and L referents is .26! From this correlation, one would infer a low relation between the referent ratings of the students and those of the random sample, a highly misleading inference. Indeed, a regression analysis showed that the regression coefficients (b's) were .98 for the C referents and .37 for the L referents. The difference is highly significant ($t = 4.43, p < .001$). The two relations, in other words, are quite different and need to be considered separately. If one takes the trouble to plot the two sets of referents of N-I and N-II and then insert the two regression lines, one sees this clearly: they are quite different. For a detailed discussion of the data of the two Dutch samples, see Kerlinger (1980b).

the individual factors under whose names they are listed. They also tell us what *may* be the hard core of conservatism and liberalism in modern Western societies. In addition, if generality is a goal of attitude measurement, these items can be the basis of scales to measure conservatism and liberalism. (Exceptions to this statement would probably be *homosexuals, childless couples,* and *"having a say"* in Table 9.6 because they were specific to the Netherlands samples and to aspects of Dutch culture. These items are excluded from the statements that follow.) Of the 17 *C* and 18 *L* items of the two tables—with the three *L* items just mentioned excluded—one can, for example, use twelve to fifteen items for *L* and the same number for *C* measurement. (This has not been tried.)

What are these "hard cores" of conservatism and liberalism? On the conservative side, they are the three first-order factors found repeatedly in different samples: Religiosity, Economic Conservatism, and Tradi-

TABLE 9.5

Referents and Factor Loadings of Factor Arrays Common to Two
or More Samples, Conservative Factors

Factor	U.S.	Spain	Neth-I	Neth-II
Religiosity				
faith in God	.66	.61	_[a]	_[a]
religion	.65	.60	.69	.68
church	.63	.32	.67	.64
Christian	.55	_[a]	.64	.64
Traditional Conservatism				
discipline	.50	.37	_[b]	.35
law and order	_[a]	.36	.39	.52
authority	.44	.31	.41[c]	.54[c]
competition	.36	.31	.37	.55[d]
Economic Conservatism				
profits	.62	.50	.56	.49
money	.50	.52	.39	.36
business	.48	.38	_[a]	_[a]
free enterprise	.31	.34	_[b]	.48
corporate industry	.44	.40	.44	.43
real estate	.43	.43	_[a]	_[a]
capitalism	.43	.27[b]	(-.43)[e]	.41
competition	_[b]	_[b]	.37	.55
private property	.35	.42	.34	.37

[a] Item was not used in this sample.
[b] Item had a low loading ($< .30$).
[c] Item somewhat different, but having similar meaning.
[d] Item did not appear on the same factor but on another related factor.
[e] Item did not appear positively, but negatively on another factor.

TABLE 9.6
Referents and Factor Loadings of Factor Arrays Common to
Two or More Samples, Liberalism Factors

Factor	U.S.	Spain	Neth-I	Neth-II
Feeling and Affection				
love	.59	.41	.35[d]	.36
human warmth	.50	_[b]	.40[d]	.45
affection	.49	.61	.45[d]	.56
feeling	.37	.50	_[b]	_[a]
Sexual Freedom				
equality of women	.60	.43	_[a]	_[a]
women's liberation	.58	.40	.31[c]	.31[c]
birth control	.31	.39	.37	.46
sexual freedom	_[a]	_[a]	.61	_[b]
homosexuals	_[a]	_[a]	.57	.50
childless couples	_[a]	_[a]	.39	.52
divorce	_[b]	.31	.38	(-.43)[e]
Social and Economic Equality				
equality	.46	_[b]	.44	.48
social equality	_[a]	_[a]	.40	.34
"having a say"	_[a]	_[a]	.32	.45
Socialism (Social Welfare)				
labor unions	.49	.46[c]	_[a]	_[b]
socialized medicine	.44	_[b]	.31[d]	.49
government price controls	.39	.64	_[b]	_[b]
social welfare	.37	.41[d]	_[a]	_[a]
government ownership of utilities	.36	.57	.33	.39
economic reform	.34	_[b]	.41	_[b]
social equality	_[a]	_[a]	.35	.34[d]

[a,b,c,d,e] See footnotes of Table 9.5.

tional Conservatism, and their main items: *religion, church, authority, competition, profits, corporate industry,* and so on. On the liberal side, they are the less stable first-order factors: Feeling and Affection, Sexual Freedom, and Socialism (or Social Welfare), with their attendant items: *love, affection, women's liberation, birth control, labor unions, government ownership of utilities,* and so on. (This omits the factor Social and Economic Equality of Table 9.6 because it is apparently the weakest of the two tables.) The description and measurement of social attitudes may well begin with these referents.

CONCLUSIONS

As we have seen, the data produced by the five samples in four countries are complex. Still, certain conclusions can be drawn from the study, and we attempt to outline them.[5]

Recall that we found in Chapter 8 substantial agreement among the factors in the different samples. The agreement among the conservative factors was strong and stable, while the agreement among the liberal factors was moderate and more labile. In this chapter we used those factors, both C and L, that appeared in the four samples and compared the factor cluster means and the C and L means of the clusters. When we did so, we found the Dutch random sample and the American sample to be the most conservative and Dutch and German student samples to be the least conservative. The Dutch and Spanish students, on the other hand, were the most liberal and the German students the least liberal. The means of the factor clusters generally followed these patterns (see Table 9.1).

The means of individual L and C referents showed interesting contrasts among the five groups. The U.S. and Netherlands-I were high on *profits,* whereas the Netherlands-II and Germany were low. Despite the American students being high on *profits,* their mean on *corporate industry* was low. *Capitalism* is low in all the samples except in the U.S. where it is relatively high. *Sexual freedom* is substantial or high in the U.S., Spain, and Netherlands-II, and consistently lower in Germany and Netherlands-I. The same is true of *women's liberation.* Surprisingly, *birth control* is high in all samples except Germany where it is lower than in the other samples. *Abortion,* another highly controversial issue, is quite different: it is high or substantial in Netherlands-II and the U.S., but low and negative in Spain and Netherlands-I. *Equality* and *freedom* are high in all samples. (See Tables 9.2 and 9.3.)

Perhaps the most important and interesting conclusion of this chapter springs from the correlations among the five samples' ratings of the means of the referents (Table 9.4). These correlations were substantial to high on the C referents, an average r of .75, and mostly substantial on the L referents, an average r of .62. Despite the often large differences in L and

---

[5]An important caveat is necessary. The comparisons and conclusions discussed above and below should by no means be generalized to the general or student populations of the four countries. While the comparisons are interesting and perhaps indicative of actual population differences, the evidence from these samples—except, perhaps, that of Netherlands-I, the random sample—certainly does not justify general statements applicable to the five populations. My experience indicates that the differences between the two Dutch samples, for example, rather accurately reflect Dutch general and student population differences, but the opportunistic sampling used forbids generalization.

C means and in factor cluster means, the five samples show substantial average agreement in their ratings of the *L* and *C* referents. This marked and unmistakable agreement seems to indicate a common value-attitude perception, similar hierarchies of social attitude and value concepts. Within the conservative referents, for example, the American students put high average values on *money* and *private property* (1.73 and 1.72) and relatively low values on *church* and *military training* (.53 and − .44). The Spanish students did the same, even though all the average values were lower (.27, .21, − .77, − 1.52). Similarly, within the liberal referents the American students gave high values to *birth control* and *equality* (2.15 and 2.49) and lower values to *labor unions* and *government price controls* (.36 and .52); the Dutch random sample's average values were similar in their rank order (1.48, 1.64, − .31, and .69).

This substantial to high agreement was unexpected. Originally, there had been no intention of calculating these correlations. In fact, it was almost an accident: the correlations were first calculated because tables of factor cluster referents and means had been set up to study the qualitative relations among the factor clusters and, almost as an afterthought, the *r*'s were calculated. It was then seen how valuable they might be, especially in those cases where the differences between *L* and *C* means were large. The substantial agreement of the samples' profiles, both when the *L* and *C* means are alike and when they are different, may indicate a common Western cultural and social attitudinal core, a common perception of social issues.

The findings of this chapter and the last chapter have provided both support and lack of support of the criterial referents theory. The major expectations, which we need not labor further, were sustained: in the factor analyses, the factor loadings indicated the underlying dualistic structure both in the first- and second-order analyses. And the expectations were sustained in different countries. While they of course differed in specifics of content, the first-order factors showed marked similarities, especially of conservative factors. And the second-order structures that appeared in the different samples are perhaps the strongest support for the theory. The predicted dualistic structure, that, with one major exception, appeared in all the samples, is of course the core of the theory. Therefore when the predicted liberal and conservative second-order factors appeared, the theory was supported.

There is, however, a major exception to the nice picture of confirmed theory. There were three and not two second-order factors in two of the four samples. The uncomfortable third second-order factors were justified, perhaps rationalized, by saying that they are complementary factors, offshoots, so to speak, of one of the two main liberal and conservative factors. Will this explanation hold up under closer scrutiny? Is it possible that with a large number of items of diverse character more than two second-order factors will appear? I think it is quite possible. If so, then do we go on explaining them away?

The results of the profile approach of this chapter also seem to support the theory. The substantial L and C correlations among the samples in the referent profile ratings are further evidence of the existence of liberalism and conservatism as latent variables underlying attitude referent responses. And the appearance in two or more samples of the same C and L referents (see Tables 9.5 and 9.6) further strengthens the assumption of the C and L latent variables. In the next chapter we turn to another approach to the data, a more rigorous multivariate approach that allows us to test more directly the empirical implications of the alternative duality and bipolarity hypotheses.

10 Analysis of Covariance Structure Tests of Duality and Bipolarity[1]

We have reached a turning point. Most of the evidence for the empirical validity of the criterial referents theory has been presented. From this point on, we study the research of others related to the theory, and, the subject of this chapter, present "direct" tests of the contrasting duality and bipolarity hypotheses. To test these alternative hypotheses, we have used a flexible, general, and powerful form of multivariate analysis: analysis of covariance structures. We used this method because it is well-suited to testing complex alternative hypotheses and because it makes it possible to include latent variables in analyses.

As we have seen in the last few chapters, the research findings have

---

[1] Much of the substance of this chapter comes from a multivariate study whose purpose was to test the duality and bipolarity hypotheses of attitude structure (Kerlinger, 1980a). I wish to thank Prof. dr. W. Saris and Prof. dr. G. Mellenbergh for critical reading of the original paper and for technical help with the interpretation of the results of the covariance structure analysis and the computer program LISREL-IV.

Some readers may experience difficulty with the technical aspects of this chapter since the mathematics and statistics are complex and different from the usual statistics. An effort will be made to explain as much as possible without going into too much tedious detail. A highly simplified explanation of analysis of covariance structures can be found in my book (Kerlinger, 1979, pp. 224ff.). Fortunately, a general conceptual understanding of the method should be sufficient for following the argument and assessing the evidence.

Some readers may also wish that I had not used Greek symbols. I agree that using ordinary letters of the English alphabet would be easier. But many readers will have to learn the LISREL system itself, and will also have to read research papers that have used analysis of covariance structures and the Greek symbols. For these reasons, I decided to retain the symbols used in the LISREL manual. They are rapidly becoming part of the behavioral research literature.

supported the criterial referents theory, though not unambiguously. The scientifically astute reader may be discontented with the relative imprecision of the conclusions stated earlier. With much, perhaps all, factor analytic research it is difficult to make statements about the results of research that are unambiguous and precise. One major problem, for instance, is the identification and naming of factors. As we have seen, the nature of the factors can change with different samples and different tests and items. How can we be assured, too, that the names we give factors are the "correct" names? The number of factors to extract and rotate is another difficult and often unclear problem. Although there are objective methods for deciding how many factors to rotate, they are not always satisfactory since they work only statistically.

Factor analysis, in other words, is a powerful method of analyzing data, but its actual use suffers from looseness inherent in certain technical problems, as suggested above, and in the interpretation of factor analytic data. Factor analytic studies are quite unlike the comforting precision of factorial experiments in which subjects have been assigned at random to experimental conditions, and analysis of variance used to provide fairly clean testing of hypotheses. During the last decade or so new multivariate methods have been devised to help solve such problems. It is now possible to set up theoretical models and to test factor analytic hypotheses with precision—though not always satisfactorily from a research point of view. Perhaps the most highly developed available method to do so is called analysis of covariance structures (Bentler, 1980; Jöreskog, 1971, 1974, 1978; Jöreskog & Sörbom, 1978).[2]

In the analyses to be reported, analysis of covariance structures was used to test the implications of the criterial referents theory. Since the method is relatively new and not generally known, we will describe it and some of the ideas behind it. Before doing so, however, let us review the problem under study by reexamining the empirical implications of the duality and bipolarity attitude hypotheses.

THE THEORY AND THE PROBLEM

Referents are names, categories, constructs that stand for sets or categories of objects, ideas, properties, or behaviors. Attitude referents are referents that can be the "objects" of attitudes: *civil rights, Russians,*

---

[2]As Jöreskog, one of the most active protagonists of analysis of covariance structures, always acknowledges, several individuals (e.g., Bock & Barman, 1966; Wiley, Schmidt, & Bramble, 1973) have developed the theory and method. Jöreskog and his colleagues have put it within reach of researchers by writing computer programs, especially LISREL, to implement the mathematical and statistical theory.

children's needs, real estate, subject matter, for example. Attitude referents are differentially relevant and important to different individuals and different sets of individuals. *Civil rights, blacks, profit-sharing, human warmth,* and *women's equality* may be important to you but not to me. To me *free enterprise, money, profits, discipline,* and *law and order* may be important. I respond favorably to these referents and to things associated with them. Although I am not necessarily opposed to *civil rights, profit-sharing,* and *women's equality,* "your" referents, I may be more or less indifferent to them. In other words, you, I, and sets of people that have similar attitudinal predilections share positive feelings, sentiments, and reactions to sets of referents. But certain sets of referents are more important, more criterial, to you and people like you, and other sets of referents are more important, more criterial, to me and people like me.

The substance of the above paragraph expresses the core of the criterial referents theory: the idea of the differential criteriality of different sets of referents and what can be called the "principle of positivity." The referents are positively criterial to individuals and sets of individuals. Referents tend in general not to be negatively criterial, except under certain conditions. I may not particularly like *equality of women* and *profit-sharing,* for example, but they are not negatively criterial for me—again, except under certain conditions. On the other hand, a defensible case can be made for the view—indeed, it is the commonly held view—that in addition to the referents that are positively criterial for me there are other referents that are negatively criterial. If I say that I detest the ideas of *women's equality, profit-sharing,* and *civil rights,* I am expressing negative criteriality. The theory says that negative criteriality is a relatively minor psychological phenomenon if many social attitudes are measured over many people. It is necessary to say why this is so, assuming that it *is* so. It is also necessary to explain an even more difficult issue: why attitudes are in general positively criterial and how they become criterial. Unfortunately, satisfactory answers cannot be given at this time. It must be admitted, then, that the criterial referents theory is deficient. A theory should give explanations of how and why things are so-and-so and such-and-such. The criterial referents theory, however, only tells how social attitudes are structured. It does not tell why they are so structured. The present chapter, then, deals only with the empirical testing of the main structural empirical implications of the theory: the contrast between the duality and the bipolarity views.

In the Western world, social attitudes and values tend largely to fall into two categories usually called liberalism and conservatism. In some Western European countries "liberalism" has a conservative connotation, as pointed out in Chapter 2. In this book, when we write "liberalism" we mean the American emphasis on freedom of the individual, constitutional participatory government and democracy, the rule of law, free negotiation, discussion and tolerance of different views, constructive social progress and change, egalitarianism and the rights of minorities, and positive government action to remedy social deficiencies and to improve human welfare. Whatever the term in other societies and cultures, this is what is here meant by "liberalism."

Conservatism, on the other hand, is a set of social beliefs characterized by emphasis on the status quo and stability, religion and morality, liberty and freedom, the natural inequality of men, the uncertainty of progress, and the weakness of human reason. It is further characterized by distrust of popular democracy and by support of individualism and individual initiative, the sanctity of private property, and the central importance of business and industry. The point being made is that these two broad sets of beliefs, two ideologies, apparently underlie most social attitudes in the Western world. Most attitude and value referents, for example, can be categorized as liberal or conservative.

The criterial referents theory accepts the "existence" of liberalism and conservatism and says, in effect, that they are two separate though related phenomena that can and should be empirically described as "relatively orthogonal," which means that they are virtually and generally independent of each other. In factor analytic language, they are two separate second-order factors derived from first-order factors each of which is basically liberal or basically conservative—but not both. We call this a duality position or hypothesis.

The bipolarity position or hypothesis, recall, is that attitudes are basically polarized, that opposition to positions not one's own is a fundamental characteristic of attitudes. Liberal issues are opposed to conservative issues, and similarly with liberal and conservative individuals and groups. The factor analytic implications of the bipolarity assumption are that first-order factors will have both liberal and conservative scales or items on them, and there will be one bipolar second-order factor with both liberal and conservative first-order factors on the second-order factor but with positive and negative loadings.

This brief review of the factor analytic empirical implications of the duality and bipolarity hypotheses should be sufficient conceptual foundation for the explanation of the testing of the two alternative hypotheses. The testing was done using twelve sets of data obtained in the studies described in earlier chapters. (See detailed description of the samples and scales under Method, below, especially Table 10.3.)

ANALYSIS OF COVARIANCE STRUCTURES

The basic preoccupation of science is to explain things. To explain something means, in large part, relating the something to other things. In research we try to explain a phenomenon by finding and studying vari-

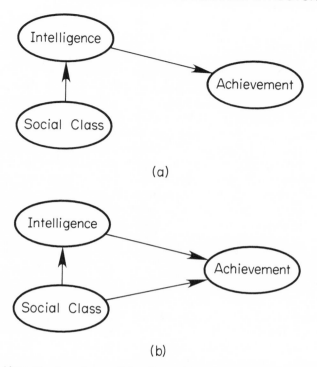

FIG. 10.1. Alternative hypotheses of the effects of intelligence and social class on achievement

ables that affect or influence the phenomenon—or that are affected or influenced by it. Take the achievement of children. We want to know why some children's reading achievement is better than other children's. We have, say, certain hunches or even hypotheses: intelligence is the chief influence on reading achievement; social class is also an influence on achievement but an indirect influence: it works through intelligence. That is, social class influences intelligence, and intelligence influences achievement. Social class, then, has no direct influence on achievement. Some social scientists, however, may be dissatisfied with this "explanation" of achievement. They may say that social class directly influences both intelligence and achievement. We have stated simple alternative hypotheses. They are diagrammed in the two path diagrams of Figures 10.1.

The arrows indicate influences. In (a), social class influences intelligence, which in turn influences achievement. Call this hypothesis I. In (b), intelligence and social class influence achievement directly, but social class also influences intelligence. Call this hypothesis II. These are of course very rudimentary hypotheses or "explanations" of achievement, itself a complex phenomenon. Nevertheless, they are alternative explanations that can be tested empirically, and one of them may be found to be better than the other in the sense that it "fits" whatever data are obtained to test the hypotheses.

Analysis of covariance structures is a mathematical and statistical procedure developed in the last decade or so by several individuals (e.g., Bock & Bargmann, 1966; Jöreskog, 1974, 1978; Wiley, Schmidt, & Bramble, 1973) for the purpose of setting up and testing theoretical models. (For an excellent review of the subject, see Bentler, 1980.) As indicated earlier, the most used procedure and computer program, LISREL, has been developed by Jöreskog and Sörbom (1978). It is a sophisticated procedure that combines factor analytic, multiple regression, path analytic, and other multivariate approaches to complex sets of data for the basic purpose of testing the empirical adequacy of theoretical explanations of phenomena. For example, a theory of achievement might specify or imply a set of dependent, or y, variables—different kinds of achievement, for example—as influenced by a set of independent, or x, variables. The relations among the x variables and among the y variables, as well as between the x and y variables, can also be assessed.

Perhaps most important, the conceptualization and use of latent variables is explicitly built into the LISREL system. In the Figure 10.1 example, intelligence and achievement are really latent or unobserved variables, presumed "entities" underlying observed variables or measures. Factors obtained in factor analysis are latent variables, as pointed out earlier. One of the method's chief features is that the relations between latent variables themselves and between latent variables and observed variables can be analyzed and assessed. Another important feature is that the "fit" of theoretical explanations can be assessed for their adequacy. This is accomplished by explicitly setting up models of theories in the form of path diagrams and algebraic equations and then testing the models statistically. In Chapter 4, an outline of the method as applied to the criterial referents theory was given. It is suggested that the reader again read the section "Analysis of Covariance Structures" in that chapter. It may help to strengthen the present explanation. The following explanation of the application of the method of the duality and bipolarity hypotheses may also help. I will try to explain both the method itself and its application to the problem at hand as we go along. For the reader unfamiliar with the mathematics and statistics involved—admittedly abstract and not easy—some grasp of the core ideas should be sufficient to follow the argument and the evidence presented.

MODELS OF THE DUALITY AND BIPOLARITY HYPOTHESES

The essence of the use of analysis of covariance structures and the LISREL computer program used to analyze the data (Jöreskog & Sörbom, 1978, 1981)[3], as already indicated, is to set up a theory in the form of algebraic equations using all or part of the LISREL system. These equations contain terms associated with measured and unmeasured, or latent, variables, and a model of the theory. The model to test the criterial referents theory is a restricted factor analytic model with correlated factors. Because it is a factor analytic model we need use only y measured variables.

The model of the duality theory is a two-factor second-order model. Its general expression is:

$$y = \Lambda_y \eta + e \tag{1}$$

where y is a vector of observations, Λ (lambda) is a matrix of factor loadings to be estimated by the program, η (eta) is an unobserved or latent variable or variables, or factors, and e is a vector of residuals.

Consider Figure 10.2, which is a specific diagrammatic expression of equation 1 for the dualistic implication of the criterial referents theory. (Later we describe an example of actual research analyzed on the lines of the diagram.) The y's are six scales or measures of liberal attitudes (y_1, y_2, and y_3) and conservative attitudes (y_4, y_5, and y_6). η_1 is a latent variable, liberalism; η_2 is a second latent variable, conservatism. These two latent variables are assumed to "influence" the observed y variables. The "influences" are indicated by the λ's: λ_1, λ_2, and λ_3 estimate the influence of η_1 on y_1, y_2, and y_3; and λ_4, λ_5, and λ_6 estimate the influence of η_2 on y_4, y_5, and y_6. They are factor loadings. The "pure" expression of the theory would prescribe the correlation between η_1 and η_2 to be zero, $\psi_{21} = 0$. In Figure 10.2, the double-headed arrow indicates correlation. This means that we let the program estimate the correlation rather than to set it at zero. (Later, we set $\psi_{21} = 0$, in strict accordance with the duality hypothesis, and compare the results with those obtained from estimating ψ_{21}. See Table 10.8 and accompanying discussion.) We presume that all the λ's, which are factor loadings, will be positive since that is an implication of the theory. This, then, is a model of the theory. We must put it specifically in matrix form, tell the computer what this is, as well as other information, for instance, the correlations among the six y's.

---

[3] When these analyses were done the version of LISREL was LISREL-IV (Jöreskog & Sörbom, 1978). Today, an improved version of the program, LISREL-V (Jöreskog & Sörbom, 1981), is available.

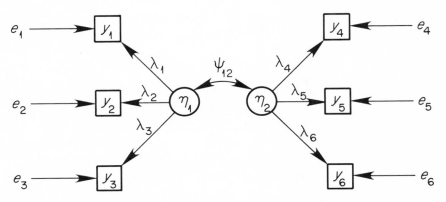

FIG. 10.2. A specific model of the criterial referents theory of attitudes. y_i: observed variables; η_1, η_2: L and C factors; χ_{21}: correlation between the two factors; λ_i: factor loadings; e_i: error terms.

The specific matrix expression of equation 1 and Figure 10.2 is:

$$
\begin{pmatrix} y_1 \\ y_2 \\ y_3 \\ y_4 \\ y_5 \\ y_6 \end{pmatrix}
=
\begin{pmatrix} \lambda_1 & 0 \\ \lambda_2 & 0 \\ \lambda_3 & 0 \\ 0 & \lambda_4 \\ 0 & \lambda_5 \\ 0 & \lambda_6 \end{pmatrix}
\begin{pmatrix} \eta_1 \\ \eta_2 \end{pmatrix}
+
\begin{pmatrix} e_1 \\ e_2 \\ e_3 \\ e_4 \\ e_5 \\ e_6 \end{pmatrix}
\tag{2}
$$

The lambda's in the first matrix on the right, λ_1, λ_2, . . . λ_6, are the hypothesized factor loadings and η_1 and η_2 are two postulated factors. One of these two factors in Λ_y should be L and the other C. We assume that three of the six y's are L and the other three C. The 0's in Λ_y are constraints put upon the system: they are "fixed" by instruction and the computer does its calculations while always maintaining these values at zero. The y's are given observations, six attitude scales, say, or, in this case, six first-order factors. (Actually, the input will be the correlations among the six factors.) $E(\eta\eta') = \psi$ (psi) is the variance-covariance matrix of factors, in this case a correlation matrix. Since there are only two factors, there is only one correlation between them, or ψ_{21}. A "pure" statement of the theory, as indicated earlier, would constrain ψ_{21} to be 0, that is, the correlation between the two second-order factors is zero since the theory is dualistic and predicts two orthogonal (uncorrelated) factors. It is advantageous, however, to estimate ψ_{21} to see how close to orthogonality the factors actually are and to provide a one-degree-of-freedom difference between the model of (2) and the bipolarity model given below. (Actually, ψ_{21} *was* set at zero in tests to be described later. See Table 10.8 and accompanying discussion, and the discussion accompanying the example that is given immediately after this section.)

The alternative bipolarity hypothesis predicts one second-order factor. There is one vector in Λ_y and η contains only the element η:

$$\begin{pmatrix} y_1 \\ y_2 \\ y_3 \\ y_4 \\ y_5 \\ y_6 \end{pmatrix} = \begin{pmatrix} \lambda_1 \\ \lambda_2 \\ \lambda_3 \\ \lambda_4 \\ \lambda_5 \\ \lambda_6 \end{pmatrix} \eta + \begin{pmatrix} e_1 \\ e_2 \\ e_3 \\ e_4 \\ e_5 \\ e_6 \end{pmatrix} \qquad (3)$$

The hypothesis assumes that three of the loadings or λ's will be substantial and positive and three will be substantial and negative since three of the y's are L and three are C. It was said earlier that the one-factor model is a special case of the two factor model. Since the number of estimated factor loadings, or λ's, is the same in both models—there are six λ's in both equations 2 and 3—and only one loading was permitted for each variable in the two-factor model, the one-factor model is a special case of the two-factor model.[4] Since the correlation between the two factors is estimated in the two-factor model, there is a one degree-of-freedom difference between the models. Thus the difference between the two models can be tested statistically by the difference in the χ^2's with one degree of freedom (see below).

The data input to LISREL is the unbiased sample estimate, **S**, for the population covariance matrix Σ, plus certain identifying information (e.g., number of cases and number of factors) and the model specifications in equations 2 and 3. (In our case, **S** = **R**, the correlation matrix.) Assuming that the error terms in the model of equation 1 are uncorrelated with each other and with the unobserved factors, the structure of the population covariance matrix is:

$$\Sigma = \Lambda_y \psi \Lambda_y' + \theta_\epsilon \qquad (4)$$

where θ (θ:theta; ϵ:epsilon) is a diagonal matrix of error variances. The scale of the factors is determined by setting their variances equal to 1, and, therefore ψ is the factor correlation matrix. Using the maximum likelihood method, LISREL estimates the parameters from the sample covariance matrix **S**. If the observed scores are multivariate normally distributed, the χ^2 statistic can be used to test the goodness of fit of a model. If the obtained χ^2 is significant at level α, the hypothesized model

---

[4]Another way to show this is to let the correlations between the two factors of the two-factor model equal 1 (see Bentler, 1980, pp. 424–425). That is, it is possible with LISREL to constrain ψ_{21} to be any value one wishes, or one can let the program estimate it. In this case, let $\psi_{21} = 1$. If this is done, the λ values or factor loadings of both models, or the λ values in equations 2 and 3, will be the same, except that three of them will be positive and three negative in the one-factor model.

is rejected. If χ^2 is not significant, the model is not rejected. (Note that this statistical test has a different meaning from the usual statistical test. Here one "wants" non-significance, so to speak.) The better the matrix S can be reproduced by the factor loadings, the correlations between the factors, and the residual variances, the better the fit of the model to the data.[5]

There is a difficult technical and scientific problem in connection with model testing in general and with LISREL in particular. This is the possibility and desirability of adjusting the model under test to help attain a better fit (Saris, de Pijper, & Zegwaart, 1979). For example, one can have the program estimate one or two values of Λ_y that were fixed at zero. But how much adjustment is permissible before one can talk about improper tinkering with the data? In the use of LISREL in the analyses to be presented, no relaxation was permitted, even though the two-factor model could sometimes have been substantially improved by relaxation. The main reason was the need for completely parallel tests of the two models. Relaxation in one model had to be accompanied by the same relaxation in the other model, and this was not possible. The basic purpose of the study of testing and contrasting the two models, then, forbids the use of relaxation, so often highly useful not only for improving the fit of models, but more important, for getting insight into limitations and possible changes in the theory under test.

An Example

To help clarify the procedure, take an actual example from the REF-I data reported in Chapters 3 and 7 and to be analyzed later with the analysis of covariance structure approach. A 50-item social attitude referents scale, REF-I, was administered to 530 graduate students of education in Texas and North Carolina (Kerlinger, 1972c).[6] The 50 items were intercorrelated and the correlations factored and six factors rotated to an approximation of simple structure. The six first-order factors in general conformed to the criterial referents theory: three factors were L and three were C; L items appeared on L factors and C items on C factors (see Tables 3.2 and 3.4). The correlations among the six factors were themselves factored and two second-order factors extracted and rotated orthogonally. (The first three eigenvalues were 1.76, 1.14, and .19, clearly indicating two factors.)

The LISREL approach was accomplished by setting up, first, a two-factor target matrix to test the two-factor hypothesis and using as a model

---

[5]One must emphasize an important difficulty. The χ^2 test is often significant with large N, even when the fit may be good. Jöreskog (1974, 1978) has said that χ^2 with large N should be interpreted cautiously. In fact, he recommends the testing of alternative hypotheses as a better procedure. We have, when possible, followed his recommendation.

[6]The details of the study were given in Chapter 3; it was also briefly outlined in Chapter 7. It is suggested that the reader glance at Tables 3.2 and 3.4 and Figure 3.1.

a matrix of 1's and 0's based on the second-order factor matrix obtained earlier. (See Table 10.2.) The program was instructed to estimate the L and C factor loadings where they occurred in the earlier analysis; all other loadings (usually low loadings) were fixed at zero. (Only one loading in each row was estimated; the other value was fixed at zero.) It was also instructed to calculate ψ_{21}, the correlation between the two second-order factors η_1 and η_2.

The same procedure was used to test the one-factor hypothesis except that Λ_y had only one factor, there was only one η, and, of course, there was no ψ_{21} to estimate. In addition to the LISREL analysis, the root mean square of the squared residuals, *rms* (Harman, 1976), the square root of the mean of the squared differences of the elements of

$$S - (\hat{\Lambda}_y \hat{\psi} \hat{\Lambda}_y' + \hat{\theta}_\epsilon),$$

where $\hat{\Lambda}_y$, $\hat{\psi}$, and $\hat{\theta}_\epsilon$ are the estimates, respectively, of Λ_y, ψ, and θ_ϵ, was calculated for each LISREL analysis. Although there appears to be no clear criterion level for *rms*'s, *rms* $\leq$ .11 was used in this study to indicate an acceptable level of residuals. This value seemed to be a sensible cutoff point because it seemed from inspection to indicate a relatively low level of residuals. Unfortunately, there appears to be no objective criterion value of *rms* that indicates a satisfactory fit. Its use, therefore is only a rough guide. Nevertheless, it can be a useful index for comparing results of different models.

The LISREL results for the present example were, for the two-factor hypothesis: $\chi^2 = 10.50$, $df = 8$, $p = .23$, and *rms* = .11. The estimated correlation between the two factors, or ψ_{21}, was $-.16$. These results alone support the theory. The two-factor model fits the data. The one-factor hypothesis results strengthen the evidence: $\chi^2 = 29.29$, $df = 9$, $p = .00$, *rms* = .19. ($p = .00$ means that $p < .005$.) The one-factor model does not fit the data. Moreover, the estimates of the six values of Λ_y were unsatisfactory in that the three L factors had low loadings, indicating that the one-factor or bipolar solution "missed" three of the six variables (factors). (See Table 10.2.)

It is possible to test the two hypotheses against each other by subtracting the χ^2 of the two-factor test (duality) from the χ^2 of the one-factor test (bipolarity). As shown earlier, this is possible since the one-factor model is a special case of the two-factor model. The difference between the χ^2's, $28.29 - 10.50 = 17.79$, is, at one degree-of-freedom, statistically significant ($p < .005$). This means that the model associated with the χ^2 of the two-factor hypothesis fits the data better than does the model of the one-factor hypothesis. Taken in conjunction, the nonsignificant χ^2 of the two-factor hypothesis, the significant χ^2 of the one-factor hypothesis, and the significant χ^2 of the difference between the two hypotheses mean that the two-factor or duality hypothesis is supported and the one-factor or

TABLE 10.1
Residuals of Two-Factor Hypothesis Solution (above diagonal)
and One-Factor Hypothesis Solution (below diagonal)

	1	2	3	4	5	6	Type
1		-.17	.17	-.09	.00	-.02	C
2	-.07		.00	-.02	-.06	-.13	L
3	.03	.42		.03	.22	.14	L
4	-.05	.39	.39		.06	-.17	L
5	.01	.05	.05	.10		.00	C
6	-.05	-.04	.01	-.13	.01		C

bipolarity hypothesis rejected. The reader can see the reason in the two matrices of residuals given in Table 10.1. The two-factor solution residuals are above the diagonal and those of the one-factor solution below the diagonal. The large *rms* of .19 of the latter is due mostly to the residuals .42, .39, and .39, which are associated with the *L* factors.

To see the results a bit better, study the original rotated factor matrix and the LISREL factor matrices for the two-factor and one-factor solutions. In Table 10.2, the original rotated factor matrix, the target matrix of 1's and 0's indicating where the substantial loadings and zero loadings should occur, the LISREL two-factor solution, and the LISREL one-factor solution, together with the *C* and *L* designations of the first-order factors are given. "Significant" loadings are italicized. It can be seen that the target matrix is merely a skeletal representation of the original matrix: 1's are where the original substantial loadings were, and 0's where the low loadings were. The LISREL two-factor matrix also faithfully reflects the original matrix—as it should. The LISREL one-factor matrix, however, shows substantial loadings only on the *C* factors. The *L* factor loadings are all low: the one-factor solution has "missed" them. The χ^2 results, the residuals, and the *rms*'s reported earlier confirm the superiority of the two-factor solution over the one-factor solution. As we will see, however, empirical data often pursue their own recalcitrant way. The results of other samples sometimes do not conform to this nice picture.

In describing the model used to test the duality hypothesis—see Figure 10.2 and accompanying discussion—it was said that ψ_{21}, the correlation between the two factors, was estimated to see how close to orthogonality the factors actually are. To test the difference between the duality and bipolarity hypotheses, moreover, there has to be a difference in degrees of freedom so that the duality model χ^2 can be subtracted from the bipolarity model χ^2. (See Jöreskog & Sörbom, 1979, p. 48.) The difference of one degree-of-freedom between the two models is due to the estimation of ψ_{21} in the duality model. That is, it is estimated in the duality

TABLE 10.2
Second-Order Factors, REF-I, Texas and North Carolina
Sample, N = 530: Original Rotated Factor Matrix,
Target Matrix, LISREL Two-Factor and One-Factor Matrices

Original Factor Matrix		Target Matrix, Two-Factors		LISREL Two-Factor Matrix[a]		LISREL One-Factor Matrix	
I	II	I	II	I	II	I	Type[b]
.71	.09	1	0	.65	0	.67	C
-.22	.64	0	1	0	.71	-.25	L
.19	.61	0	1	0	.54	.12	L
-.13	.65	0	1	0	.63	-.15	L
.78	.04	1	0	.87	0	.83	C
.68	-.12	1	0	.63	0	.65	C

[a]The 0's were fixed by the program.
[b]C: conservatism; L: liberalism.

model, but, of course, not in the bipolarity model. Therefore, to test one model against the other, ψ_{21} must be estimated in order to provide a difference in degrees of freedom between the models.

In a strict sense, test of the duality hypothesis, however, ψ_{21} would be set at zero since the theory says that the two factors are orthogonal. Although in the tests of the duality hypothesis reported below ψ_{21} was estimated—the correlation between the factors was calculated rather than set at zero—the analyses were all repeated but with ψ_{21} fixed at zero. If the results are significantly worse than when ψ_{21} is estimated—the χ^2 is significantly larger, for instance—it means that the two factors are not orthogonal. In the present case, χ^2 was 10.61, which at 9 degrees-of-freedom is not significant. The difference between the two χ^2's was .11, also not significant.

METHOD

Subjects and Scales

The educational and social attitude scales described in earlier chapters were constructed and used in the period 1965–1975, though a few of them date from earlier years. In any case, the results obtained with two educational attitude and four social attitude scales were used in the present review and hypothesis-testing study. The scales were administered mostly to graduate students of education in the U.S. (see Chapter 4 for justification for using such students) and university students in Spain and

The Netherlands and to a random sample of citizens of The Netherlands. These samples were described in earlier chapters. The names of the scales, where they were administered and to how many subjects (Ss), and numbers of items are given in Table 10.3. There were eight separate samples, but the scales and the samples are not congruent because the same scale was administered to different samples and different scales were administered to the same sample.

As described earlier, two kinds of items were used in the scales: statements and referents. A statement item is the usual sentence to which Ss indicate degree of agreement or disagreement, for example, "The well-being of a nation depends on its business and industry." A referent item is a single word or short expression—*labor unions, capitalism,* and *discipline,* for example—that epitomizes the "object" of an attitude or succinctly expresses an attitudinal principle.

All scales were of the 7-point summated-rating (Likert) type. It had been found in earlier research that such items were best for factor analytic purposes. The instructions to the Ss were to indicate agreement or disagreement with statement items and positive or negative feelings to referent items. It would have been desirable to have used the same instructions with statement and referent scales, but it was not possible to do so for two reasons. First, responses of agreement-disagreement, a "natural" form of response to attitude statements, are not possible with

TABLE 10.3
Tests, Scales, Samples, and Numbers of Subjects and Items

Test[a]	Scale[b]	Sample	N[c]	k
1a,b	SA	N.Y.	666	40
2a,b	ES-VI	N.Y.	344	46
3a,b	ES-VII	Tex. & N.C.	530	30
4a,b	REF-I	Tex. & N.C.	530	50
5a,b	REF-IV	N.Y.	237	76
6a,b	REF-VI	N.Y. & Va.	500	78
7a,b	REF-VI	Spain	427	78
8a,b	REF-VI	Neth-I	685	72
9a,b	REF-VI	Neth-II	270	72
10a,b	SAREF	Texas	227	—
11a,b	SAREF	N.C.	206	—
12a,b	Values	N.Y.	237	—

[a] a,b: two tests: a = 2 factors; b = 1 factor.
[b] SA: Social Attitudes Scale; ES-VI and ES-VII: educational attitudes scales; REF-I, REF-IV, REF-VI: social attitude referent scales; SAREF: six social and educational attitude scales; Values: two values statement scales and one attitude referent scale.
[c] N: number of subjects; k: number of items.

referents. And second, the instructions with the statement scales ante-dated those of the referent scales. The difference may have caused possible mean differences, but seems to have had little effect on factor structures, which were similar in the statement and referent scales.

The reliabilities of all scales were satisfactory: the L and C alpha coefficients of one social attitude statements scale for four samples in different parts of the U.S. ranged from .72 to .82, with averages for the L and C subscales of .79 and .77. Average reliability coefficients of the L and C subscales of a referents scale of 50 items were .84 and .88. Similar coefficients were obtained in Spain, The Netherlands, and Germany: average L: .82; average C: .91. The scales had between 30 and 78 items.

The American samples of subjects were obtained in New York (five samples) and Texas, North Carolina, and Virginia (one sample each). The Texas and North Carolina sample data were merged to form one large sample, except in one case: so were one of the New York and the Virginia samples. The European samples were obtained in Spain (one sample) and The Netherlands (two samples, one of students and the other a random sample of the country). The scale names and the location of the samples were given in Table 10.3.

Earlier Analyses

After studying the psychometric characteristics of the L and C subscales of each scale—means, standard deviations, item-total correlations, L items with L totals and C items with C totals, and L and C reliabilities—the items of a scale were intercorrelated and factor analyzed with the principal factors method (Harman, 1976, Ch. 8) with, in most cases, R^2's as estimates of communalities (Harman, 1976, p. 87) and both orthogonal (varimax) and oblique (promax) rotations of the factors.

To determine the "correct" numbers of factors to rotate, varied numbers of factors were rotated and four criteria used. (1) Eigenvalues greater than 1 indicated factors for consideration, but this did not necessarily eliminate factors with eigenvalues less than 1. (2) The unrotated factors were studied for size of loadings: in general, if two or more loadings were greater than .30, the factor was a candidate. (3) Solutions that yielded factors consistent with earlier solutions were favored. And (4), solutions had to be, as far as could be checked, consistent with the R matrices. For example, if a solution yielded a certain factor that had, say, one or two items seemingly not consistent with the other items of the factor, the r's among the items were studied to check their "agreement" with the factor loadings.

A crucial step in testing the theory was the extraction and rotation of second-order factors from the correlations among the obliquely rotated factors (promax method: Hendrikson & White, 1964). These correlations were also factored with the principal factors method, but the factor rotations were orthogonal. The "correct" number of second-order factors was determined much as the number of first-order factors, except that it was much easier to make the determination because of far fewer variables and because it was usually obvious that there were two or three second-order factors.

RESULTS

The results are presented in four parts. The first part consists of the results obtained from analysis of the statement scales; they are given in Table 10.4. The first part of the tabled results, tests 1a and 1b, are those obtained from the social attitude scale of 40 items, 20 L and 20 C, described in Chapter 7. (Although results obtained with this scale have not been published, results obtained with its successor have been published. See Kerlinger, 1970a. The items of the latter scale appear in Shaw & Wright, 1967, pp. 313–324, and in Robinson et al. 1968, pp. 98–101.) The remainder of the table, tests 2a, 2b, 3a, and 3b, contains the LISREL results for two educational attitude scales, ES-VI and ES-VII of 46 and 30 items respectively, half the items of each scale progressive (P) and half traditional (T). For descriptions of both scales, see Chapter 6. The a tests

TABLE 10.4
Social and Educational Attitude Statement Scale Results
and Alternative Hypotheses Tests[a]

Test	k^b	χ^2	df	p	rms^c	ψ_{21}
1a	40	22.58	34	.93	.08	-.20
1b	40	38.92	35	.30	.13	
1b - 1a		16.34	1	.00[d]		
2a	46	19.82	19	.41	.10	-.29
2b	46	31.07	20	.05	.14	
2b - 2a		11.25	1	.00		
3a	30	7.06	8	.53	.12	-.62
3b	30	10.12	9	.34	.13	
3b - 3a		3.06	1	.08		

[a] See Table 10.3 for characteristics of the scales and samples. 1a: criterial referents (duality) theory hypothesis test; 1b: bipolarity hypothesis test; 1b - 1a: test of duality vs bipolarity hypotheses.
[b] k = number of observations used in χ^2 test (number of items in scales).
[c] rms: root mean square of residuals; ψ_{21}: correlation between L and C or P and T second-order factors.
[d] p = .00 means $p < .005$.

are the two-factor hypothesis tests, and the b tests are the one-factor hypothesis tests.

The χ^2's of none of the a and b tests is statistically significant, though one (2b) is almost significant ($p = .0543$). Considering only these χ^2 tests, both models fit the data. But which of them fits the data better? Two of the three rms's of the two-factor tests (1a and 2a) are .10 or less, while one (3a) is .12. The correlations betwen the two second-order factors (ψ_{21}) of 1a and 2a, $-.20$ and $-.29$, are in accord with the theory, but that of 3a, $-.62$, is very high. Thus tests 1a and 2a support the model, but test 3a does not. (The rms of .12 and the ψ_{21} of $-.62$ of 3a were caused by one substantial negative factor loading, $\lambda_{11} = -.53$, in the original analysis. When this loading was estimated by the LISREL program instead of being fixed at 0—a relaxation of the "pure" model—$rms = .09$ and $\psi_{21} = -.29$, both acceptable values.) The rms's of 1b, 2b, and 3b are .13, .14, and .13, all greater than the criterion of .11. The χ^2's of two of the contrast tests, 1b-1a and 2b-2a, are highly significant, but that of 3b-3a is not significant. The results, then, are mixed. The tests of 1 and 2 favor the two-factor hypothesis, but the tests of 3 do not differentiate the two hypotheses. Although the original second-order solution did not show it— except for the one loading of $-.53$ mentioned above—evidently there was enough bipolarity in the data to weaken the two-factor model.

Tables 10.5 and 10.6 contain the LISREL results of the analysis of the data of the social attitude referent scales, REF-I, REF-IV, and REF-VI. (For a description of REF-I, see Chapter 3. Results obtained with REF-IV have not been published. A description of REF-VI is given in Kerlinger et al., 1976, and in Chapter 8.) The data of all the samples were tested similarly: two second-order factors for the duality hypothesis and one second-order factor for the bipolarity hypothesis. In the study in which REF-VI was used (Kerlinger et al., 1976), three instead of two second-order factors were extracted and rotated. Although the theory predicts only two second-order factors, one associated with liberal first-order factors and the other with conservative first-order factors, it was found in two of the samples (of four), as pointed out in Chapter 8, that extracting and rotating only two factors resulted in the "loss" of one or two first-order factors in the rotated solutions. "Loss" means that the two factor loadings of a first-order factor in a two-factor solution are small, but if a three-factor solution is used, the first-order factor has a substantial loading on the third second-order factor. In other words, there were clearly three factors in two of the samples, and it was decided at the time to rotate three factors in all four samples to maintain consistency in the samples to which REF-VI had been administered. The same policy was followed in the covariance structures analysis (Kerlinger, 1980a: see Table 5 of that report). The third factor was in each case a factor complementary to one of the other two factors (see discussion in Chapter 8).[7]

In the covariance structure analyses of this chapter, however, it was decided to proceed in strict accordance with the duality hypothesis in all samples. This means that only two second-order factors were extracted and rotated. It also means that the duality and bipolarity hypotheses can be tested against each other with all scales and all samples. Thus, unlike the analysis of covariance structure tests of the published study (Kerlinger, 1980a), the present report uses the same duality and bipolarity tests in all samples.

The summary LISREL results with REF-I are given in lines 4a and 4b of Table 10.5. These results were discussed earlier and need not be discussed again, except to say that the two-factor hypothesis is supported and the one-factor hypothesis not supported. Tests 5a and 5b come from the analysis of the data of the 76-item referent scale, REF-IV, administered to 237 graduate students of education in a study of the relations between attitudes and values. (Other data from this study are given below, tests 12a and 12b.) Its L and C subscales had alpha reliabilities of .85 and .92. Factor analysis of its item intercorrelations yielded ten factors. The correlations among the ten factors were the data analyzed. The duality hypothesis matrix was the resulting two second-order factors obtained from the factor analysis of the 10-by-10 correlation matrix. The LISREL results are given in lines 5a and 5b of Table 10.5: the χ^2's are both significant, and both rms's are large. Evidently the fit of neither model is good. The two-factor hypothesis achieves a better fit than the one-factor

TABLE 10.5
Social Attitude Referent Scales Results and Alternative
Hypotheses Tests[a]

Test	k	χ^2	df	p	rms	$\sqrt{21}$
4a	50	10.50	8	.23	.11	-.16
4b	50	28.29	9	.00	.19	
4b - 4a		17.79	1	.00		
5a	76	61.57	34	.00	.15	.03
5b	76	85.16	35	.00	.17	
5b - 5a		23.59	1	.00		

[a] For definitions of symbols, see footnotes a, b, and c of Table 10.4.

---

[7] The finding of three second-order factors instead of two in two of the samples of course forces alteration of the theory (see Kerlinger et al., 1976). If the third factor is always a "complementary" factor (Cattell, 1952)—a factor that expresses some aspects of one of the two main factors—then the duality hypothesis is still valid. If not, then the theory may require more radical change—or it may even have to be scrapped.

TABLE 10.6
Social Attitude Referent Scales Results: U.S.,
Spain, Netherlands-I, and Netherlands-II Samples[a]

Test	k	χ^2	df	p [b]	rms	ψ_{21} [c]
6a	78	108.10	43	.00	.15	.11
6b	78	148.48	44	.00	.18	
6b - 6a		46,38	1	.00		
7a	78	103.72	53	.00	.15	.12
7b	78	116.72	54	.00	.15	
7b - 7a		13.00	1	.00		
8a[d]						
8b	72	40.54	20	.00	.13	
9a	72	48.94	43	.25	.11	-.30
9b	72	69.14	44	.01	.12	
9b - 9a		20.20	1	.00		

[a] For definitions of symbols, see footnotes a, b, and c of Table 10.4.
[b] $p = .00$ means $p < .005$.
[c] ψ_{21} is the correlation between the two factors in the duality solution.
[d] The data of the "pure" duality model of this sample could not be analyzed because of unknown specification errors. See text.

hypothesis, as indicated by the difference χ^2 test in the line 5b-5a: the χ^2 is significant. The relatively poor performance of the two-factor test is for virtually the same reason as that given in the discussion of test 3a, above: there was one negative loading, $\lambda_{21} = -.42$, that was not estimated (it was fixed at zero). When the model was relaxed and λ_{21} estimated, $\chi^2 = 42.71$, $df = 33$, $p = .12$, and $rms = .12$. So, rms is still too high, even though χ^2 is not significant. While negative correlations between factors were moderate to low, there was enough bipolarity in the data to muddy the two-factor hypothesis test. Yet the one-factor solution again "missed" the L factors: the LISREL-estimated Λ_y had only substantial loadings for C factors.

The results of the LISREL tests of the duality and bipolarity hypotheses tests with REF-VI of the U.S., Spain, Netherlands-I, and Netherlands-II samples, given in Table 10.6, favor the duality hypothesis.[8] The test of the Netherlands-I random sample data (8a and 8b) could only be used with the bipolarity test, 8b; the duality second-order solution, 8a, resisted adequate solution because of unknown specification error. Thus no comparison of the two models was possible. Except for the duality test

[8] The instruments used in the three countries were of course not identical since they were in different languages and were also adapted to the social and cultural conditions of the countries.

of the Netherlands-II student sample, 9a, which indicated that the model fitted the data (χ^2 = 48.94, df = 43, p = .25, rms = .11), none of the tests indicated that the models fit: all the χ^2's were significant, and the rms's, except that of 9a, exceeded the criterion of .11. The reason is that three second-order factors are evidently necessary to achieve adequate fits to the data, even though the third eigenvalues were comparatively small. In the original report, where three factors were used in the LISREL tests, the fits were satisfactory (see Kerlinger, 1980a, Table 5). The three tests of the duality versus the bipolarity hypotheses that were possible, however, clearly favored the duality hypothesis: the χ^2's of the three differences were statistically significant (see lines 6b-6a, 7b-7a, and 9b-9a of Table 10.6). Moreover, the bipolarity or one-factor solutions, with one exception, again yielded unsatisfactory solutions: the factor loadings of the liberal first-order factors were low; the solutions "missed" these first-order factors. The one-factor solution of Netherlands-II, the University of Amsterdam sample with substantial numbers of radical students, was the exception. The one-factor pattern was the nearest to a legitimate bipolar solution in the sense that the liberal first-order factors had substantial negative loadings. (Recall that earlier it was predicted that radical samples would produce bipolarity: see Chapter 3, section "Bipolarity" and the addendum to the chapter.) Nevertheless, the two-factor solution provided a better fit than the one-factor solution.

The results of the final set of tests, 10a through 12b, given in Table 10.7, are in two important respects different from the results of Tables 10.4, 10.5, and 10.6. The N's used in the χ^2 tests of Tables 10.4, 10.5, and 10.6 were all based on N being the number of items in the scales; the tests of Table 10.7, however, are based on N's in the usual sense of number of persons.[9] The consequence is that the χ^2 values of Tables 10.4, 10.5, and

---

[9]The tests of Tables 10.4, 10.5, and 10.6 were applied not to the usual correlations calculated between variables (items) over persons. They were calculated from the transformation matrix used to rotate the first-order factors obliquely (Thurstone, 1947, Ch. XVIII, especially pp. 432–433). They are therefore in effect correlations calculated over the first-order factors, which makes the N for the χ^2 test the number of variables or items and not the number of persons. Even if N as the number of persons had been used in the χ^2 tests of the tables, virtually the same conclusions would have been reached because all statistics except χ^2 and p would have been the same and the difference tests would have had much larger χ^2 differences and still only one degree-of-freedom. An undesirable consequence of using the relatively low N's of the numbers of items is that the maximum likelihood parameter estimates are less stable than they might be. The important differences between the two-factor and one-factor tests, however, seem not to have been vitiated: the two-factor model in most cases fits the data better than the one-factor model (see below).

A reviewer of the research paper on which this chapter is based said that there is no justification for using the χ^2 tests as strict statistical tests because the second-order correlation matrices do not meet the assumptions of the model. I agree. The "statistics" are more

TABLE 10.7

Total Scale Scores Analysis: Social and Educational Attitudes, Statements and Referents (10 and 11) and Values and Referents (12) Scales[a]

Test[b]	N	χ^2	df	p	rms	ψ_{21}
10a	227	56.47	8	.00	.08	-.33
10b	227	176.10	9	.00	.19	
10b - 10a		119.53	1	.00		
11a	206	67.10	8	.00	.08	-.33
11b	206	151.02	9	.00	.16	
11b - 11a		83.92	1	.00		
12a	237	104.86	8	.00	.09	-.45
12b	237	302.27	9	.00	.20	
12b - 12a		197.41	1	.00		

[a] The scales were: SA (26 statement items), L and C; ES-VII (30 statement items), progressive and traditional; REF-I (50 referent items), L and C. (See Table 10.3.) Values-I and Values-II: statement values scales. See Table 10.4, footnotes a, b, and c for explanation of symbols.
[b] These tests (χ^2) use N, the number of subjects, N's of 227 and 206 for tests 10a and 10b and 11a and 11b and 237 for tests 12a and 12b. See footnote 9.

10.6 are lower than those of Table 10.7. Note that all the χ^2's of Table 10.7 are statistically significant. The second and more important difference is that the correlations being analyzed are correlations among total scores of scales and not correlations among factors. In other words, the results of Table 10.7 were obtained from the usual factor analysis of the correlations among scales calculated over all subjects in a sample.

In each of tests 10a and 10b (Texas sample, $N = 227$) and 11a and 11b (N.C., $N = 206$), six scales were used. The first two were social attitude statement scales, L and C; the third and fourth were educational attitude statement scales, P (progressive) and T (traditional); and the fifth and sixth were the L and C subscales of REF-I, described earlier. The two-factor and one-factor tests are the same as those used earlier. The difference is that the covariance structure analysis is applied to the correlations among the six attitude scales instead of to the correlations among obliquely rotated factors. For tests 10a and 10b, the results favor the two-factor hypothesis. Although both χ^2's are significant, that of 10b is much larger than that of 10a. So is the one-factor rms of .19 much larger than the

decision rule guides, as the reviewer pointed out. Moreover, instead of the first-order confirmatory factor model used to analyze the second-order correlation matrices, a better way would have been to use a second-order model directly, that is, start with the original data and derive the first-order factors and then the second-order factors. Limitations of computational time and expense and unavailability of the original data, however, made such analyses impossible.

two-factor *rms* of .08. Tests 11a and 11b are much the same: compare the *rms*'s: .08 versus .16. Again, the results favor the two-factor hypothesis.

Tests 12a and 12b are based on two social values statement scales, VAL-I (Values I) and VAL-II (Values II), and a social attitude referent scale, REF-IV, mentioned earlier (tests 5a and 5b; see Chapter 7). The main purpose of the original study in which these scales were used was to explore the possible similarity of attitude and value factor structures. Even though more bipolarity is to be expected with values than with attitude scales, the tests were made. The results are similar to those of tests 10 and 11 except that the χ^2's are much larger. In short, the values tests support the two-factor hypothesis more than the one-factor hypothesis—as do tests 10a through 11b—but, strictly speaking, we must say that neither set of data fits the model, even though the *rms* of 12a was .09. The marginality of 12a, the two-factor test, seems to be due to greater bipolarity in the data. Evidently the values scales produce this greater bipolarity. (The comparatively large negative correlations between the *L* and *C* factors are discussed below.)[10]

After describing the results obtained with the LISREL analysis applied to the REF-I data of the Texas and North Carolina sample, above, it was said that in a strict test of the duality hypothesis ψ_{21}, the correlation between the two factors, should be set at zero. The question, then, is: Had it been possible to test the duality and bipolarity hypotheses against each other with $\psi_{21} = 0$, would the results have been different? The results of the LISREL analyses of the duality hypothesis with (a) ψ_{21} estimated, and (b) $\psi_{21} = 0$ are given in Table 10.8, together with the differences between the two χ^2's and the statistical significance of the differences.

Again, the results are mixed. In 7 of the 12 cases, the differences are not significant. One, 3a, is marginal. In another case, 8a, the LISREL parameter values of the "pure" duality hypothesis could not be computed because of specification (of model) error. In the last three cases, however, χ^2's of the differences are highly significant. These results are much the same as described earlier for 10a, 11a, and 12a: there is more bipolarity in these data. (More bipolarity was expected in 12a, the values scales.) On balance, however, the 11 valid tests indicate that the correlations between the two factors tend to be low negative: even with the substantial negative

---

[10] It should again be said that the marginality of some of the results can often be removed by relaxing the model. For example, if there are one or two negative factor loadings whose magnitudes have not been estimated, the model can be relaxed to estimate them. An example is test 6, Table 10.6. By estimating two of the correlations between residuals, χ^2 dropped from 63.50 ($p = .01$) to 49.56 ($p = .07$). There was little change in the *rms*, however.

TABLE 10.8
Comparison of Duality Hypothesis Models:
(a) Correlation between Factors Estimated;
(b) Correlation between Factors Set at Zero

Sample	(a) χ^2: ψ_{21}	Est. $\psi_{21}{}^a$	(b) χ^2: $\psi_{21}=0$	Diff.: (b) - (a)	p
1a	22.58	-.20	23.32	.74	n.s.
2a	19.82	-.29	18.27	1.55	n.s.
3a	7.06	-.62	12.52	5.46	.05
4a	10.50	-.16	10.61	.11	n.s.
5a	61.57	.03	61.69	.03	n.s.
6a	102.10	.11	102.66	.56	n.s.
7a	103.72	.12	104.13	.41	n.s.
8a[b]	. . . .				
9a	48.94	-.30	51.43	2.49	n.s.
10a	56.47	-.33	71.76	15.29	.001
11a	67.10	-.33	86.48	19.38	.001
12a	104.86	-.45	142.98	38.12	.001

[a] ψ_{21}: correlation between duality hypothesis factors.
[b] The values of Sample 8a, Netherlands-I, could not be estimated. See text.

r's of two of the eight samples, the average r, via z was $-.31$. In sum, setting the correlations between the factors in the duality tests to zero, in strict accord with the orthogonality hypothesis, does not change the import of the results as discussed earlier. Thus, the use of the duality model with the correlation between the two factors estimated yields much the same results had it been possible to set the correlations equal to zero.

DISCUSSION

The results of the analysis of covariance structure tests of the implications of the two-factor hypothesis of the criterial referents theory of social attitudes and the one-factor bipolarity hypothesis support the former more than the latter. In all cases, the χ^2's and the rms's (measures of the average magnitude of residuals) associated with the two-factor tests were smaller than those associated with the one-factor tests. On the other hand, the results of the separate χ^2 tests of fit were mixed. Four of the five χ^2 two-factor tests of Tables 10.4 and 10.5 were not statistically significant, while two of the five one-factor tests were not significant. (Recall that non-significance means a good fit of the model to the data.) Of the four χ^2 tests of the three-factor tests of Table 10.6, two were not significant. The two-factor tests of Table 10.7 were all significant, as were the one-factor tests. Accepting this evidence at face value, the theory is not unambiguously supported: only six of twelve χ^2 tests were not significant.

It must be remembered that the tests used were severe since no relaxation of the models was permitted, and the χ^2 tests have to be interpreted cautiously (Jöreskog, 1978, p. 448). Both Bentler (1980) and Jöreskog (1978) stress the importance of specifying and testing alternative models, which in this study are the two-factor and one-factor models or the a-b tests in the tables. Seven of the eight χ^2 differences between the models were significant, indicating better fits of the two-factor model. Thus the weight of this evidence is for the criterial referents theory and against the bipolarity theory. Study of the factor solutions supports this conclusion. The two-factor solutions were satisfactory: the factor loadings were positive, substantial, and where they were supposed to be. The one-factor solutions were consistently unsatisfactory since the λ estimates of the liberal factors or scales were too low and the residuals larger.

The correlations between the second-order factors, estimated by LISREL and given in the tables, are an important part of the evidence. The criterial referents theory predicts correlations from 0 to $-.30$ between L and C. In Tables 10.4, 10.5, and 10.6, these r's (ψ_{21}) are, with one exception (3a), low: $-.20$, $-.29$, $-.62$, $-.16$, $.03$, $.09$, $-.02$, $-.04$, and $-.12$. In Table 10.7, however, they are larger: $-.33$, $-.33$, and $-.45$. Taken at face value the latter cast doubt on the theory. Estimates obtained from promax rotations, however, were: $-.05$, $-.06$, and $-.06$, quite different. (Promax rotations seem to stay as close to orthogonality as possible.) If we accept some value between the extremes, we can reasonably conclude that the orthogonal nature of the L and C second-order factors is upheld by the data, though the exceptions must be carefully noted.

Evidently the two-factor model of the criterial referents theory fits the attitude scale data discussed in this chapter better than the one-factor model of the bipolar assumption does. Does this mean that the bipolar model is never applicable to social attitudes? No such claim is made. The claim is more modest: the two-factor model fits better. It is also claimed that assuming social attitudes always to be bipolar is misguided. The evidence of this review study indicates that social attitudes are perhaps fundamentally dualistic. Bipolarity appears to be a lesser phenomenon.

11 The Research of Others

In this chapter we report research done by other investigators that is directly or indirectly related to the criterial referents theory. Some few studies were done specifically to test the theory; other studies, although not done to test the theory, produced evidence pertinent to it. For the most part, the results of these studies support the theory. Some studies do not support it. In addition, we cite several researchers that used variables other than attitude variables but whose results may be suggestive for reexamination of the assumptions of the measurement of important psychological variables.[1] The chapter is admittedly thin. This is either because there has been little research done that is relevant to the theory, or because research that might be considered relevant was done in such a way that adequate assessment is difficult or impossible. One cannot assess the evidence of a study adequately, for example, if its methodology is either questionable or incompletely reported. Examples are older factor analytic studies in which factors were not rotated and more recent studies in which the measurement was compromised by assuming that attitudes are necessarily bipolar. Still others are investigations in which too few items were used to represent the social attitude domain.

---

[1]Recall that we earlier mentioned a computer search of the literature relevant to the attitude problems of this book. We assume that the search was reasonably thorough, even though its focus was on recent research. (Some of the studies cited in the book did not appear in the computer printouts.) In any case, most of the studies turned up were not relevant to our purposes. Some few were and we cite them in this chapter.

SUPPORTIVE RESEARCH

Most of the research done specifically by others to test the criterial referents theory has been done using educational attitudes. In only two studies were social attitudes measured. Marjoribanks and Josefowitz (1975) administered three social attitude scales to 460 17-year-old students from six secondary schools in England and Wales. The proposition that guided the study was that duality and not bipolarity "is a basic feature of social attitude structure." Through factor analysis of the items of the three scales, eight measures were derived: Racial Prejudice, Nationalism, Patriotism, Social Conservatism, Disrespect for Authority, Sexual Freedom, Modern Art, and Political Activism. The correlations among these measures were factor analyzed, and two clear orthogonal factors emerged. The first four of the above measures were substantially and positively loaded on the first factor, and the second four on the second factor. There were no substantial negative loadings. The authors concluded that the criterial referents theory was supported.

The second study of social attitudes, although not specifically done to test the criterial referents theory, did in fact test it. Ziegler and Atkinson (1973) tested the hypothesis that constraint or consistency of liberalism-conservatism increases as knowledge of political affairs increases. This is reminiscent of Converse's notion of the attitudes of elites and masses (see later). Perhaps more important, the authors hypothesized that liberalism and conservatism are *not* independent dimensions. They used a 113-item conservatism scale, which they subdivided into 17 "aspects." (They noted that 75 of the 113 items were worded in a conservative direction and 38 in a liberal direction.)

The authors factor analyzed the correlations among 16 of the 17 conservatism aspects. They expected to obtain one factor "to be interpreted as a liberalism-conservatism factor." They found four and five factors for the high and low information groups, the first of which was a "general" conservatism factor and the second a "general" liberal factor—for both high and low information groups. Their expectation was thus not fulfilled. They concluded that liberalism and conservatism tend to be independent, but that the political attitudes of the better informed students were more consistent and tend more toward bipolarity.

The remaining studies of this section focused on educational attitudes. Bell and Miller (1979) studied the relations between the educational attitudes of progressivism and traditionalism and the philosophic viewpoints of pragmatism and realism. As predicted, they found substantial positive correlations between progressivism and academic and applied pragmatism (.50 and .77) and between traditionalism and academic and applied realism (.40 and .58). ("Realism" is philosophical realism.) The correlation between progressivism and traditionalism, the educational attitudes, was .08. The correlation between *academic* pragmatism and realism was .04, while the correlation between *applied* pragmatism and realism was .61! Bell and Miller factor analyzed their six measures (two each for pragmatism and realism, academic and applied philosophies, and progressivism and traditionalism) and obtained a clean two-factor structure. The only exception to an almost perfect two-factor simple structure was Applied Realism, which had substantial positive loadings on both factors. The results, in short, were consistent with the duality hypothesis.

Some of the best evidence—"best" because of the wide range of issues studied and the method of analysis—on the duality of educational attitudes is found in a study of Wolfe and Engel (1978). They administered 18 statements from the Minnesota Teacher Attitude Inventory and 52 Wehling and Charters items to 364 education majors of the University of Delaware. They used image component analysis,[2] and concluded that their results agreed ("rather compelling," they say) with the results on educational attitudes reported earlier in this book. Their main factors were: Traditionalism, Progressivism, and a factor on children's need for emotional support—which they say was relatively unimportant.

Similarly, McAtee and Punch (1977) found the progressivism and traditionalism two-dimensional structure in their study of 841 teachers in a random sample of 46 Western Australian secondary schools. They used ES-VII (see Chapter 6) and factor analyzed the correlations among the 30 items of the scale. The resulting solution conforms almost perfectly to earlier American solutions. They also found little relation between progressivism and traditionalism and sex or age. Bledsoe (1976) also used ES-VII. Using 20 of the scale's 30 items, he made up two scales of ten items each (five *P* and five *T*). He factor analyzed the two forms separately and in each case obtained the usual two-factor structure.

Further corroboration of the dual structure of educational attitudes comes from Israel. Zak and Birenbaum (1980) specifically tested the criterial referents theory using 34 educational attitude referents (in Hebrew) and a radial parcelling analysis and factor analysis.[3] Their subjects were

---

[2] Image analysis is based on the *image* of a variable, which means its multiple regression on all other variables of a set, and the *anti-image,* the error of estimate of the multiple regression. The method presumably solves one or two long-standing problems of factor analysis, e.g., specification of the common and unique parts of variables and the calculation of factor scores. See Harmon's (1976, pp. 221–228) and Mulaik's (1972, pp. 186–196) excellent but rather difficult discussions.

[3] Radial parcel analysis (Cattell & Burdsal, 1975) is essentially a cluster analysis, which finds one, two, or more clusters or parcels of variables (items, tests) by systematic search for variables that covary with each other and not with other variables. That is, clusters or

713 individuals in Israel: mostly teachers and student teachers, plus a smaller number of other subjects. Factor analyses were done on two randomly selected groups of 348 and 365 individuals and on the total sample. The results showed that the dualistic theory was supported. The results of the radial parcel analysis yielded similar results. In addition, Zak and Birenbaum added much-needed direct analysis of the criteriality claim of the theory. They used a criteriality scale in which the subjects were asked to check only those concepts relevant to them when relating to education. Analysis of the response patterns showed that responses to criterial referents were J-shaped and responses to noncriterial referents were diffused; they showed no discernible pattern. That is, the subjects' responses to the criterial referents were systematically distributed (the J curve), whereas the responses to the noncriterial referents exhibited no systematic or identifiable distribution.

In a later study, Birenbaum and Zak (1982) tested the criterial referents theory against Eysenck's (1975, 1976) theory of social attitudes. The latter conception predicts two basic factors of social attitudes, both of which are bipolar: Conservatism versus Radicalism and Toughmindedness versus Tendermindedness. Since the results and the authors' conclusions were given earlier (Chapter 5, footnote 5), it need only be said here that the results supported the duality hypothesis of this book and did not support Eysenck's conception.

Hofman (1970) tested the criterial referents theory and an idea similar to Zak and Birenbaum's: the notion that progressives in education will structure progressive referents more, and traditionalists will structure traditional referents more. By "structure" Hofman meant that subjects will respond to attitude referents differentially: the more differential the responses, the greater the structure. The idea is that, to obtain clear factors, responses to attitude items must be differentiated by the individuals of a group. He hypothesized that progressive referents, if they are criterial to progressives as the theory states, should be differentiated by progressives but not by traditionalists, and similarly with traditional referents and traditionalists. Factor analyses of progressives' data, of traditionalists' data, and of the combined data were much alike, however. While he obtained the usual dual structures, Hofman took the similarity of the structures to mean that the criterial referents theory was found wanting. His point is well-taken. Much more research explicitly on the criteriality issue is needed. Zak and Hofman have started such research.

Baggaley (1976), in a study of values of students of a two-year college,

---

parcels of variables are found that presumably reflect the underlying factors without the necessity of factor rotation. Zak and Birenbaum used the method to compare the results to a conventionally rotated oblique factor matrix.

administered along with his value measures, REF-I, the referents social attitudes scale described in Chapters 2 and 6. He intercorrelated and factor analyzed the values measures and included the REF-I L and C subscales in the analysis. C's loading on factor I was .67; some of the value items also with positive loadings were *spirituality* (.64), *reverence* (.78), *loyalty* (.60), *order* (.44), *salvation* (.72), and *righteousness* (.75). The REF-I L loading on factor II, in contrast, was .34. Also on factor II were *spontaneity* (.47), *sensory awareness* (.60), *flexibility* (.52), and so on. The appearance of the C and L subscales on different factors is further evidence that conservatism and liberalism are separate attitudinal entities. The nature or content of the value items on the factors, moreover, supports the construct validity of conservatism and liberalism. For example, *spirituality, loyalty,* and *order* are conservative concepts, and *spontaneity* and *flexibility* are progressive educational ideas.

DUALITY IN OTHER AREAS

The results of several investigations with other than attitude variables lead us to speculate that duality may sometimes characterize other psychological phenomena and variables. Zak (1973, 1976) did research in the United States and in Israel in which he found duality rather than commonly assumed bipolar unidimensionality. In the United States, he administered a Jewish-American Identity Scale to 1006 Jewish Americans between the ages of 17 and 25. Part of the problem was this: Is the identification of Jews with the Jewish group in conflict with their identification with the American group? Zak points out that a number of observers have said that there is such conflict. If so, then measurement of the two identities should yield bipolar results. Zak, however, believed differently. He thought that Jewish-American identity was dualistic, composed of two relatively orthogonal components, one reflecting the Jewish identity and the other the American identity.

Zak factor analyzed the correlations among the 20 items of his scale for four samples: (1) students of a Hebrew language department in New York; (2) other Jewish students in New York City; (3) Jewish college students in Greater Boston; and (4) students who had visited Israel in 1968, 1969, or 1970. The N's ranged from 206 to 280. He found similar results in the data of the four samples: two orthogonal factors. He also repeated the analysis with the total sample of 1006: the factor structure was again dualistic. The American identity items appeared on factor A, the Jewish identity items on factor B. There was little bipolarity, and the correlation between the factors (obtained from an oblique rotation) was $-.10$. Zak concludes his report: "The findings . . . raise questions about one of the myths concerning ethnic groups, that is, that the preservation of the ethnic group structure leads to disloyalty toward the larger social unit, the United States" (p. 899).

Zak's second study dealt with Arab-Israeli identity. Are the two identities of Arab students in Israel in conflict or are they complementary? Zak used an Ethnic Identity Scale, with nine items on Arab identity and eight items on Israeli identity. The scale was administered to 532 Israeli-Arab students throughout Israel. Most of the students were Moslem, and Zak limited his analysis to their data ($N = 418$). (He also used a self-esteem scale, but it does not concern us here.) The results of factor analysis of the items were clear-cut: the Israeli identity items appeared on one factor, and the Arab identity items on another factor.

"In the experimental research on cooperation and competition, the two variables are often treated as if they were opposite ends of a single dimension," write Johnson and Ahlgren (1976, p. 99), in a study of attitudes toward schooling of over 2000 school children, grades 2 through 12. They found, however, that this was not so. A canonical correlation analysis yielded two significant sources of variance, one related to cooperation and the other to competition. In different school grades, moreover, they found that the correlations between the two variables ranged from .02 to .07.

Interest in the conceptualization and measurement of masculinity and femininity has recently increased. Evidently the two concepts have been assumed to be a bipolar continuum. Constantinople (1973), however, questioned the validity of conceptualizing masculinity-femininity as bipolar and suggested that the two should be conceived and measured as separate dimensions. Myers and Gonda (1982) also questioned the assumed bipolarity of masculinity and femininity and measurement that is based on the assumption.

Perhaps the most impressive and surprising evidence on the duality of a psychological variable commonly thought to be bipolar comes from Bradburn's (1969) study of positive and negative affect in the sense of well-being. Bradburn used personal interviews in National Opinion Research Center samples in Detroit, Chicago, Washington, D.C., and a mixture of the ten largest metropolitan areas in the country. Analysis of his ten feeling-state items (*ibid.,* p. 56, Table 4.1) yielded two independent clusters, one of positive affect and the other of negative affect. Moreover, the two affects correlated differently with other variables. Other investigators' data support Bradburn's findings. Costa and McCrae (1980) found that extraversion correlated positively with Bradburn's positive affect measure and neuroticism with his negative affect measure. Cherlin and Reeder (1975), in a large random samples of the Los Angeles area in 1972 and 1973 found clear two-factor structures and r's of $-.07$ and $-.09$

between positive and negative affects. Warr, Barter, and Brownbridge (1983) obtained essentially the same results in a study of an English sample of 520 undergraduates. They also used another kind of response mode in addition to the conventional mode (asking numbers of events in a recent period) and obtained a negative correlation between positive and negative affects. It seems, however, that the negative correlation was an artifact of the mode of response, an ipsative procedure that produced spurious negative correlation because positive and negative affect responses were *within a fixed sum framework*. (See Chapter 4, Footnote 2, for a definition of ipsative measurement.) The evidence seems clear: affect is a dualistic phenomenon: positive affect and negative affect seem to be independent psychological dimensions. Perhaps we should not be surprised by the dualistic nature of liberalism and conservatism.

RESEARCH INIMICAL TO THE THEORY

It can be said that most of the research studies on the structure of attitudes, or related to the structure of attitudes, is based on the bipolarity assumption. We have discussed this research in earlier chapters and need not recapitulate it here. Comparatively little research has been free of the assumption. In this section we report research in which bipolarity seems to be a legitimate outgrowth of the data.

One of the studies potentially most damaging to the dualistic hypothesis that of Sontag and Pedhazur (1972), who compared structures yielded by analyzing together the data from two completely different measurement instruments. They used ES-VII, the author's scale of educational attitudes described in Chapter 6, and Oliver and Butcher's (1962) *Survey of Opinion About Education,* which has three scales influenced by Eysenck's attitude factors: Radicalism-Conservatism, Tendermindedness-Toughmindedness, and Naturalism-Idealism. (See Chapter 6 and the summary in this chapter of the Bell and Miller study.) The Oliver and Butcher study seemed to be methodologically sound, but it is virtually impossible to judge the adequacy of their factor interpretations because the scale items are not given with the factors. In any case, Sontag and Pedhazur intercorrelated the five subscales of both scales: ESA (Progressivism), ESB (Traditionalism), Naturalism, Radicalism, and Tendermindedness. They also factor analyzed the correlations among the 63 items of both scales and obtained seven factors, which they subjected to a second-order factor analysis that yielded two factors.

Two of the first-order factors were bipolar, but both factors are puzzling: the loadings of all the items of both should logically be positive. For example, an OB (Oliver and Butcher) item on factor II, "Reason(s) for religious instruction: it instills a sense of duty" ($-.498$), and an ES-VII item, "Schools should teach children dependence on higher moral values" (.485), seem to be expressing similar moral or religious sentiments. Factor III is similar: an OB item, "Argument for corporal punishment: Some children will not respond to any other form of discipline" (.596), and an ES-VII item: "Children need and should have more supervision and discipline than they usually get" ($-.442$), also seem to be expressing similar sentiments. Is the scoring of the OB items different from that of the ES-VII items? The second-order structure has a clear bipolar factor. I confess that I am baffled. Even more perplexing are the correlations among the subscale total scores. Two of the OB subscales are correlated negatively and substantially with the ES-VII traditionalism scale ($-.624$ and $-.642$). This may be "true" bipolarity, but why these high negative correlations between different measurement instruments? Is this similar to the previously noted substantial negative cross-correlations between statement and referent scales encountered in Chapter 7? The results of this methodologically well-executed study, in any case, raise serious questions about the criterial referents theory.

Using an original pool of 123 Likert-type items, Rambo (1972) constructed a liberalism-conservatism scale. He used item discrimination procedures basically characterized by the known-groups method and successive winnowing of items, and then by factor analysis of different samples of individuals. Two samples exhibited no bipolarity, but one sample yielded three of four factors that were bipolar. It is difficult, however, to judge the results because details on scoring were not given (reversed scoring was probably used: see Rambo, 1972, p. 465), nor were the factor arrays given. The study is cited because its results indicate substantial bipolarity in at least one sample.

Comrey and Newmeyer's (1965) study of "radicalism-conservatism" used a somewhat different approach to attitude structure. They defined 30 attitude variables and wrote four items to measure each of them. The 120-item scale was administered to 212 subjects. (Apparently reversed scoring was used for some of the items.) They then factored the 120 items (note the unfavorable subject-variable ratio: 212/120) and used the results to create 25 attitude variables. These variables were factor analyzed (a more favorable subject-variable ratio) yielding nine factors, five of the arrays of which the authors report. Of the five factors two are clearly bipolar. Moreover, of the 36 correlations among the nine variables, seven were substantial and negative. Factor analysis of these 36 correlations yielded one factor which was strongly bipolar. Comrey and Newmeyer say that this second-order factor is radicalism-conservatism.

Taken at face value, this study is damaging to the criterial referents theory. Its methodology—aside from the unfavorable initial subject-variable ratio, reverse scoring, and the underlying assumption of bipolarity—is perhaps the best of the many studies influenced by the bipolarity assumption. Again, it is difficult, if not impossible, to judge the empirical validity of the findings because the authors sometimes report all the loadings of a factor with negative signs and use reversed scoring. Moreover, there is what appears to be an inconsistency of some of the correlations among the factors, for example, the correlation between second-order factors 4 and 7 is reported as −.60, but both factors, as labeled, are conservative: Nationalism and Religious Attitudes. The study is well-enough done, however, to warrant serious attention. If, indeed, the strong negative correlations among the first-order factors and the one bipolar second-order factor arose from completely adequate methodology, the criterial referents theory is in serious trouble. To date, however, I have had no such results from many and varied studies. Bipolarity of attitudes has almost always been a relatively minor phenomenon, except with radical samples. I must therefore wonder about Comrey and Newmeyer's complete methodology. There is sufficient evidence in the study, however, and sufficient opposing evidence to indicate that the structure of social attitudes is still not understood!

LIBERALISM, CONSERVATISM, AND ATTITUDE STRUCTURE IN MASS PUBLICS

There is an influential point of view that, if valid, casts serious doubt on the research and conclusions of this book. This is that liberalism and conservatism are abstractions that have little or no basis in the reality of people's attitudes. Converse (1964), for example, says that the elites of a society have well-formulated and structured attitudes, but the attitudes of mass publics are unstructured, amorphous, virtually nonexistent. Moreover, he decries the "liberalism-conservatism idea." It is "a rather elegant higher-order abstraction, and such abstractions are not typical conceptual tools for the 'man in the street'" (p. 215). To support his argument, Converse cites research findings from national samples of the people of the United States, part of which are correlations among attitude items. These correlations are substantial for elite samples and low for the mass public: for example, the average correlation within domestic issues for elites is .53, but only .23 for the mass public.

There is little doubt of the influence of this view. Nie, Verba, and Petrocik (1976), for instance, in their book, *The Changing American Voter,* put heavy weight on Converse's conclusions. And, while it has been severely criticized, the basic findings appear to be valid—but not quite as Converse states them. Evidently the correlation between social beliefs and other variables increases with more education (Bishop, 1976; Wray, 1979). So correlations are larger in educated samples than in relatively uneducated samples. But this does not mean that the mass public has little or no structure of attitudes (see Knitzer, 1978; Luttbeg, 1968). The correct conclusion, I believe, is that the attitude structure of elites is more defined and consistent than is that of the public at large. Yet, to deny structure and ideological concern to public attitudes is too sweeping.

Methodology is especially important in this case. To draw an important conclusion, the methodology used must provide measurement and sampling conditions that are capable of supplying the data to warrant the conclusion, whatever it is. And this is precisely the difficulty with the Converse conclusion: the data on which it is based are inadequate to warrant the conclusion. In the surveys that supplied the data Converse used, relatively few social issues were used. In these surveys large representative samples of the public are asked many questions, but comparatively few of them directly measure social attitudes. Perhaps the most complete and authoritative source of such questions and items asked over the years by the Survey Research Center of the University of Michigan is contained in a section of Robinson, Rusk, and Head's (1968, pp. 485–669) anthology of measures of political and social attitudes. The questions for all the surveys cited cover a large number of issues, but those in any one survey are necessarily limited because only a few such questions can be asked in any one interview. The researchers, moreover, deliberately focused such questions primarily on issues related to the government and its relationship to citizens.

The point is this: to study attitude structure adequately the same individuals have to be presented with a large number and a wide variety of social issues so that the correlations among them can be studied. Valid answers to structural questions on the attitudes of mass publics and on liberalism and conservatism can only be obtained in this way. In other words, if the attitudinal items presented to samples are limited, they may be useful for survey purposes but they are not adequate for structural methods of analysis like factor analysis.

Let us now reexamine data specifically collected to study attitude structure. In the Dutch studies reported earlier in Chapters 8 and 9, there is evidence of the similarities and differences in attitude structures of a large random sample of the mass public of The Netherlands and a smaller elite (university student) sample. The factor structure of the students, as shown earlier, was clearer and more coherent than that of the public. Nevertheless, the public yielded an interpretable and coherent factor structure. It can hardly be said that the mass public of The Netherlands has "no" attitude structure. (See Tables 8.6, 8.7, and 8.8.)

There is more evidence in the Dutch data, data that were not reported

TABLE 11.1
Correlations Between Liberal (L) and Conservative (C) Subscales
of REF-VI and "Ideological" Identifications,
Dutch Student and Random Samples

	Conservative	Traditional	Right	Left	Socialist	Progressive[a]
Student Sample						
L	-.25	-.26	-.35	.47	.44	.47
C	.41	.47	.47	-.44	-.35	-.28
Random Sample						
L	-.19	-.16	-.20	.22	.36	.38
C	.32	.44	.41	-.34	-.29	-.15

[a] "Progressive" in Dutch ("Progressief") is almost the same as "Left," though it seems to have a more general meaning.

in earlier chapters. Because my Dutch colleague and I wanted to know if both the students and the public were "aware" of their own ideological predispositions—recall that Converse denied such awareness of the mass public—we asked the subjects of both samples to what extent they identified themselves with Conservative, Left, Traditional, Socialist, and other "ideologies," and then we correlated these responses with the individuals' liberal and conservative scores of Referents-VI (REF-VI), our attitude scale. Some of the data is given in Table 11.1. The meaning of the correlations is as follows. If students, for instance, were high on liberalism (L), then they tended to identify themselves with Left, Socialist, and Progressive, and not with Conservative, Traditional, and Right, and the converse for students high on conservatism (C). In every case the correlations are higher for the students than for the Dutch public. But it can also be seen that the Dutch public's identifications are all consistent and correlated "as they should" with liberalism and conservatism.

Whether conservatism and liberalism are typical conceptual tools for the man-in-the-street is not the central point. For the scientist, too, liberalism and conservatism are abstractions like any other abstract concepts he works with: introversion, intelligence, radicalism, achievement, political development and the like. To be sure, most people don't recognize their abstract nature and certainly don't use them as social scientists do. Nevertheless, they *are* quite familiar with their behavioral and environmental manifestations. Does this mean that they are unimportant in behavioral science and research? Liberalism and conservatism are useful abstractions that express identifiable and measurable clusters of beliefs that correlate positively with each other. They also happen to agree rather well in their behavioral and research manifestations with informed scholarly accounts of liberalism and conservatism such as we summarized in Chapter 2. One of the difficulties of the social sciences, of course, is that they often have to deal with concepts that are also part of our mental baggage. Liberalism and conservatism are such concepts. Still, if we find good agreement between philosophical descriptions of liberalism and conservatism, on the one hand, and on the other, the empirical clustering of items that express aspects of the descriptions (referents), then we have some assurance of the empirical validity of the descriptions, the items (referents), and the clustering—and, ultimately, of the legitimacy of the abstract concepts liberalism and conservatism.

CONCLUSIONS

The research of others cited in this chapter yields a mixed verdict. Most of it supports the duality hypothesis, but there is enough evidence of bipolarity to cloud the picture. The data of the Sontag and Pedhazur and the Comrey and Newmeyer studies, for example exhibited substantial bipolarity. Whether this is "real" bipolarity or the result of artifact or other extraneous source of variance is unknown. It is sufficient to cause uneasiness and to be a spur to further research—and emendation of the theory.

An influential viewpoint potentially threatening to the criterial referents theory, the denial of attitude structure of mass publics and the concomitant denial of the existence and usefulness of liberalism and conservatism, was seen to be based on questionable evidence. The denial of the attitude structure of mass publics was backed by research that could not bear the full weight of the conclusions drawn, though the conclusion of the difference between the structures of mass publics and elites was supported. The inability of the research to support the full conclusion was a function mainly of inadequate sampling of the attitude domain: the survey research cited was necessarily limited in its attitude scope (no reflection on the quality of the research, of course). The categorization of liberalism and conservatism as higher order abstractions as far as the man-in-the-street is concerned was countered by research using a random sample of The Netherlands, where the factor structure of attitude issues and items was seen to be similar to those of other samples, though suffering from less clarity and definition of factors. Data from The Netherlands also showed that both students and a random sample of the Dutch population were at least to some extent aware of their attitudes as conservative and liberal.

The evidence of a few studies (not many, to be sure) indicates that certain psychological variables ordinarily assumed to be bipolar may in fact not be bipolar. The variables in the studies cited include cooperation and competition, self-identification of American Jews and Israeli Arabs, positive and negative affect, and masculinity-femininity. Other candidates for research examination might be introversion and extroversion (see Stephenson, 1953, who found evidence of duality), field dependence and independence, and self-other perceptions. In any case, there is enough evidence to indicate that assumed polarities must be questioned and demonstrated before measurement can be considered valid.

ADDENDUM

There is a missing patch in the quilt of reasoning and research of this book that some readers may have detected: discussion of response set and its relation to the measurement instruments used. Because summated-rating scales seem to be particularly vulnerable to response styles (Guilford, 1954, p. 451), some observers may say that special precautions must be taken with them. Special precautions have not been taken with the attitude scales used in the research reported in this book (except care with instructions) for three reasons. (1) There is little evidence that response style explains more than a fraction of the variance of attitudes (Nunnally, 1978, p. 672). (2) If response style is a significant source of variance, response style factors should appear in factor analysis of attitude items. Such factors have never appeared in the dozens of factor analyses done over the years. (3) A major form of attitude measurement used in the research, scales with referent items, would seem to be less subject to such tendencies as agreement response because agreement and disagreement can obviously not be used and because the difficulties presumably associated with statements are effectively avoided.

To obtain evidence, however, that response set is or is not a factor in the results reported in the book, three studies were done. The results of the studies indicated that, with one exception, social desirability, agreement response tendency, and social acquiescence did not correlate substantially with either the statement or the referent measures of liberalism and conservatism used in the research. A description of the studies and a summary of their results are given in Appendix C at the end of the book.

12

The Structure and Content of Social Attitudes: A Perspective

This book began with the idea of "attitude man," following Fleming's intriguing conception of the place and importance of attitudes in this century. Recall that Fleming said that a revolution had taken place in man's conception of himself, and that this revolution centered in the attitude concept. Human beings have persistent organized psychological tendencies acquired from previous experience to react consistently and predictably to social objects. Attitudes, in this conception, are a significant part of personality and psychological functioning that is at the juncture of personality and the social environment. And this part is thus highly important social psychologically not only because it acts as a psychological mediator between the person and the social environment, but also because the capacity to form and use attitudes is a vital part of human functioning. As Fleming says, human beings are supremely attitudinal organisms.

This radically new and different conception of man was probably born in the nineteenth century as a result of the beginning and growth of classical liberalism. Classical liberalism became the conservatism of today (Girvetz, 1963); socialism and certain precepts of classic liberalism, especially freedom of the individual, led to modern liberalism, especially in America (Smith, 1968). Do these two large views of the world, conservatism and liberalism, really "exist"? How much empirical basis do they have? What is their nature and structure? When we ask questions about the nature and structure of social attitudes, are we in fact asking about conservatism and liberalism?

One of the major goals of this book was to learn something of "attitude man." The position taken was that historical, sociological, psychological, and political scientific accounts of attitude man are epitomized by modern conceptions of liberalism and conservatism. Attempts were made to answer three complex questions, first enunciated in Chapters 1, 2, and 3.

What is the nature and structure of social attitudes? Are attitudes bipolar as commonly assumed and believed? Or are they dualistic, as maintained in this book? Does the content (nature) of social attitudes reflect liberal and conservative positions and issues?

Do liberalism and conservatism underlie social attitudes in the sense that people, issues, and social attitude referents can be categorized as one or the other? Are sets of beliefs accurately categorized as liberal and conservative?

Are referents of social attitudes differentially criterial to different individuals and groups of individuals?

In addition, two operational questions were asked:

Can social attitudes be measured reliably and validly using only social attitude referents? How do statement and referent scales and items compare psychometrically?

Are attitude first-order factors liberal or conservative but not both? Are there two relatively orthogonal second-order attitude factors, one of them liberal and the other conservative?

FINDINGS AND CONCLUSIONS

Recall from earlier chapters that the criterial referents theory implies a number of empirical outcomes. Since these have been spelled out in previous chapters, we forego repeating them here (see, especially, Chapter 3). Instead, we summarize and comment upon the findings. In doing so, we also try to give the essence of the structure and content of social attitudes in a visual way. To summarize the nature and content of the factors we give samples of items that appear to be the most representative, the most prototypical as cognitive psychologists would say, of the factors that were common to two or more samples.

Major Factor Analytic Findings

The first and most important finding is that social attitudes are multifactored at the first order and dualistic at the second-order. The individual factors resulting from the factor analysis of attitude statement and referent items consistently exhibited the same pattern in different samples: liberal items appeared positively and substantially on certain factors, and conservative items on other factors. The two kinds of items did not usually appear together on the same factors. Factor bipolarity sometimes appeared, but it was a relatively uncommon phenomenon. The same was true of the results obtained from factor analysis of attitude subscales: liberal subscales loaded together on one factor and conservative subscales on another factor.

The second-order factor analysis of the correlations among the first-order factors in general yielded two second-order factors, one with liberal first-order factors and the other with conservative first-order factors. Bipolarity appeared in some solutions, but it was infrequent. In some samples, three second-order factors appeared, with the third factor either liberal or conservative and appearing to be "complementary" to one of the two "main" factors. This is of course not congruent with the theory that predicts two second-order factors, one liberal and one conservative.

Another important finding of the book is that liberalism and conservatism seem to be general ideologies that pervade most social beliefs and attitudes in different parts of the United States and in three countries of Western Europe. While the content and details of the liberal and conservative first-order factors differed in the United States, Spain, and The Netherlands, a number of factors that emerged in different places with different people of different societies and cultures were similar. This was especially so of conservative factors. Three or four conservative factors and three or four liberal factors appeared in two or more samples (Chapters 7, 8, and 9). The conservative factors were: Religiosity, Economic Conservatism, Traditional Conservatism, and, less strong, Morality. The liberal factors were Civil Rights, Social Liberalism, Sexual Freedom, and Feeling and Affection. These factors may be the multivariable expressions of important facets of liberal and conservative views of contemporary social issues that are broadly common to many people in Western society. But most striking and surprising was the ubiquitous emergence of the two second-order factors of liberalism and conservatism from the first-order factor diversity.

Closely related to the pervasiveness and emergence of the liberalism and conservatism second-order factors was the similar emergence of progressivism and traditionalism as second-order factors of educational attitudes. The evidence for this finding is not nearly as strong as that for the more general liberalism and conservatism, but it was supported by the similar dualistic structures that were found in different samples with both R and Q approaches. Even more important, however, was the finding that the educational attitude factors of progressivism and traditionalism seemed to be subsets of the more general liberalism and conservatism.

That is, while progressivism and traditionalism are evidently second-order educational factors, they are also aspects of liberalism and conservatism, progressivism a facet or aspect of liberalism and traditionalism a facet or aspect of conservatism.

Attitude bipolarity appeared as a relatively minor phenomenon in most of the research reported in the book. This is a difficult conclusion to state accurately. What is meant is that negative correlations and factor loadings appeared, but infrequently and at a low level compared to the prevailing positive correlations and factor loadings. Only very small proportions of correlations between liberal and conservative items were greater than $-.30$ (in absolute value), and only a few factor loadings of first- and second-order factors were negative and substantial.

It was said earlier that attitude bipolarity should occur under three conditions or circumstances: the preponderance of radicals of the right or the left or both in a sample, the salience at a particular time or over a long period of time of social issues that are important and controversial, and technical aspects of measurement, such as scoring of items and scales. The second of these, salience of issues, is very difficult, if not impossible, to test systematically, nor was it tested in the studies reported. The third, which can be called "artifacts," was also not systematically tested in the studies. Only evidence for the first, sample characteristics, was available and "tested." The conclusions reached from the limited data, mainly the data of the two Dutch samples, was that considerably more bipolarity appeared with a radical student sample than with a sample of the population. From the evidence available, however, this is hardly a firm or strong conclusion. The conditions of attitude bipolarity deserve further thought and research.

Structure and Content: A Representative Illustration

A diagrammatic "summary" of the structure and content of the view of social attitudes presented in this book is given in Figure 12.1. The figure is based on the usage and conventions of analysis of covariance structures (see Chapter 10). The rectangular boxes are meant to be items. Obviously in any analyses there would be many more than sixteen items. The items chosen for this illustration are representative of the referent items used in a number of studies. Those on the left are liberal items: *civil rights, racial equality, socialized medicine,* and so on. Those on the right are conservative items: *religion, church, profits,* and so on. The circles represent first-order factors. CR is Civil Rights, with items *civil rights* and *racial equality,* R is Religiosity, with items *religion* and *church.* Each factor, then, is defined by two items. The factor abbreviations are given below the figure. As can be seen, there are four liberal factors and four conservative factors. In the analysis of covariance structures system, the rectan-

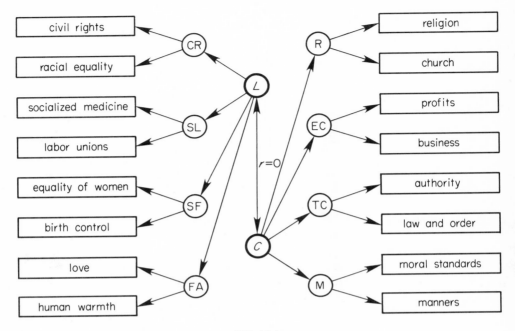

FIG. 12.1

First-Order Factors:
  CR: Civil Rights
  SL: Social Liberalism
  SF: Sexual Freedom
  FA: Feeling and Affection

  R: Religiosity
  EC: Economic Conservatism
  TC: Traditionalism Conservatism
  M: Morality

Second-Order Factors:
  L: Liberalism   *C:* Conservatism

gles represent observed variables and the circles unobserved or latent
variables. The arrows from the latent variables or factors to the observed
variables or items mean "influence" or "underlies." CR, Civil Rights, for
example, underlies *civil rights* and *racial equality*.

The heavy circles, L and C, represent the second-order factors,
Liberalism and Conservatism. These are, of course, higher-order latent
variables. One can call them latent entities underlying the first-order latent variables or factors. The arrows from these second-order factors to
the first-order factors, like those from the first-order factors to the items,
also indicate "influence" or "underlies." That is, Conservatism presumably underlies Religion, Economic Conservatism, Traditional Conservatism, and Morality. Conservatism, then, is the presumed entity behind
these four first-order factors. The double-headed arrow, labeled "$r = 0$,"

simply indicates the correlation between the two second-order factors, as the theory dictates.[1]

Figure 12.1 is both a model or graphic expression of part of the criterial referents theory and an oversimplified expression of the findings of the studies reported in this book. As a model it can be and has been tested for its congruence with actual attitude data using first- and second-order factor analysis (Chapters 6, 7, and 8) and analysis of covariance structures (Chapter 10). In general, the model and the data are congruent, as we have seen. But, as we have also seen, the congruence is far from perfect.

To make the model more realistic and "data-driven," I have prepared Figure 12.2. It was constructed from Figure 12.1, but contains departures from the model. Actual data will "produce" a diagram more like Figure 12.2 than Figure 12.1. The departures from the model are mostly not serious, however; they are like the usual results of factor analysis. These departures are marked with asterisks on the arrows. If readers will take a minute or two to study the departures and to compare the two figures, they may get a more concrete idea of how actual data depart from a model.

First and most important, the coefficient of correlation between L and C, the two second-order factors, is $-.20$ and not 0, as in the original model. Remember that the "pure" model predicts two orthogonal second-order factors, which of course means $r = 0$. $r = -.20$, however, is within the usual criterion of $r \leq -.30$ (in absolute magnitude). So L and C are "relatively" orthogonal, as repeatedly said in earlier discussions. Remember, too, that if the bipolarity model were correct, $r = -1.00$, which really means that there are not two second-order factors, L and C, but only one second-order factor.

Second, five paths from the first-order factors to the items are marked with asterisks. (If nothing else appears on an arrow, the sign of the loading is taken to be positive and substantial.) These mean that the items have loaded on more than one factor. For example, note the arrow with an asterisk from CR to *equality of women*. *Equality of women* is loaded on SF (Sexual Freedom), and is also loaded on CR (Civil Rights). Such departures from the model (double loadings) occur fairly frequently in factor analysis. More serious departures are the paths marked both with an asterisk and a minus sign from the second-order factors, L and C, to first-order factors. There are two of these: one from L to TC (Traditional Conservatism) and one from C to SF (Sexual Freedom). These indicate some bipolarity in the data. C, for example, is negatively "influencing"

---

[1] Strictly speaking, there should be error terms for each of the items and disturbance terms for the latent first-order factors. They have been omitted because Figure 12.1 is only an illustration and not an actual tested model.

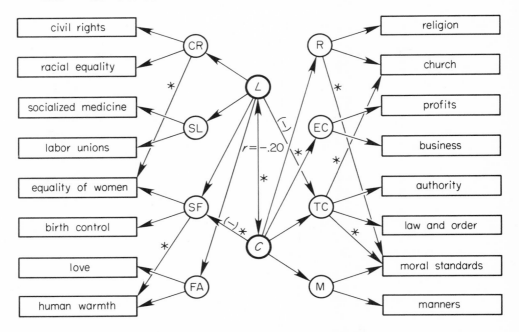

FIG. 12.2   Asterisk indicates departure from model of Figure 12.1

Sexual Freedom, or there is a negative relation between Conservatism and Sexual Freedom. These two departures may be serious, depending on the magnitudes of the coefficients associated with the arrows. They were inserted into the model for illustrative purposes. Actual departures like these, however, have been rare. One such departure has occurred in some samples, as we saw in earlier chapters, but two or more such departures only rarely.

Reliability and Validity of Referent Scales

A conclusion not related to the criterial referents theory but of considerable attitude measurement interest is that attitudes can be measured reliably and validly using only the referents of attitudes—*civil rights, children's interests, religion, free enterprise, equality of women, law and order,* for example. Scales using such referent items have exhibited high reliability: in the .80's and .90's, somewhat higher than those obtained (in these studies) with statement scales. And factor analysis of referent item intercorrelations have consistently yielded readily interpretable first-order factors and clear second-order factors. The factors were similar to those yielded by statement social attitude scales (see Chapter 7, Table

7.7). The correlations between the comparable *L* subscales and the *C* subscales of the statement and referent scales were also positive and substantial—a range from .46 to .66 in one study, and from .51 to .70 in another study (see Tables 7.9 and 7.10)—especially when one takes the different modes of measurement into consideration.

Evidently the measurement instruments used, especially the referent scales, were reliable, more often than not highly so (.80,s and .90's for the *L* and *C* subscales: see Tables 3.1, 7.3, and 8.1.) While most of the reliability coefficients were of the internal consistency kind, repeat reliability estimates were also calculated. They, too, were substantial to high.

Validity, as usual, is a much more difficult question. The evidence for the validity of the referent scales is mostly factor analytic. That is, the *L* and *C* subscales of the referent scales had factor validity in the sense that much the same factors were yielded in study after study, and the factors were congruent with historical and sociological descriptions of liberalism and conservatism. Minor evidence on validity was obtained with the Dutch samples. The subjects assessed their own ideological positions, and these assessments were correlated with *L* and *C* subscores (see Chapter 11, Table 11.3). The correlations were "as they should be": between measured *C* and subject assessment of themselves being traditional, for example, the correlation for the student sample was .47 and for the random sample of the population .44. Between measured *L* and subject assessment of themselves as "progressive" the correlation for the student sample was .47 and for the random sample .38. And, of course, evidence of the construct validity of the scales is furnished by the repeated confirmation of the theoretical predictions.

Attitude Structure and Memory: An Experimental Failure

The results of an unsatisfactory experimental study mentioned in Chapter 1 must be reported. A colleague (Dr. B. Meuffels) and I did two experiments, one in The Netherlands and the other in the U.S., primarily to test the hypothesis that attitude structure affects recall and recognition memory. A second hypothesis was that measured liberalism and conservatism are positively correlated with recall and recognition of liberal and conservative referents. In these experiments, attitude structure was experimentally varied by presenting subjects with sets of predominantly liberal and sets of predominantly conservative referents, referents that had been found to have high factor loadings in the factor analyses described in earlier chapters. The experimental instructions were directed toward having the subjects remember the referents. Recall and recognition of the presented referents were contrasted with recall and recognition of sets of referents that presumably lacked attitude structure. Attitude structure was defined as follows: High structure was defined as sets of either liberal or conservative referents, the referents having had high factor loadings in the research reported in earlier chapters. Liberal and conservative referents were not mixed in the high structure referents. Low structure (or lack of structure) was defined as sets of referents that had had low factor loadings or were not attitude-related (e.g., *education, tolerance, culture, foreign aid*). These latter neutral referents constituted control conditions. Another control condition was presenting subjects with mixed liberal and conservative referents. It was assumed, following an implication of the criterial referents theory, that mixing liberal and conservative referents would be equivalent to a lack of structure, or at least to a muddying of structure.

Subjects in the high structure condition recalled and recognized better than they did in the low structure or control condition in both the Dutch and the American experiments. (In the Dutch experiment, the referents were presented via a recorder; in the American experiment, the subjects read the referents.) There was little doubt that the sets of liberal and the sets of conservative referents were remembered better than the sets of control referents. Evidently liberal referents that had high factor loadings on liberal factors in the factor analyses and conservative referents that had high factor loadings on conservative factors "produced" high structure that aided their recall and recognition. It was also found that subjects "recognized" referents that had *not* been presented to them in the experiments if the referents had high loadings on liberal and conservative factors. We called this "reflected recognition."

The testing of the second hypothesis yielded disappointing results: the correlations between subjects' scores on liberalism and conservatism statement scales especially designed for the research and their liberal and conservative referent recall and recognition scores were low and not statistically significant. Even with these results, which, taken at face value, were not encouraging to believers in the criterial referents theory, we thought that the results of the tests of the first hypothesis, as reported above, *were* encouraging. Unfortunately, they did not directly bear on the theory. They showed that subjects, *regardless of their own attitudes,* remembered attitude referents better when liberal referents were presented together and when conservative referents were presented together. Evidently memory was influenced by structure if structure can be assumed to be produced by presentation of attitude materials that reflected the factor analytic results. This led us to speculate that there may be a relation between the consensual structure as defined by liberal and conservative factors obtained from analysis of the responses of many people to attitude material, on the one hand, and the "structure in the heads of individuals," on the other hand.

As interesting as the results were, especially the intriguing notion of some sort of relation between the consensual factors obtained from the responses of many people and the cognitive attitude structure of individuals, the research *did not really address the basic implication of the criterial referents theory,* namely that liberals should better remember liberal referents and conservatives should better remember conservative referents. For this reason I have only summarized the research here and not reported it in detail in an earlier chapter.

Even though the research did not really test the crucial relation just mentioned, I think that the obtained relation between the attitude structure of liberal and conservative referents and memory is a significant finding. But even more significant—and maybe more significant psychologically—is the relation that was not really tested in the research: the possible correspondence between the social attitude structure as obtained consensually from many people, the liberal and conservative factors found in the research reported in this book, and the intrapersonal structures or attitude schemata of individuals. In most of the studies reported earlier, "structure" means the factor structure obtained from the responses of many individuals to many items. "Structure" is thus abstracted from the responses of many people. When cognitive psychologists talk about "structure," however, they seem to mean something quite different: structure in the head of the individual. This is seen clearly, for example, when Atkinson and Shiffrin (1976) say, "It seems inescapable that the human memory system is organized in such a way that information is arranged in meaningful, useful structural units" (p. 118). Or note Rosch's (1973) assertion: ". . . most real categories are highly structured internally . . ." (p. 112).

Perhaps a question on the relation between social structure and intrapersonal structure is unanswerable. One cannot help but wonder, however, whether a certain attitude factor structure found from the responses of many individuals has some sort of representation in the cognitions of individuals. My colleague and I thought that the liberal and conservative attitude factors might be "generated" or "activated" in individuals. But the results of our studies were only suggestive and only weakly supported the idea of the conjecture. Nevertheless, it confirmed to some small extent the "validity" of liberalism and conservatism as latent variables, and also lent some small weight to the criterial referents theory since only the highly structured liberal and conservative referents presented separately enhanced remembering. At the very least, we thought, attitude theory and research into the relation between the consensual attitude factors and the cognitive structures of individuals may be encouraged and stimulated. Such an outcome of our efforts would after all be more desirable than satisfactory results of our own research.

The Research of Others

The limited amount of research of other investigators whose specific purpose was to test the criterial referents theory supported the theory. Most of this research, however, concentrated on educational attitudes. In only two studies were social attitudes measured. A handful of studies of other variables found the dual structure characteristic of the social attitude studies described in this book. These variables included American-Jewish identity, Arab-Israeli identity, cooperation and competition, and positive and negative affect. On the negative side, two well-done studies by others reported substantial bipolarity. On balance, studies by others support the theory but not completely. More interesting psychologically, the duality notion may apply to psychological variables other than social attitudes. It may be that a number of presumed polarities may not really be polarities.

Response Set

The results of studies of response set in relation to the social and educational attitude measures used in the research reported are given in Appendix C at the end of the book. The scales used seem not to be contaminated with response set, at least the response sets measured by four of the principal extant instruments. None of the liberalism or progressivism measures correlated significantly with any of the response set measures—with one exception. The one source of significant correlations with the response set measures was conservatism, which twice correlated significantly with Bass' Social Acquiescence Scale and once with the Marlowe-Crowne Social Desirability Scale. It was believed, however, that both these scales may have content related to conservatism. The Bass scale's cliches and homilies smack of conventionalism. The Marlowe-Crowne has some of the same flavor, but with an additional dash of virtue. This interpretation was strengthened by the lack of correlation of conservatism with the other measures of response set. So, the summated-rating type scales used in these studies, usually believed to be particularly vulnerable to response set, fared rather well in the few tests made.

Q Studies

Q studies have not often been used in attitude research, especially to test hypotheses and explore theories, despite Stephenson's (1953) strong advice to do so. In this series of studies, Q sorts with both statements and referents were used to study educational and social attitudes. Three studies were of educational attitudes (see Chapter 6) and one of social attitudes (Chapter 7). Although only one social attitude Q study was done, its results were strengthened by the use of two entirely different Q sorts, one with statement items and the other with referent items.

The basic approach used to test the theory was the "known groups" and "known individuals" methods. Whenever possible, individuals were selected whose educational or social attitudes were known either by the author or others. When this was not possible, professional or other identifications were used. From this knowledge, factor analytic and analysis of variance predictions were made, for example, that "known" liberals would appear on one factor together and "known" conservatives on another factor. The predictions generally held up: duality of attitude structure was evident, and there was comparatively little bipolarity.

The third Q study (Kerlinger, 1972a) used two entirely different kinds of Q sorts: one with statement items and the other with referent items. The rotated factors of the separate factor solutions were highly similar, as judged by the usual visual comparison of the loadings of the factor matrices and by the more objective statistical analyses used (see Table 7.11 and accompanying discussion in Chapter 7). And the factor solutions were in general accord with the expectations of the theory. It is gratifying that the results of a Q approach in which persons' responses are correlated and factor analyzed led to similar conclusions as those that emerged from an R approach.

Q methodology has potential for studying the problem discussed earlier of the attitude structure of individuals, or intrapersonal structure. As has been repeatedly said in this book, structure is operationally defined by the factors obtained from the responses of many individuals to many attitude items; it was called consensual or social structure. Part of the virtue of Q is its potential for studying the attitude structures of individuals. Stephenson (1953) pointed this out many years ago, but his suggestions have been largely ignored. One of the suggestions was that theories can be embodied in Q sorts using analysis of variance model designs. For example, if a theory or hypothesis can be expressed in a research design fashion—a factorial design, for instance—a Q sort that embodies the design can be constructed in accordance with the factorial design, and properly selected individuals can be asked to respond to it in Q fashion (see Kerlinger, 1973, Ch. 34, and Ch. 7, above, for examples.) Although Q's ability to express and test theories and hypotheses is considerably more limited than Stephenson's original sweeping proposals, it may have the potential for bridging the gap between consensual and individual attitude structures. Earlier, for example, Q was used to test the empirical validity of consensual duality findings in a Q manner by building the consensual factors into the Q sorts used. The Q or persons factor results should parallel the consensual factor results if the theory built into the Q sorts is valid (see

Chapters 6 and 7). The approach can perhaps be used, however, to explore intraindividual psychological structure.

The study of positive and negative affect mentioned in Chapter 11 is a good example. As usually conceived, affect is seen as bipolar. But Bradburn (1969), to his own surprise, found it to be dualistic. Items expressing positive and negative affect can be incorporated in Q sorts and the sorts administered to individuals with the express purpose in mind not only of testing the duality and bipolarity notions but also of studying the structure of affect in individuals. To my knowledge this has not been done. Certainly it seems worth trying. The Q studies described in earlier chapters were partly successful: they showed, even though weakly, that there seemed to be a parallel between consensual and intrapersonal attitude structures. Perhaps such a Q approach can stimulate and enrichen a psychology of attitudes and attitude structure.

DEFICIENCIES AND WEAKNESSES

We have emphasized positive evidence bearing on the criterial referents theory, though occasionally negative evidence and potential weaknesses have been mentioned. We now summarize and briefly discuss possible deficiencies and weaknesses of the evidence and of the argument for the theory.

Evidence for bipolar factors has been strong in the studies of Comrey and Newmeyer (1965), Eysenck and Wilson (1978), Ferguson (1973), Sontag and Pedhazur (1972), and Wilson (1973). The possible reasons for this bipolarity were discussed in earlier chapters and need not be repeated here. Unfortunately, it cannot be said that the negative correlations reported in these studies are or are not "legitimate." The best conclusion seems to be that the results of the studies raise doubts as to the generality of the criterial referents theory. What is needed is a strong further research effort specifically directed at resolving the bipolarity issue. The weight of the evidence reported in this book favors the theory, but the negative evidence cited earlier leaves room for doubt. At the very least, however, the massive faith in the bipolarity assumption should have been shaken.

Another possible weakness of the studies and the evidence is that insufficient effort was made to control response set or style. This issue, too, was discussed earlier. (See Chapter 11 and Appendix C.) It must be admitted that more research could have been done, perhaps especially using the methods of Edwards (1958), Edwards and Walsh (1964) and Bentler (1969), rather than merely correlating the liberalism and conservatism measures with measures of response set. There is another and perhaps more potent defense. If response set was a significant source of variance, then one or more response set factors should have appeared. At no time did such a factor or factors emerge from the analyses. Response set, then, is probably not a weakness of the research.

A third possible weakness or criticism is the use of referents as attitude items. It can legitimately be said that such items lack real meaning and validity because meaning depends in good part on the contexts in which concepts appear and referent items have no contexts. The first results with referent items surprised us on two counts: reliability and factor structure. Both were highly satisfactory and have been consistently satisfactory. Moreover, the correlations between referent and statement scales, as noted earlier, were substantial. Evidently the referent scales are to a substantial extent measuring the same things as the statement scales. Naturally, referent items cannot be as rich, complex, and subtle in meaning as statement items. But they measure liberalism and conservatism efficiently, reliably, and validly, and they are well-suited to the study of the structure of social attitudes.

The emergence of three second-order factors in two of the sets of REF-VI data raises difficulty for the theory, which predicts two second-order factors. In most of the second-order analyses, there was a sharp drop in the eigenvalue of the third factor. (For example, in the REF-I study the three eigenvalues were 1.76, 1.14, and .19, and in the REF-VI, Netherlands-II data, the Dutch random sample, they were 1.29, .91, and .33.) And more than three second-order factors was never justified. Research directed specifically at this point seems needed, especially using an analysis of covariance structures approach and specific testing of alternative hypotheses.

In a critique of the criterial referents theory and the research supporting it, Zdep and Marco (1969), said, among other things, that the finding of two sets of criterial referents "may be item-bound rather than nature-bound." At the time of their writing, this criticism had validity. But since then many more items have been used and the same structure found. Zdep and Marco (p. 736) also said that my rotations to simple structure "precluded bipolarity." In effect, this means that it is possible to get rid of disagreeable bipolarity by rotation. But if bipolarity is in the data, it will appear in rotated matrices. It has in general not appeared. Moreover, factor analytic methods that do not depend on rotation (see Chapter 10) have also been used with similar results. (See Kerlinger, 1970b, for a more detailed answer to Zdep and Marco.)

It may be, as said in an earlier chapter, that the items used in the attitude scales of the research reported in this book are not representative of the social attitude domain, that the factor structure obtained is due to item selection and writing consciously or unconsciously influenced by the theory's predictions. Items that perhaps may have produced substantial negative correlations with other items were somehow not selected or were discarded. While care was taken to include among the referents a wide range of concepts, it is still possible that bias operated. The major remedy is for other researchers to produce attitude referents and to study their characteristics extensively and intensively.

Another related difficulty is that it has been virtually assumed, if not directly stated, that liberalism and conservatism underlie *all* social attitudes. Is this actually so? Generally so? Is it possible that item generation and selection were biased to include mainly referents that were manifestly related to liberalism and conservatism? Again, further research is needed to explore the problem in depth.

The last weakness of the research of this book to be mentioned is one of the most serious. No attempt was made to study the criteriality of attitude referents directly. The theory says that referents are differentially criterial for different individuals and different groups. It was assumed that if people were asked to react to referents and factor analysis of these reactions showed mostly positive manifold that this was evidence for the differential criteriality notion. And it is, but only indirectly. A more direct test would be, as Zdep and Marco pointed out, to assess the criteriality of referents for each individual and then, perhaps, to correlate the liberal and conservative measures with the criteriality measures. This has not been done, unfortunately. Another possibility is to manipulate criteriality in experiments.

Zak and Birenbaum (1980), in a study cited in Chapter 11, measured the criteriality of educational referents. They had their subjects check "those concepts that were relevant to them when relating to education." They then plotted the percentage of mean responses to criterial and noncriterial referents separately—and for progressive and traditional referents separately. For criterial referents they obtained J curves for both progressive and traditional referents, but for noncriterial referents they obtained a more diffuse pattern (especially for the traditional referents). They say that the only systematic source of variance emerged from the criterial referents, and they thought that these results supported the theory.

Hofman (1970), in another study cited in Chapter 11, on the other hand, obtained results that he thought did not support the theory's criteriality notion. He administered an educational attitude referent scale and also had his subjects rate 13 educational concepts on a 12-adjective bipolar semantic differential. On the basis of the attitude scale he set up a group of progressives and a group of traditionalists and intercorrelated the 13 educational concepts for each group separately and for the total group.

The three factor analyses yielded much the same results: two orthogonal factors with traditional concepts on one factor and progressive concepts on the other factor. Hofman concluded that differential criteriality as an explanation of factor independence received no support. Thus, with these two studies we are back where we started. The familiar admonishment is: More research is needed!

FURTHER RESEARCH

It is not hard to find and list areas of needed attitude research. One or two such areas were mentioned earlier. We now list and discuss areas of social attitude research that need to be studied. The emphasis will be methodological rather than substantive. Some of these areas and problems have hardly been touched. Research and theory of attitude change have been plentiful (McGuire, 1969), sometimes with insufficient attention paid to the measurement of the attitudes being changed. But research on the structure of social attitudes and on attitude measurement itself has been limited, at least during the last decade. And there is little recent research on liberalism and conservatism. A fundamental general question underlying our suggestions is: Are the dissertations on liberalism and conservatism of political and social thinkers like Girvetz (1963), Rossiter (1968), Smith (1968), and Watkins (1957) accurate and valid in the sense that the content of their descriptions actually reflect the beliefs of people in contemporary society?

First, the measurement of social attitudes. As I said above, there has been little recent research on the measurement of social attitudes. After the creative work of Thurstone, Likert, and others, methodological interest seems to have waned. By now the reader will realize that the structure of social attitudes is at least an interesting area of research. To study the measurement of attitudes we have to study structure. In addition to technical measurement problems, we need to know, for example, how valuable for social research in general are the attitude factors found in factor analysis of social attitude scales and items. We need to know much more than we do about educational attitudes. Are the factors discussed in Chapter 6 good bases for educational attitude measurement? Measurement involves much more, of course, than technical problems. To study measurement adequately is to probe the nature of social arrangements and human reactions to the arrangements. To probe the validity of the measures we use is a psychological, sociological, and philosophical exercise of large scientific importance.

Certain concepts or phenomena repeatedly mentioned in this book need to be studied—criteriality, for instance. Is it as central and important as the present monograph says it is? It has been insufficiently studied, even in the research reported in this book. Indeed, as pointed out earlier, its importance has been assumed and not itself directly attacked! Bipolarity as a technical issue and as a social psychological phenomenon needs analysis and research. Perhaps the most important bipolarity problem is under what conditions it occurs. It has been said that it is a relatively minor aspect of social attitudes that probably occurs only under certain conditions. Is this really so?

A fruitful and much easier area for research is the study of the relations between attitude statement items and referent items. When we use referent items, for instance, how much of the essential substance of social attitudes do we capture? The use of referents as attitude items was successful, even highly successful, in the studies described earlier. They were reliable and they produced clear first- and second-order factors. Referent L and C subscales also correlated substantially with statement L and C subscales (see Tables 7.9 and 7.10), indicating that they measure the same things, despite the totally different kinds of items used.

The economical aspect of measuring attitudes with referents is enticing. Think of how much more can be accomplished with referents as items. Perhaps fifty referents can be responded to in the same time it takes to respond to twenty statements.[2] It is obvious that the bare use of referents cannot tap certain attitudinal ideas. How much do the referents miss— from a measurement point of view? It is clear from the evidence that they do not miss liberalism and conservatism. But do they measure other aspects of attitudes that might be important in research? It is also clear that the use of attitude referents in experimental attitude research—for example, as in the two experiments outlined earlier—may be highly profitable.

Another research possibility is the most obvious: the use of liberal and conservative scales in research in which other variables are the major focus of interest, for example, voting studies, studies of legislative and board of education decisions, content analysis studies of communication media, studies of leadership styles and effects and of organizational conflict. In any case, research in which liberalism or conservatism or both are correlated with other variables should add to our knowledge of conservatism and liberalism themselves.

More important, technical methodology is now available for conceptualizing and analyzing complex problems in which latent variables like conservatism and liberalism are used. Many theoretical and research

---

[2] In the study in which REF-VI was administered to a random sample of The Netherlands (Netherlands-I, Chapter 8), for example, REF-VI, a referents instrument with an original 86 items, and an "ideology" scale were administered along with the weekly survey questions of the Netherlands Institute of Public Opinion. A statement attitude scale of 86 items is hardly possible as part of a survey.

problems in psychology, sociology, political science, and education can be more potently conceived by using conservatism and liberalism or progressivism and traditionalism (in education) as latent variables influencing both manifest or measured variables and other latent variable. For example, one can conceive of an educational research problem in which one or two factors of educational attitudes are used as latent variables influencing not only the items of the factors but also other pertinent latent variables like expectation and achievement. Similarly, liberal and conservative factors can be used in social psychological research—on anti-Semitism, say—as latent variables influencing other latent variables, which influence anti-Semitic tendencies and behavior. As Huba and Bentler (1982, p. 609) say, in arguing for the use of latent variable models in psychology, "We wish to have a science of constructs, not a science of test-specific results." The same argument was elaborated earlier when we discussed analysis of covariance structures in Chapter 10. My hunch is that liberalism and conservatism and factors of both will be found to be indirect influences on latent variables like attitude change and achievement. Such complex relations can be studied using standard methods like multiple regression and path analysis and analysis of variance, of course, but I think it is much more likely that a latent variables approach in analysis of covariance structures will produce more interesting scientific and practical results.

The last area of research to be mentioned is both important and difficult: experimental research. One of the first questions we ask of a variable is: Can it be manipulated? Can conservatism, for instance, be manipulated? One can think immediately of a number of possibilities. But is the manipulated variable the same variable as the measured variable? Hardly. Another question researchers have to ask of a variable, if not explicitly, is: Can it be used as a dependent variable? Liberalism and conservatism, of course, are not good candidates because it is assumed that they are deep underlying variables not easily changed. Nevertheless, Newcomb (1943) reported that Bennington College evidently changed the liberalism and conservatism of its first students, but over a relatively long time period (two or more years). And the changes lasted (Newcomb, Koenig, Flacks, & Warwick, 1967).

In the unsuccessful experimental studies described earlier, "structure" was manipulated by presenting sets of referents that had been heavily loaded on liberal or on conservative factors as contrasted to sets of referents that had not been heavily loaded, had not appeared at all on attitude factors, or whose structural properties were muddied by mixing *L* and *C* referents. For example, the set *money, profits, law and order, business,* and *real estate* has high structure, whereas the set *education, civilization, foreign aid, world government,* and *modern society* has low structure. This is, in effect, a manipulation of conservatism.

The evidence for the validity of a variable and for its place in a theory is greatly strengthened when the variable can be both measured and manipulated. A large problem, as said before, is that they are never the same variable. But in many cases there should be a relation. The variable "liberalism," for instance, is ordinarily a measured variable. But it can be manipulated—with verbal materials, as in vignettes of "characters" presented to subjects to study and react to in prescribed ways (e.g., Pedhazur, 1969). Social attitude study can profit from experimental research in which such manipulations are used.

Another use of conservatism and liberalism in experimental research is as "interacting" variables. An experimenter might be interested in the effects of an experimental variable to change attitudes, say, but realizes that the experimental variable may work differently with high and low conservatives. An experimental factorial design is set up in which the experimental variable and conservatism are the independent variables that are conceived to interact in their effect on attitude change, the dependent variable. This idea opens up possibilities in psychological, educational, and political science research. From the viewpoint of this book, such research can also illuminate the study of social attitudes because the more knowledge of how a variable relates to other variables, the more one learns of its own nature.

RETROSPECT

The evidence presented, analyzed, and evaluated in this book supports the criterial referents theory of social attitudes. Most of the factor analytic evidence, both at the first and second orders, supports interpretation and assessment congruent with the theory. Conservative and liberal beliefs are evidently not opposites. They are simply different. The person who espouses liberal beliefs does not necessarily condemn conservative beliefs. One can of course carry such generalizations too far. Obviously there are many liberals who actively and systematically condemn conservative beliefs and many conservatives who loathe liberal beliefs. The conclusions, then, are very much "in general." If nothing else, however, the criterial referents theory is useful if it does nothing more than arouse skepticism about social attitude polarity.

The major emphasis throughout this book has been on structure. Much less emphasis has been put on the nature or content of social attitudes. The reason is obvious: the criterial referents theory is basically a structural theory. It is of course impossible to talk about attitude structure without at the same time talking about content. After all, liberalism and conservatism can only be inferred from their constituents, single beliefs and sets of beliefs expressed in some verbal way. It is fitting, therefore, that this book end on a content-of-attitude note.

To do so, I have prepared Tables 12.1 and 12.2. All similar tables in the book have been based on the results of specific factor analyses and solutions. These tables, however, are based on a sifting of experience with the results of many factor analyses of the items of referent scales. They are supposed to express the nature of three conservative and five liberal first-order factors. These factors have been found repeatedly in three or more samples with three referent scales, REF-I, REF-IV, and REF-VI. They are, in other words, my impression of the nature of the main factors of social attitudes. It should be clearly understood, however, that I am *not* saying that these factors are *the* factors of social attitudes. They simply express the essence of the results of a number of factor analyses of referent scales. There are undoubtedly more social attitude factors. Indeed, at least four or five more factors were found in the research studies. For example, certain other factors were found in Spain and The Netherlands. In The Netherlands, a factor called Militant Social Action was found in both Dutch samples. It could of course not appear in other samples because the items were only in the Dutch attitude instrument. In Spain, a factor, Foreign Influence *(America, Soviet Union, Jews, United Nations),* appeared. It is apparently limited to the Spanish students who responded to the instrument.

When I prepared the "factors" in the tables, I wanted equal numbers of factors in each table, but gave up because I could not find enough conservative factors that were consistent across samples. Is this due to truly fewer conservative than liberal factors "out there"? Perhaps the sample bias—most of the samples were graduate students of education who tend to be more liberal than conservative—accounts for the difference. A more likely explanation is that conservative social attitudes may not be as multifaceted as liberal factors. That this makes sense, though not necessarily truth, can be understood from the very nature of conservatism and liberalism.

TABLE 12.1
Conservative Factors and Referents

Religiosity	Economic Conservatism	Traditional Conservatism
religion	profits	discipline
church	money	law and order
Christian	business	authority
faith in God	free enterprise	family
teaching of spiritual values	corporate industry	tradition
	real estate	
	private property	
	capitalism	
	competition	

TABLE 12.2
Liberal Factors and Referents

Civil Rights	Social Liberalism	Sexual Freedom
civil rights	Social Security	equality of women
blacks	socialized medicine	women's liberation
racial integration	poverty program	birth control
desegregation	economic reform	abortion (liberalized abortion, free abortion)
	government ownership of utilities	
	social welfare	
Human Warmth and Feeling	**Progressivism**	
love	child-centered curriculum	
human warmth	children's interests	
affection	children's needs	
feeling	pupil personality	
	self-expression of children	

Conservatism emphasizes the past, the existing order, the "eternal verities," and resistance to change. If this is so, one does not expect "new" and different factors emerging from factor analyses. There should be relatively few factors based on the substance of different sets of important beliefs: religious, economic, moral, for instance. Liberalism, on the other hand, should be more protean. There should of course be factors based on the substance of different sets of important beliefs: social welfare, belief freedom, civil rights. In addition, however, factors should change with changing times and changing issues. Human Warmth and Feeling and Sexual Freedom, for instance, may be the result of contemporary social movements. In 1920, perhaps, there would have been no such factors, whereas Social Liberalism, or some form of it, should have emerged in factor analyses. In other words, the commitment to change of liberalism may itself make for proliferation of factors, whereas the belief in a fixed social order and morality of conservatism should make it unlikely that new and different factors will appear.

The three conservative factors of Table 12.1 emerge clearly from conservative doctrine. Religion was a cornerstone of Burke's thinking. In *Reflections on the Revolution in France* (Burke, 1790/1955), he said, "We know, and what is better, we feel inwardly, that religion is the basis of civil society and the source of all good and of all comfort" (p. 102). And religion is emphasized by modern conservative thinkers, like Kirk (1960; see Rossiter, 1962, pp. 42–46).

Economic Conservatism is part of the foundation of modern conservatism. It started with classic liberalism and its espousal of laissez-faire economic policy (Smith, 1968). It is still vigorous today. Recently, the people of the United States and England, for example, elected governments committed to conservative economic policies. An outstanding economic conservative, who recently won a Nobel Prize, has had (at this writing) a book on the New York Times best seller list for many weeks.

Traditional Conservatism, or simply Traditionalism, was also emphasized by Burke who said, "There is no qualification for government but virtue and wisdom . . ." (p. 57), and "The levelers . . . only change and pervert the natural order of things" (p. 55). Various themes suffuse Traditionalism; the referents of Table 12.1 express five of these (see Rossiter, 1962, pp. 198–199). The traditionalism of the conservative is particularly stimulated by education. Education is a conserving and civilizing force: children should learn the inherited wisdom of the race, how to lead a moral disciplined life, and to love order and respect authority (Rossiter, 1962, p. 26). What may be most interesting about this factor is its apparent close relation to authoritarianism. Adorno et al. (1950) mention conventionalism and authoritarian submission as part of the authoritarian complex. Indeed, this factor may be a link to the study of conservatism as a personality trait rather than as a set of attitudinal predispositions. A major contribution of *The Authoritarian Personality* was its assertion that political, economic, and social beliefs are related to deep-seated personality characteristics.

The liberal referents of Table 12.2 express contemporary ideas of progress, social amelioration, and human rights. Sexual Freedom seems to be centered on women's rights, and Civil Rights on the rights of blacks (and perhaps other minorities). The Social Liberalism referents express social amelioration: initiate and implement programs to improve life. Progressivism, the only educational attitude factor among these factors—perhaps because there were insufficient educational referents to permit other educational factors to emerge—centers strongly on the child's needs, interests, and personality. Finally, Human Warmth and Feeling expresses concern for love, affection, and feeling. It is a source of common factor variance that appears to be relatively new. Factors like this one have not been mentioned in treatises on liberalism.

"Attitude" is one of the great concepts of contemporary social science. No one who reads Fleming's fine essay on attitudes can escape feeling their extraordinary importance and relevance in modern social research. Indeed, Fleming concludes his essay: "This, in many ways greatest of all revolutions in modern man's conception of himself, is encapsulated in the triumphant progress of the concept of attitude" (1967, p. 365). The concept is important, first, because it is a bridge between the person and the environment. The essence of the idea of "attitude man" lies in the power of attitudes to amalgamate cognitions and feelings. It is a positive and productive alternative to "irrational man," a conception dominated by feeling and distortion. Fleming says:

> Man . . . is an organism oriented by cravings and aversions toward the objects of cognition and perception—neither purely cognitive nor purely affective, but an indissoluble compound of thinking and feeling, knowing and wanting. In this conception, the intellectual dimension of man remains intact but not inviolate. Knowledge of things . . . is seen to be inextricably compounded with emotional evaluations, orientations toward and away from, for and against, the objects of experience" (*ibid.,* pp. 359–360).

It would be hard to improve on this statement.

A second reason for the importance of "attitude" is that it has become the common property of the academic social scientist and the man-in-the-street. Although the latter may be vague about its meaning, there is no doubt of the broad popular currency of the term and related terms and the ideas connected with them. Attitude, in other words, has become a bridge between social science and the popular mind, particularly the responses of the latter to attitude objects or referents.

The third and fourth reasons for the importance of the attitude concept are scientific. The concept is so rich and at the same time so amenable to definition and measurement that it has stimulated much research. It is likely to go on doing so. Starting in the 1920s and 1930s with the gifted inventions, contributions, and analyses of Thurstone, and especially with his classic essay, "Attitudes Can Be Measured" (Thurstone, 1959, Ch. 19) and his monograph with Chave (Thurstone & Chave, 1929), the stream of research on attitudes has never stopped. Now, with the development of more powerful multivariate methods for testing theory, we should see even more research on attitudes, both experimental and nonexperimental.

These methods and the explicit inclusion of latent variables in attitude research should significantly and salubriously affect both basic and applied research on social and educational attitudes. Latent variables are of course not new in social science. Lazarsfeld (1959; Lazarsfeld & Henry, 1968) pioneered latent structure analysis. But Lazarsfeld talked about latent structures and not latent variables, though he probably had latent variables in mind. The most advanced method or approach to latent variables and their influence on each other and on measured or manifest variables is analysis of covariance structures (Jöreskog, 1978; Jöreskog & Sörbom, 1978, 1981). As recent as the method is, it has already been used in attitude study (see Chapter 9; Bagozzi & Burnkrant, 1979; Bentler &

Speckart, 1979; Kerlinger, 1980a), and there is little doubt that it will continue to be so used.[3]

Attitudes can be viewed as cognitive organizations or structures that are predispositions to action and that use repositories of previous learning and experience to orient human beings to their social environment. We have in this book emphasized the structure of attitudes. Our major interest was in liberalism and conservatism and their relations to social attitudes. These ubiquitous, general, and weighty concepts—ideologies, if you will—encapsulate much of the essence of the beliefs of people in modern society. They carry heavy attitude freight. When we say that a man is conservative or that a social policy is liberal, we pretty much know what we mean, even though there are rough edges and ambiguities in our understanding of the many and varied social phenomena with which we must deal. Liberalism and conservatism are invented concepts that express not only the content of our social attitudes; they also imply the relations among social attitudes and thus their structure. We have tried to show, among other things, that liberalism and conservatism are second-order social attitude factors that underlie the multiplicity of first-order attitude factors and the specific issues and referents of such factors.

The criterial referents theory of attitudes is of course a structural theory in which attitude referents are conceived as the most important parts of attitudes. They are the core of the cognitive component of attitudes. Being basically cognitive and structural, the theory neglects the evaluative (in the semantic differential evaluative factor sense), emotional, and motivational components of attitudes. These latter components may be more important than the cognitive component in actual influence on behavior. But the behavior is in large part triggered by and directed toward referents. That is, the emotional, motivational, and evaluative aspects of attitudes cannot work without the cognitive substance, the referents.

A more encompassing and general theory must take all attitudinal components into account. One fate of the criterial referents theory, then, may be absorption into a larger more general theory. Before that happens, of course, the theory will no doubt have to be amended, altered, even re-

---

[3]It is wise to temper enthusiasm for analysis of covariance structures and computer programs to implement it with continuous critical assessment of its use and value in actual research studies (see Cliff, 1983). That it will be misused is obvious: new methodologies that promise much are always enticing and always subject to misuse. To counsel avoidance of complex methods because they are misused, however, is poor advice. Blaming methods for questionable practice confuses the essentially neutral means to accomplish desired ends with users of the means. It is like the frequent but ignorant criticism of experiments as artificial and limited because they can't do what they were never meant to do.

jected. If its fate is like the fate of most theories in science, and especially in psychology, we must expect changes, additions, even complete upset. The theory's further testing and subsequent change, however, may help to increase our knowledge of the structure and content of social attitudes, provide better explanations of those potent and ubiquitous latent variables, liberalism and conservatism, and justify the effort of this book in probing the complexities of social attitudes.

Appendix A

Factor Analysis

Factor analysis, with its many facets and its controversial problems, is often a subject of conceptual and scientific difficulty. Since it is the main statistical method used to analyze the social attitude data of this book, we define and explain enough of factor analysis itself and certain key concepts and ideas so that readers can follow the arguments and the factor analytic evidence presented in the chapters. In what follows it is assumed that readers have at least elementary statistical background and some knowledge of psychological measurement.

DEFINITION AND PURPOSE

Factor analysis determines the number and nature of the variables, or factors, that underlie larger numbers of variables, measures, tests, scales, or items. Succinctly, it is a method for determining k underlying variables or factors from n sets of measures, k being less than n. It can also be categorized as a method for extracting common factor variances from sets of measures. Factor analysis is essentially a method driven by the needs of parsimony: it reduces multiplicities of tests or measures to greater simplicities. It tells us, in effect, what tests or measures belong together: which ones measure the same thing and how much they do so. In Q methodology, it tells us which persons cluster together in their responses to a Q sort.

A *factor* is a construct, a hypothetical entity, that is assumed to underlie tests, scales, items, and, indeed, measures of all kinds. A factor, in other words, is a latent variable, an expression we use a good deal in this book. A *latent variable* is an unobserved variable that presumably underlies certain observed measures. For instance, a factor called Economic Conservatism has been found in a number of factor analyses. This is a latent variable that is thought to underlie many people's responses to attitude referents like *profits, capitalism, money, private property,* and *free enterprise*. These referents are all positively and substantially correlated, and factor analysis, using these correlations, determines the degree to which each of them reflects the latent variable Economic Conservatism. "Economic Conservatism" is a name given to the latent variable or factor by the analyst. There is nothing in the method that "finds" this name. Indeed, the factor might have been called "Economics," or "Ecodogism," or even just "A" or "B."

The data commonly analyzed in factor analysis are correlation coefficients. The correlations among all the variables to be analyzed—there are $n(n - 1)/2$ of them, where n is the number of variables—are calculated, and the resulting correlation matrix, **R,** is then factored by any one of a number of methods. This is a process of finding which variables belong together as determined by the magnitudes of the correlations among the variables. The main method used in this book is called the principal factors method; it is essentially a procedure for solving a large number of simultaneous linear equations. ("Linear" means that all the terms of each equation are of the first order or power. That is, no terms are squared, cubed, and so on.)The result of a principal factors factor analysis is a set of roots of the equations, called eigenvalues, and a set of so-called factor loadings, called eigenvectors.

Rotated and Unrotated Factors

The main outcome of such a factor analysis is a set of factor loadings, which when presented together for the different factors constitutes an *unrotated* factor matrix. A *factor loading* can be viewed as a weight, as a regression coefficient, or as a correlation between a particular variable and the factor. In any case, it is an index of the degree of relation between the variable and the underlying factor or latent variable. If, for example, a test of vocabulary has a factor loading of .70—factor loadings have the same range as correlation coefficients: from $-1.$ through 0 to $+1.$—this can be interpreted as a substantial relation between the vocabulary test and the underlying factor, say Verbal Ability.

In order to interpret factors, to determine their nature and substance, rotation is almost always needed. We define and illustrate rotation of factors and then examine why rotation is both necessary and desirable. *Rotation* of factors means rotation of the axes to which the factor loadings

TABLE A.1
Correlations Among REF-I, ES, and SA Scales, Texas
Sample, $N = 227$

	REFL[a]	REFC	ESA	ESB	SAL	SAC
REFL	1.000	-.066	.459	-.161	.534	-.373
REFC	-.066	1.000	-.022	.553	-.145	.544
ESA	.459	-.022	1.000	-.086	.323	-.183
ESB	-.161	.553	-.086	1.000	.060	.648
SAL	.534	-.145	.323	.060	1.000	-.093
SAC	-.373	.544	-.183	.648	-.093	1.000

[a] REFL: Referents I, or REF-I, Liberalism; REFC: REF-I, Conservatism; ESA: Education Scale ES-VII, Progressivism; ESB: ES, Traditionalism; SAL: Social Attitudes II, or SA-II, Liberalism; SAC: SA-II, Conservatism.

are referred (and on which they can be plotted). So that we have something to work with, we will use the results of a factor analysis of six attitude scales, or subscales. The six scales are: the Liberalism *(L)* and Conservatism *(C)* subscales, REFL and REFC, of a referents social attitudes scale, Referents I, or REF-I; the Progressivism *(P)* and Traditionalism *(T)* subscales of an educational attitudes scale, ESA and ESB, Education Scale VII, or ES-VII; and the *L* and *C* subscales, SAL and SAC, of a statement attitude scale, Social Attitude Scale II, or SA-II. The correlations among the six scales are given in Table A.1. The scales' names have been abbreviated as noted above and in the table. Part of the results of a factor analysis produces the unrotated factors, which are the two columns of numbers given on the left of Table A.2, labeled I and II. The factor analysis of the correlation matrix of Table A.1 showed that there were two factors with the unrotated factor loadings in the columns I and II.

The principal factors method of factor analysis (Harman, 1976, Ch. 8) obtains roots of simultaneous equations, called eigenvalues, and the factor loadings, called eigenvectors, given on the left of Table A.2, as said earlier. A basic characteristic of the method is that the source of the greatest amount of variance in the correlation matrix is extracted first and the eigenvectors calculated, then the next source of variance, which is orthogonal to (independent of) the first source, is extracted and the eigenvector calculated, and so on for as many factors as there are.[1] These

---

[1] In the table under "Unrotated Factors" is the symbol Σa_i^2, which is the sum of squares of the factor loadings of a column of the table. These are the eigenvalues; they are also the variances of the factors. It can be seen that the variance of the first factor is considerably larger than that of the second factor (1.909 and 1.073). After rotation, these values of course change (in this case to 1.673 and 1.310).

TABLE A.2
Unrotated and Rotated Factors: REF-I, ES, and SA Scales,
Texas Sample, N = 227

| | Unrotated Factors | | Rotated Factors[a] | | |
	I	II	A	B	h^{2b}
REFL	-.543	.545	-.170	.750	.591
REFC	.596	.329	.680	-.039	.463
ESA	-.338	.408	.069	.526	.281
ESB	.658	.398	.769	-.014	.592
SAL	-.338	.548	.005	.644	.414
SAC	.773	.208	.765	-.235	.641
$\Sigma\, a_i^2 {:}^c$	1.909	1.073	1.673	1.310	2.982

[a] Significant loadings are italicized ($>$.35).

b_h^2: communality: sum of squares of the factor loadings in a row.

c $\Sigma\, a_i 2$: sum of squares of the i factor loadings in a column: variance of the factor.

eigenvector values are the so-called unrotated factor loadings. They may or may not have psychological meaning, usually not. The result of this procedure characteristically produces one factor with all positive loadings and the remaining factors with half positive and half negative loadings, even if all the correlations of the correlation matrix are positive. These half-and-half factors are an artifact of the procedure; they do not usually have psychological meaning.

The argument over rotated versus unrotated factors has thrived for many years. In early attitude research, English investigators did not rotate attitude factors, whereas American investigators did. Part of the argument for unrotated factors was that the factor with all positive loadings is a general factor and should be preserved. Even if this were true—and it is not—the remaining factors are perforce bipolar, whether or not the data and the correlation matrix are truly bipolar. The argument for rotated factors is based on the idea of invariance. Invariance means that the same factors emerge with different samples and different measures of the same variables. The unrotated factors are not invariant. If, for example, we add two or three more attitude scales to the example just given, all the factor loadings and the pattern of the unrotated matrix will probably change. With appropriately rotated factors, on the other hand, the same structure will tend to appear, whether there are six or ten scales, the factor loadings will exhibit much the same pattern, and the results will be legitimately interpretable. (See Guilford, 1954, pp. 500–501; Harman, 1976, pp. 93–94, 278ff.; Mulaik, 1972, Ch. 14.)

Let's return to the example. The results of a principal factors factor analysis, then, yielded the unrotated factors on the left of Table A.2. It can be seen that factor I is bipolar—half the loadings are positive and the other half negative—and factor II has all positive loadings. This is the characteristic unrotated factor pattern yielded by the principal factors method. The unrotated factor loadings of the two factors have been plotted in Figure A.1. For example, REFC is plotted .596 on I and .329 on II. For now, disregard the axes marked I' and II'; concentrate on the axes marked I and II. Note that the C scales form a cluster on the right and the L scales another cluster on the left. We want a more parsimonious portrayal of the structure. To obtain one, we rotate I and II in such a manner that they are simultaneously placed as near as possible to the plotted points of the two clusters. Ideally, we want I to go through REFC, ESB, and SAC and II to go through REFL, ESA, and SAL. Since we also want to keep the two axes at right angles, or orthogonal, to each other, we cannot achieve this wish perfectly. But we do the best we can. Rotating the two axes rigidly counterclockwise through an angle of 32 degrees is about the best we can do. (We could have done better, of course, if we had allowed the axes to have an oblique angle between them. This would then have been what is called an oblique rotation in contrast to the rotation of Figure A.1, which is an orthogonal rotation.)

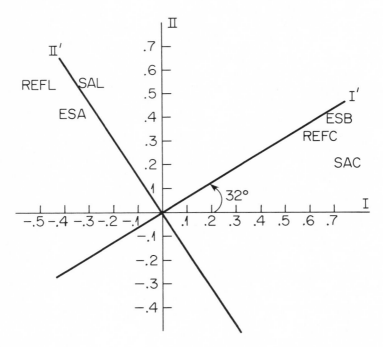

FIG. A-1

The required rotation is also shown in Figure A.1. The new axes are marked I′ and II′. It can be seen that the three C subscales are near I′ and the three L subscales near II′. The set of principles behind such a rotation, essentially formulated many years ago by Thurstone (1947), is called simple structure.[2] The basic idea, as the name suggests, is to find the simplest possible factor structure given the data. This means, as Thurstone pointed out, the smallest number of substantial entries in each row of the factor matrix, or, most succinctly put, the greatest number of zero or inconsequential entries in the factor matrix. If, of course, we reduce some entries in a row to zero, then we must at the same time increase other entries, since the variance in any row is the same before and after rotation. This can be seen in the unrotated and rotated matrices of Table A.2. In the unrotated matrix, most of the loadings are substantial—there are no zero or close-to-zero loadings—whereas in the rotated matrix there is usually only one substantial loading and one loading near zero in each row. The rotated factors in this table are a good, if elementary, example of simple structure. It is not always possible, however, to achieve "good" simple structure, especially with many factors and complex tests or scales.

The calculations of the rotated factors do not concern us. Readers may want to know, however, that one way to obtain them is to read them from the rotated axes I′ and II′. For example, I cut a strip of paper, marked the axis values on it, laid it on I′, and read off REFC as .70, − .05 and ESB as .77 and − .02. This rough procedure yields fairly accurate values. Most important, note that the liberal subscales, REFL, ESA (Progressivism has been found to be a liberal factor in other research), and SAL, have substantial positive loadings on one rotated factor, and the conservative subscales, REFC, ESB, and SAC, have substantial positive loadings on the other factor. The rotated matrix has been plotted anew in Figure A.2. The new axes have been labeled A and B to conform to the column headings of Table A.2. L and C labels have been added in parentheses because the subscales on A express conservatism and those on B express liberalism. In any case, one sees the relatively orthogonal structure clearly, almost dramatically.

FIRST- AND SECOND-ORDER FACTOR ANALYSIS

Although first- and second-order factor analysis were explained to some extent in Chapter 4, as were other factor analytic matters, we have an urgent need to understand second-order factors and factor analysis. So

---

[2]Thurstone actually discussed simple structure in conjunction with oblique factors. The idea applies, however, to orthogonal factors, though less satisfactorily.

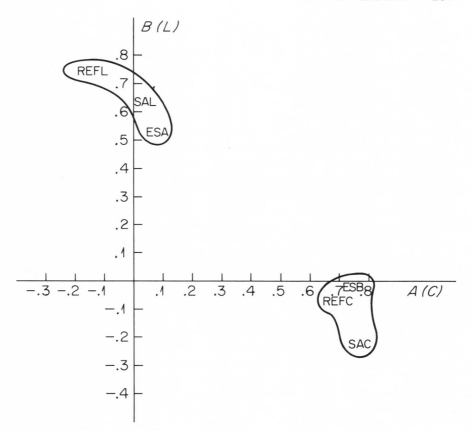

FIG. A-2

we reexamine this important but seldom explained and little understood aspect of factor analysis.

The factors obtained from the direct factor analysis of tests, scales, items, and variables in general are called first-order factors. The factors reported in Table A.2 were obtained directly from the correlations of Table A.1. They are first-order factors. In this book many first-order factors are reported and discussed. They are the main fruits of factor analysis. Most of the factor analyses reported in research studies are first-order factors. Sometimes, however—rarely, to be sure—second-order factors are reported. In this book second-order factors have fairly often been reported and interpreted. Without them, in fact, the evidence for the criterial referents theory would be much weaker than it is.

If we wished, we could have rotated the unrotated factors of Table A.2 obliquely. If, in Figure A.1 for example, we put the I′ axis through the middle of REFC, ESB, and SAC and the II' axis through the middle of REFL, ESA, and SAL, we would have an angle of about 103 degrees between I' II' instead of an angle of 90 degrees. The two axes would have been rotated separately, as it were: I through an angle of about 25 degrees (from axis I) and II through an angle of about 38 degrees (from axis II). This is an oblique rotation because the angle between the two rotated axes is greater than 90 degrees. (It can of course be less than 90 degrees.) This means that there is a low negative correlation between the two factors. (Had the angle been less than 90 degrees the correlation would have been positive.) A similar procedure—actually we do not physically rotate the axes; the procedure is analytic: the computer does the work for us—can be used with any number of factors, and the correlations among all the factors calculated.

If we follow such a procedure we will have a matrix of correlations among all the factors. This correlation matrix can then be factor analyzed in the usual way, and its factors rotated orthogonally or obliquely. The resulting factors, unrotated and rotated, are called second-order factors; they are presumably the latent variables behind the latent variables. If we factor analyzed a number of ability tests we would expect all or most of the factors to be positively correlated. A factor analysis of such a correlation matrix may yield one factor. This might be the well-known "g", a general factor. Indeed, this is the proper way to determine if there is a general factor in studies of abilities or of attitudes. To take the first principal factors factor (or principal components factor[3]) and, because it accounts for more variance—often much more—than any other factor, to call it a general factor is a mistake. It may happen to be a general factor,

---

[3]Principal components analysis is accomplished in much the same way as principal factors factor analysis. The difference is that 1's are inserted in the diagonal of the correlation matrix instead of estimates of communalities. Communalities, symbolized by h^2 (See Table A.2), are the sums of squares of the factor loadings (in any row). h^2 indicates the variance that any test shares with all the other tests. In Table A.2, for instance, SAC has a communality of .641: SAC, then, shares more variance with all the other subscales than any other subscale does. In this book estimated communalities are always used, usually estimated by R^2, the squared multiple correlation between each variable and all the other variables. Principal components analysis extracts all the variance in a correlation matrix, whereas principal factors and similar methods extract only what are known as common factors. Common factor variance is the variance of a factor shared by two or more tests. The variance of a test is assumed to be composed of common factor variance, specific variance or variance specific to that test, and error variance. (See Guilford, 1954, pp. 354–357, for a brief but good discussion.) Specific variance and error variance together make up unique variance. Common factors and principal factors factor analysis are preferred by most behavioral researchers since their interest is not so much in prediction or in reproducing the correlation matrix as it is in learning the factors or latent variables underlying observed variables.

but more likely it will not be. A characteristic of rotation is that it tends to spread the common factor variance over many factors. When the first factor is rotated with the other factors much of its variance "spreads" to other factors. If a factor withstands rotation, that is, if after rotation it keeps its appearance as a general factor, then it may indeed be a general factor. If, however, a good deal of its variance is shifted to other factors, then it almost certainly is not a general factor.

Factor analysis is a powerful method. One of the major problems of science is the categorization and measurement of variables. Factor analysis is a fundamental approach to the solution of this problem. But it is also a complex method, or rather, set of methods. It is suggested that readers will profit from study of Nunnally's clear exposition (Nunnally, 1978, Chs. 10 and 11) and from Harman's excellent text (Harman, 1976). Thurstone's (1947) book on the subject, while old, is still timely. More important, it is a classic!

Appendix B

Social and Educational Attitude Scales

The purpose of this appendix is to file the attitude scales used in the research described in this book, and to provide social and educational scales (and items) for research use.[1] There are two kinds of scales: educational attitude and social attitude. In addition, there are two kinds of items used in the scales: statements and referents. For the most part fairly substantial data were given in the text on the scales' origins, psychometric characteristics, and factor characteristics, Therefore such information need not be repeated here. We will, however, refer to the chapter and the tables in which research data are given. There is one exception: data on one of the educational attitude scales, ES-VII (see below), were not given in the text. They will be given in this appendix.

The first two statement scales, Education Scale VI, or ES-VI, and Education Scale VII, or ES-VII, measure attitudes toward education. ES-VII was actually constructed from the "best" items of ES-VI: 30 of ES-VI's 46 items were chosen so that a shorter instrument would be available. In this appendix, only ES-VI is given. The items of ES-VI used in ES-VII are marked with an asterisk. If users wish the shorter scale, they can easily extract the items from ES-VI. The instructions are the same except that the "46" in the ES-VI instructions should be changed to "30."

As can be seen from the instructions, the responses use a 7 point scale:

---

[1]The scales and items given below can be freely used in any way researchers wish. The only restriction on use is commercial: the scales and items cannot be sold or otherwise used for commercial purposes.

TABLE B.1
ES-VII: Means, Standard Deviations, Reliability Coefficients,
and the Correlations Between A and B Subscales

Sample	N	A				B			$r_{AB}{}^b$
		M	s	$r_{tt}{}^a$		M	s	r_{tt}	
Long Island	298	5.54	.69	.79		4.34	.85	.78	-.15
Indiana	322	5.51	.60	.76		4.24	.65	.69	.02
Michigan	400	5.79	.61	.80		3.93	.73	.76	-.20
North Carolina	428	5.61	.59	.71		4.03	.87	.82	-.20
New York	257	5.75	.61	.76		3.74	.73	.73	-.19

$^a r_{tt}$: alpha reliability coefficients.

$^b r_{AB}$: correlations between A and B subscales.

from +3, Agree Very Strongly, through −3, Disagree Very Strongly. (All the scales in this appendix use the same system.) "No response" is scored 0. For convenience users can add a constant of 4 to all responses, thus obtaining scale responses from 7 through 1. Twenty-three of the items of ES-VI (15 of ES-VII) are progressive items; the remaining 23 items (15 in ES-VII) are traditional items. The progressive items are marked A, and the traditional items B. *Each subject receives two scores, an A score and a B score.* These are either the sum of the A items and the sum of the B items, or the mean of the A items and the mean of the B items. I recommend using mean scores because they reflect the original scales and enhance the comparability of different scales with different numbers of items (like ES-VI and ES-VII).[2]

The reliabilities of ES-VI are substantial: from .79 to .86 with three samples (alpha coefficients). The correlations between the A and B subscales were, as expected, low negative. (See Table 6.4 in Chapter 6 and accompanying discussion.) As said earlier, data on ES-VII were not reported in Chapter 6. ES-VII means, standard deviations, reliability coefficients, and the correlations between the A and B subscales of five samples in different parts of the United States are given in Table B.1.[3] The means reflect the progressive bias of the samples, graduate students of education. The standard deviations are unremarkable. The reliabilities are satisfactory, if not as satisfactory as those of ES-VI, which were in the .80's. The correlations between the A and B subscales are low negative. This is not surprising, however, since the items were chosen on the basis

---

[2]Note that items 13 and 30 are virtual duplicates of each other. They were included for a special research purpose. They can be left as they are with little loss.

[3]These data were obtained in research on the relations between attitudes toward education and perceptions of desirable characteristics of teachers (Kerlinger & Pedhazur, 1968).

of high factor loadings and high item-total correlations. In short, the scale is satisfactory for use in research. If high reliability is important, however, it would be better to use ES-VI.

Education Scale VI[a]

Instructions: Given below are 46 statements on educational ideas and problems about which we all have beliefs, opinions, and attitudes. We all think differently about such matters, and this scale is an attempt to let you express your beliefs and opinions. Respond to each of the items as follows:

Agree Very Strongly:	+3	Disagree Very Strongly:	−3
Agree Strongly:	+2	Disagree Strongly:	−2
Agree:	+1	Disagree	−

For example, if you *agree very strongly* with a statement, you would write +3 on the short line preceding the statement, but if you should happen to disagree with it, you would put a −1 in front of it. Respond to each statement as best you can. Go rapidly but carefully. Do not spend too much time on any one statement; try to respond and then go on.

B   1. *Schools of today are neglecting the three R's.

B   2. The backbone of the school curriculum is subject matter; activities are useful mainly to facilitate the learning of subject matter.

A   3. Teaching should be based on the present needs of the child.

A   4. *The public school should take an active part in stimulating social change.

A   5. The traditional moral standards of our culture should not just be accepted; they should be examined and tested in solving the present problems of students.

B   6. *The curriculum should contain an orderly arrangement of subjects that represent the best of our cultural heritage.

A   7. *The healthy interaction of pupils one with another is just as important in school as the learning of subject matter.

B   8. The mind of the child must be well-trained if it is to perform its function properly later in life.

A   9. Children should be allowed more freedom than they usually get in the execution of learning activities.

A   10. *Right from the very first grade, teachers must teach child at his own level and not at the level of the grade he is in.

B   11. *Learning is essentially a process of increasing one's store of information about the various fields of knowledge.

B   12. Many schools waste time and money on fads and frills: activity programs, driver education, swimming pools, social services, and the like.

A   13. *Education and educational institutions must be sources of new

social ideas; education must be a social program undergoing
continual reconstruction.

___A___ 14. *The learning of proper attitudes is often more important than
the learning of subject matter.

___A___ 15. *Learning experiences organized around life experiences rather
than around subjects is desirable in our schools.

___B___ 16. It is essential for learning and effective work that teachers outline in detail what is to be done and how to go about it.

___B___ 17. *The true view of education is so arranging learning that the
child gradually builds up a storehouse of knowledge that he can
use in the future.

___B___ 18. *Teachers need to be guided in what they are to teach. No individual teacher can be permitted to do as he wishes, especially
when it comes to teaching children.

___A___ 19. *Emotional development and social development are as important in the evaluation of pupil progress as academic achievement.

___A___ 20. *It is more important that the child learns how to approach and
solve problems than it is for him to master the subject matter of
the curriculum.

___A___ 21. *Learning is experimental; the child should be taught to test
alternatives before accepting any of them.

___B___ 22. *The curriculum consists of subject matter to be learned and
skills to be acquired.

___B___ 23. *Each subject and activity should be aimed at developing a particular part of the child's makeup: physical, intellectual, social,
moral, or spiritual.

___A___ 24. *Teachers should encourage pupils to study and criticize our
own and other economic systems and practices.

___B___ 25. *Since life is essentially a struggle, education must emphasize
competition and the fair competitive spirit.

___A___ 26. *True discipline springs from interest, motivation, and involvement in live problems.

___A___ 27. *We should fit the curriculum to the child and not the child to the
curriculum.

___B___ 28. *The organization of instruction and learning must be centered
on universal ideas and truths if education is to be more than
passing fads and fancies.

___B___ 29. *Teachers should keep in mind that pupils have to be made to
work.

___A___ 30. Education and educational institutions must be sources of new
social ideas.

___A___ 31. Teachers should be free to teach what they think is right and
proper.

___B___ 32. *Schools should teach children dependence on higher moral
values.

  B   33. *What is needed in the modern classroom is a revival of the authority of the teacher.

  B   34. It is unrealistic to expect education to be like real life; it is more a preparation for life.

  B   35. One of the basic purposes of education is to conserve and transmit the values and standards of the society of which it is a part.

  A   36. *The goals of education should be dictated by children's interests and needs, as well as by the larger demands of society.

  A   37. Subjects like communism and capitalism should be studied in the public schools.

  B   38. The modern public school is sacrificing too much of our cultural heritage in its preoccupation with life-adjustment and group living.

  B   39. *One of the big difficulties with modern schools is that discipline is often sacrificed to the interests of children.

  B   40. *Subjects that sharpen the mind, like mathematics and foreign languages, need greater emphasis in the public school curriculum.

  A   41. *Children should be taught that all problems should be subjected to critical and objective scrutiny, including religious, moral, economic, and social problems.

  B   42. The movement to substitute "activities" for subjects in the curriculum of the modern school will operate against the best interests of American education.

  A   43. *Standards of work should not be the same for all pupils; they should vary with the pupil.

  B   44. *Children need and should have more supervision and discipline than they usually get.

  A   45. Education is not so much imparting knowledge as it is encouraging and prompting the child to use his potentialities for learning.

  A   46. In a democracy, teachers should help students understand not only the meaning of democracy but also the meaning of the ideologies of other political systems.

---

[a]ES-VII items are marked with an asterisk. *A:* Progressivism; *B:* Traditionalism.

SOCIAL ATTITUDES: STATEMENT SCALE

We append here only one statement scale, Social Attitudes II, or SA-II. For a description of the construction of this 26-item scale, see Chapter 7 and Kerlinger (1970a). The Liberalism *(L)* and Conservatism *(C)* means, standard deviations, alpha reliability coefficients, and correlations between the *L* and *C* subscales of samples of graduate students of education in New York, Texas, and North Carolina are given in Table 7.3. Evidently the subscales are reliable. The other characteristics and the results of item factor analyses were discussed in the text.

L and *C* scores for each individual are calculated as described earlier: sum the *L* scores and the *C* scores separately.[4] That is, each subject receives two scores. (Again, I recommend dividing the total scores by the number of items to yield mean *L* and mean *C* scores for each subject.) The *L* and *C* items are so marked.

Readers should bear in mind that SA-II is about 15 years old and can probably bear revision. Researchers should feel free to delete and add items as they see fit. A review of the items seems to indicate, however, that most of them are still timely and appropriate. Adding items on abortion, women's rights, conservation, and other contemporary issues should improve the scale.

(SA-II)

Social Attitudes Scale

Instructions: Given below are statements on various social problems about which we all have beliefs, opinions, and attitudes. We all think differently about such matters, and this scale is an attempt to let you express your beliefs and opinions. There are no right and wrong answers. Please respond to each of the items as follows:

Agree very strongly:	+3	Disagree very strongly:	−3
Agree strongly:	+2	Disagree strongly:	−2
Agree:	+1	Disagree:	−1

For example, if you agree very strongly with a statement, you would write +3 on the short line preceding the statement, but if you should happen to disagree with it, you would put −1 in front of it. Respond to each statement as best you can. Go rapidly but carefully. Do not spend too much time on any one statement; try to respond and then go on. Don't go back once you have marked a statement.

   C   1. Individuals who are against churches and religions should not be allowed to teach in colleges.

---

[4] SA-II is given in Shaw and Wright (1967, pp. 322–324) but with incorrect instructions, which say to reverse the scoring of conservative items. Presumably one emerges with one score per subject instead of two. Robinson, Rusk, and Head (1968, pp. 98–101), who include the scale in their anthology and who specifically and correctly recommend two scores, as recommended above, nevertheless include a footnote with the scale: "These are conservative items whose weights should be reversed for scoring purposes." (The items referred to were marked with asterisks.) Such is the power of the bipolarity assumption!

___L___   2. Large fortunes should be taxed fairly heavily over and above income taxes.

___L___   3. Both public and private universities and colleges should get generous aid from both state and federal governments.

___C___   4. Science and society would both be better off if scientists took no part in politics.

___L___   5. Society should be quicker to throw out old ideas and traditions and to adopt new thinking and customs.

___L___   6. To ensure adequate care of the sick, we need to change radically the present system of privately controlled medical care.

___C___   7. If civilization is to survive, there must be a turning back to religion.

___C___   8. A first consideration in any society is the protection of property rights.

___C___   9. Government ownership and management of utilities lead to bureaucracy and inefficiency.

___C___ 10. If the United States takes part in any sort of world organization, we should be sure that we lose none of our power and influence.

___L___ 11. Funds for school construction should come from state and federal government loans at no interest or very low interest.

___C___ 12. Inherited racial characteristics play more of a part in the achievements of individuals and groups than is generally known.

___L___ 13. Federal Government aid for the construction of schools is long overdue, and should be instituted as a permanent policy.

___L___ 14. Our present economic system should be reformed so that profits are replaced by reimbursements for useful work.

___L___ 15. Public enterprises like railroads should not make profits; they are entitled to fares sufficient to enable them to pay only a fair interest on the actual cash capital they have invested.

___C___ 16. Government laws and regulations should be such as first to ensure the prosperity of business since the prosperity of all depends on the prosperity of business.

___L___ 17. All individuals who are intellectually capable of benefiting from it should get college education, at public expense if necessary.

___C___ 18. The well-being of a nation depends mainly on its industry and business.

___L___ 19. True democracy is limited in the United States because of the special privileges enjoyed by business and industry.

___L___ 20. The gradual social ownership of industry needs to be encouraged if we are ever to cure some of the ills of our society.

___C___ 21. There are too many professors in our colleges and universities who are radical in their social and political beliefs.

___C___ 22. There should be no government interference with business and trade.

___C___ 23. Some sort of religious education should be given in public schools.

  L   24. Unemployment insurance is an inalienable right of the working man.

  C   25. Individuals with the ability and foresight to earn and accumulate wealth should have the right to enjoy that wealth without government interference and regulations.

  L   26. The United Nations should be whole-heartedly supported by all of us.

SOCIAL ATTITUDES: REFERENT SCALES

Three social attitude referent scales are given below: Referents I, IV, and VI, or REF-I, REF-IV, and REF-VI. Although there is duplication of items in the three scales, they are given in their entirety so that researchers can use the scale that suits their needs. The instructions given with REF-I can be used with REF-IV and REF-VI. They are a bit long because the task of the respondent is unusual. If shorter instructions are desired, the second paragraph can be used alone. For data on REF-I see Chapter 3, Tables 3.1, 3.2, 3.3, and 3.4 and Figure 3.1. Data on REF-IV are given in Chapter 7—Tables 7.6, 7.8, and 7.10. American REF-VI data are given in Chapters 8 and 9, Tables 8.1, 8.2, 8.3, 9.1, 9.2, 9.3, 9.4, 9.5, and 9.6.

The scales as given are shorter than the original scales because the originals included items used for other purposes. For example, REF-I originally had 50 items; it now has 48 items, 24 L and 24 C. REF-IV originally had 80 items; it now has 54 items, 27 L and 27 C. The deleted items were psychometrically questionable—low item-total correlations or low factor loadings—or were duplicates.

REF-VI is the American version of the scale used in the cross-cultural research described in Chapters 8 and 9. It had 78 items of which 60 could be clearly categorized as L and C for estimating subscale reliabilities. The 18 items not included among these are those not marked L or C. The 60-item scale can be used for measurement of the L and C dimensions. (At the time of scale construction, we were not sure of the categorization of the marked items. As usual, researchers should adapt the scale to their needs and purposes.) The results of the factor analyses reported in Chapter 8 included all 78 items—see Tables 8.2 and 8.3. Routine scale data are reported in Table 8.1. Note that the United States sample data were based on the 60 items, 30 L and 30 C mentioned above. Also note the high reliabilities of the L and C subscales.

It is emphasized that researchers may want to construct their own scales using items from the above referents scales and adding their own referent items. To be sure, researchers may wish to use a scale that has data to back it up. Then one of the scales can be used as it is. Sometimes, however, users may wish longer or just different *L* and *C* scales. One of the virtues of referent attitude measurement is the considerable flexibility that is possible.

The writer has constructed two additional referent scales to measure liberalism and conservatism as efficiently as possible: REF-IX and REF-X. REF-IX was constructed by taking the best 50 items, 25 *L* and 25 *C*, from previous research, based on the magnitudes of factor loadings and item-total correlations, *L* items with *L* totals and *C* items with *C* totals. REF-X is a short version of REF-IX. The seemingly best 30 items, 15 *L* and 15 *C*, were taken from REF-IX and set up in a "new" scale. These items have been marked with an asterisk in REF-IX. Unfortunately, these scales have not been used; so there are no data on them. Because of the method of selection—only the items that "did well" in earlier analyses were selected—REF-IX should yield satisfactory reliabilities and factorial validity. But REF-X is more problematical because of the considerably fewer items used.

(REF-I)

Social Concepts

Ideas confront us on all sides. And these ideas affect our ways of thinking and behaving. The notions *equality* and *moderation,* for example, to some extent affect us and the way we think about ourselves and react to other people. Notions like *love of country* and *women* have rich meanings for us, meanings that are bound up with our beliefs and opinions. Of course, different people react differently to many concepts. Some people, for instance, will feel positively while others will feel negatively toward a word like *Medicare.*

This instrument has been designed to help us study the meanings and feelings associated with concepts. More specifically, we are studying people's reactions to a wide variety of words and phrases that express or imply economic, political, religious, educational, and social ideas. A number of these words and phrases are given below. People react differently to such concepts or ideas, as we said above, and we are trying to find out how their reactions differ. We would like you to indicate your positive or negative feeling about each of the words or phrases as follows:

Highly positive:	$+3$	Highly negative:	-3
Very positive:	$+2$	Very negative:	-2
Positive:	$+1$	Negative:	-1

Suppose for example, you are reacting to the word *insurance,* and you are very favorable to insurance for yourself and for others. You might respond with $+3$ or $+2$. On the other hand, you may disapprove strongly of, or feel negatively about, insurance. In this case, you would write a -3 or a -2 in front of the word. A third alternative is that your feeling about the word may be rather weak: you may approve it (or disapprove it), but only mildly or slightly. In such a case, you would write a $+1$ (or -1) before the word.

You may, of course, have reservations about many of the concepts. For example, you may feel that your response would depend on the way a word or phrase is used or the context in which it is used. Try to think of the *general* significance and meaning of the words and phrases. That is, how do you feel about them *in general*?

There are no right or wrong responses in a thing like this. Respond as best you can—and respond to all the items, even if you're sometimes not too sure of your feeling. Go rapidly but carefully. Once you have responded, do not go back. We want your first careful reactions.

REF-I

C	1.	private property
L	2.	scientific knowledge
C	3.	religion
C	4.	racial purity
L	5.	economic reform
L	6.	child freedom
L	7.	poverty program
C	8.	patriotism
C	9.	moral standards in education
L	10.	Social Security
L	11.	separation of church and state
C	12.	national sovereignty
L	13.	Jews
C	14.	family
L	15.	self-expression of children
C	16.	homogeneous grouping
C	17.	school discipline
L	18.	racial integration
C	19.	church
L	20.	social change through education
L	21.	children's needs
C	22.	neighborhood schools
L	23.	civil rights
L	24.	federal aid to education
L	25.	Negroes
L	26.	United Nations
L	27.	pupil personality
C	28.	subject matter
C	29.	education as intellectual training
C	30.	trusted leaders
L	31.	academic freedom
L	32.	child-centered curriculum
C	33.	transmission of the cultural heritage
C	34.	Christian
C	35.	the three R's
L	36.	Supreme Court
C	37.	capitalism
C	38.	teaching of spiritual values
L	39.	social planning
C	40.	religious education
L	41.	activity program in schools
L	42.	desegregation
L	43.	socialized medicine
L	44.	children's interests
C	45.	tradition
C	46.	real estate
C	47.	free enterprise
C	48.	faith in God

REF-IV

L	1.	poverty program
L	2.	pupil personality
C	3.	discipline
L	4.	women's liberation
C	5.	religion
L	6.	collective bargaining
L	7.	open admission to college
C	8.	free enterprise
L	9.	sexual freedom
L	10.	socialized medicine
L	11.	child-centered curriculum
C	12.	the three R's
C	13.	Christian
C	14.	private property
L	15.	Negroes
C	16.	money
C	17.	competition
L	18.	trade unions
L	19.	children's interests
C	20.	law and order
C	21.	cultural heritage
L	22.	equality of women
C	23.	manners
L	24.	economic reform
L	25.	civil rights

L 26. federal housing projects
C 27. religious education
L 28. liberalized abortion laws
C 29. patriotism
C 30. profits
L 31. human personality
L 32. equality
C 33. church
C 34. corporate industry
C 35. capitalism
C 36. moral standards
L 37. racial equality
L 38. social change through education
L 39. freedom
C 40. social stability
C 41. subject matter
C 42. national sovereignty
L 43. social planning
C 44. morality
L 45. racial integration
C 46. real estate
C 47. business
L 48. desegregation
L 49. children's needs
C 50. economic stability
L 51. social welfare
C 52. tradition
L 53. Social Security
C 54. authority

REF-VI

L 1. human personality
_ 2. duty
C 3. teaching of spiritual values
C 4. national sovereignty
L 5. pupil personality
_ 6. objective tests
C 7. business
C 8. cultural heritage
_ 9. affection
L 10. labor unions
_ 11. achievement
L 12. sexual freedom
C 13. real estate
C 14. capitalism
_ 15. individual effort
C 16. military training
C 17. family
_ 18. teachers
C 19. manners
C 20. Christian
C 21. moral standards
L 22. liberalized abortion laws
_ 23. feeling
L 24. social planning

C 25. religion
L 26. children's interests
C 27. private property
C 28. tradition
_ 29. scientists
L 30. economic reform
C 31. America
L 32. civil rights
L 33. Jews
_ 34. psychological testing
L 35. birth control
C 36. social stability
L 37. equality of women
C 38. money
C 39. morality
_ 40. love
C 41. faith in God
L 42. sex education
_ 43. divorce
C 44. church
C 45. corporate industry
_ 46. human warmth
L 47. United Nations
C 48. free enterprise
C 49. patriotism
L 50. social change through education
L 51. children's needs
L 52. scientific research
_ 53. Soviet Union
L 54. government ownership of utilities
C 55. law and order
_ 56. rationality
C 57. discipline
C 58. competition
L 59. socialized medicine
L 60. government price controls
L 61. international cooperation
L 62. freedom
C 63. loyalty
_ 64. consideration for others
_ 65. individual initiative
C 66. profits
L 67. racial equality
_ 68. privacy
L 69. scientific theory
_ 70. professors
L 71. women's liberation
C 72. authority
L 73. social welfare
L 74. world government
L 75. equality
L 76. collective bargaining
C 77. work
L 78. reason

Note. The items labeled *L* and *C* were those used in the American analysis to calculate *L* and *C* statistics. Some of them, however, have been found not to be among the better items: 8, 33, 52, 69, 78. One, 8, is a *C* item; the others are *L* items. They can be omitted without loss, or other items can be substituted for them. On the other hand, the following items, not labeled *L* or *C,* have been found to be satisfactory *L* and *C* items: *L:* 9, 23, 40, 43, 46; *C:* 2, 11, 15, 65. These items can either be added to the scale or used to substitute for other items.

REF-IX

L	1. economic reform
C	*2. social stability
L	*3. feeling
L	4. women's liberation
C	5. real estate
C	*6. discipline
L	*7. government price controls
L	*8. freedom
C	*9. business
C	*10. authority
C	*11. faith in God
L	12. racial integration
L	*13. free abortion
L	*14. sexual freedom
C	*15. corporate industry
C	*16. obedience of children
C	17. morality
C	18. respect for elders
L	19. liberalized abortion laws
L	20. social equality
L	*21. collective bargaining
L	*22. socialized medicine
C	23. church
C	*24. law and order
L	*25. racial equality
C	*26. private property
L	27. birth control
C	*28. capitalism
C	29. money
C	*30. social status
C	31. religious education
L	*32. social change
C	*33. moral standards
C	*34. patriotism
C	35. profits
L	*36. equality
C	37. education as intellectual training
L	38. federal aid to education
L	*39. social planning
C	40. competition
L	41. human warmth
C	42. family
C	*43. free enterprise
L	*44. civil rights
L	45. world government
C	*46. religion
L	*47. children's interests
L	*48. labor unions
L	*49. equality of women
L	50. United Nations

Note. REF-X items are marked with an asterisk.

Appendix C

Response Set Research

To ascertain whether response set might be influencing the social attitude summated-rating scales used in the research reported in this book, four small studies were done early and late in the research. In essence, the research consisted of administering to varied samples of students and nonstudents liberalism *(L)* and conservatism *(C)* statement and referent scales together with well-known measures of response set. If response set or style influences the social and educational attitude measures, then scales designed to measure different kinds of set should correlate significantly with the attitude measures. In the first and most important study, a number of other psychological variables were also used as a "control." The social attitude *L* and *C* measures should for various reasons correlate substantially with three of these measures but not with the response set measure. That is, the first study was an effort to obtain evidence on the construct validity of the *L* and *C* attitude scales as well as a check on the possible influence of response set.

The *L* and *C* subscales of SA-II (Social Attitudes II, SAL and SAC), the 26-item (13 *L* and 13 *C*) 7-point summated-rating scale described in Chapter 7 and reproduced in Appendix B, three measures of response set, and four psychological measures were administered to 161 graduate students of education (Kerlinger, 1970a). The response set measures were Edwards' (1958) Social Desirability Scale, Bass' (1956) Social Acquiescence Scale, and Couch and Keniston's (1960) Agreement Response Scale. The psychological measures were the Wonderlic Personnel Test (1961), a short intelligence test, Gough's (1957) rigidity scale, the F Scale (Adorno, Frenkel-Brunswik, Levinson, & Sanford, 1950), and the D (Dogmatism)

TABLE C.1
Correlations of Social Attitudes, L and C, with F and D Scales,
Rigidity, Intelligence, and Three Response Set Measures;
Rotated First Factor Loadings of All Variables, $N = 161$[a]

| Measure | Correlations | | Factor |
	SAL	SAC	Loadings
F Scale	-.05	.74*	*.82*
D Scale	.27*	.38*	*.49*
Rigidity	.11	.50*	*.63*
Intelligence	.07	-.20*	-.21
Social Desirability	-.11	-.02	-.05
Social Acquiescence	.02	.51*	*.66*
Agreement Response	.17	.14	.20
SAL	1.00	-.26*	-.14
SAC	-.26*	1.00	*.86*

[a] SAL: Social Attitudes, Liberalism; SAC: Social Attitudes, Conservatism; Rigidity: Gough-Sanford Rigidity Scale; Intelligence: Wonderlic Personnel Test; Social Desirability: Edwards Social Desirability Scale; Social Acquiescence: Bass Social Acquiescence Scale; Agreement Response: Couch-Keniston Agreement Response Scale. Significant loadings ($\geq .35$) are italicized.
*Significant at at least the .05 level.

Scale (Rokeach, 1960). The nine measures were intercorrelated and factor analyzed with the centroid method. Graphic orthogonal rotations were used.

The correlations between the three response set measures and the four psychological measures and the L and C measures (SAL and SAC) are given in Table C.1, together with the rotated factor loadings of the rotated first factor of the factor analysis. It was expected that SAC would correlate positively and substantially with F, D, and rigidity, but not with the response set measures nor with intelligence. SAL's correlations with the other variables could not be predicted. If anything, it might correlate positively and modestly with one or more of the response set measures.

It can be seen from the table that SAC correlates highly (.74) with F and moderately with D (.38) and Rigidity (.50). But it also correlates substantially with Bass' Social Acquiescence Scale (.51). Can it be that Bass' scale, with its "good-sounding" cliches, measures conservatism to some extent, or is SAC contaminated with social acquiescence? SAL correlates with almost nothing, except low correlations with the D Scale (.27) and with SAC ($-.26$). The factor loadings in the third data column of the table succinctly summarize the relations. SAC has the highest loading (.86) with F a close second (.82). The factor is either Conservatism or Authoritarianism. Which? It is possible that conservatism permeates all the variables with substantial positive loadings. In any case, the conservative dimension of the SA Scale correlates with these measures and loads on

TABLE C.2
Correlations Among REFL, REFC, M-C, AR, SA, and SD;
$N = 87$, Above Diagonal; $N = 32$, Below Diagonal[a]

	REFL	REFC	M-C	AR	SA	SD
REFL	1.00	.05	.12	.13	.08	.01
REFC	-.25	1.00	.37*	.01	.25*	.16
M-C	.01	-.07	1.00	-.12	.17	.43*
AR	-.09	.04	-.36*	1.00	.49*	-.49*
SA	.29	.15	-.08	.45*	1.00	-.24*
SD	.04	-.26	.50*	-.41*	-.32*	1.00

[a]REFL: REF-I-L; REFC: REF-I-C; M-C: Marlowe-Crowne Social Desirability Scale;
  AR: Couch-Keniston Agreement Response Scale; SA: Bass Social Acquiescence Scale;
  SD: Edwards Social Desirability Scale.
*: Significant at at least the .05 level.

the factor "as it should." (See Adorno et al., 1950, Chs. V, VII, et passim; McClosky, 1958). It is not possible to say much or anything about SAL except that it appears to be virtually independent of the other measures.

In a similar study done about ten years later (unpublished), REF-I L and C and four response set measures were administered to 87 California undergraduates and 32 California non-students. The response set measures were: Edwards' Social Desirability Scale, the Marlowe-Crowne (Crowne & Marlowe, 1964) Social Desirability Scale, the Couch and Keniston Agreement Response Scale, and Bass' Social Acquiescence Scale. The correlations among the six measures for the $N = 87$ sample are given above the diagonal of Table C.2. The same correlations for the $N = 32$ group are given below the diagonal. The correlations among the response set measures are consistent; they need not be discussed. REFL correlates with nothing else; REFC, however, is significantly correlated with the Marlowe-Crowne scale and with Social Acquiescence (Bass). These correlations will be discussed later.

REF-I and the Marlowe-Crowne Scale were administered to 83 graduate students of education in North Carolina; measures of political preference (Democrat = 1; Republican = 0) and sex (Female = 1; Male = 0) were also obtained. REF-I was also administered a second time, about two or three weeks later. Neither REFL nor REFC, first or second administrations, correlated with the Marlowe-Crowne Scale. REFC, however, correlated with Democrat-Republican in both administrations of REF-I. Correlations with Sex were negligible. (The r's between the first and second administrations of REF-I were high: .88 and .86.)

Evidently response set is not much of a threat to the social attitude scales. The only consistent correlation was between SAC and the Bass Social Acquiescence Scale. As suggested earlier, this may be due to "virtue" variance common to the two scales: individuals who agree with the cliches of the SA Scale tend also to agree with conservative statements. In a later check on social desirability, the Marlowe-Crowne Scale and two recent social attitudes referents scales, REF-VII and REF-VIII, of 40 items each, written to be alternate forms with no items in common, were administered to 87 students of Pace University in New York.[1] The correlations between both scales' L subscales and the Marlowe-Crowne scale were low and not significant, but both C subscales' correlations with the Marlowe-Crowne were significant at the .01 level (.42 and .30). An examination of the Marlowe-Crowne Scale items seems to indicate, again, a "virtue" component—"I never hesitate to go out of my way to help someone in trouble"; "I am always courteous, even to people who are disagreeable." Perhaps this component and the traditional and conventional flavor of the conservative referents—*church, moral standards, social status, respect for elders,* and the like—are what produce the correlations. That it is not social desirability, in and of itself, is indicated by the lack of correlation between the liberal referents and the Marlowe-Crowne Scale and by the lack of correlation between REFL and REFC and Edwards' Social Desirability Scale (see Tables C.1 and C.2).

This excursion into response set and its possible influence on the attitude scales used in the research reported in this book seems to indicate, in general, that it has little or no such influence—at least the response set measured in the studies just reported. There were two exceptions: the significant correlations between Bass' social acquiescence and conservatism and between Marlowe-Crowne's social desirability and conservatism. Rather than social desirability or social acquiescence, however, it is believed that the virtuous-sounding cliches of both scales are measuring, in addition to response set, an aspect of conservatism, perhaps conventionalism (see McClosky, 1958). This is of course speculation, which can become more than speculation only by research specifically directed to the possibility mentioned. In any case, the weight of the evidence attests to the validity of the L and C social attitude scales uncontaminated by response set.

---

[1] I am grateful to Professor Paul Echandia, Pace University, for his help in obtaining the data of which the above is a part.

References

Adorno, T., Frenkel-Brunswik, E., Levinson, D., & Sanford, R. *The authoritarian personality*. New York: Harper & Row, 1950.

Allport, F. *Theories of perception and the concept of structure*. New York: Wiley, 1955.

Allport, G. Attitudes. In C. Murchison (Ed.), *A handbook of social psychology*. Worcester, Mass.: Clark University Press, 1935.

Allport, G. The historical background of modern social psychology. In G. Lindzey (Ed.), *Handbook of social psychology* (Vol. 1), Reading, Mass.: Addison-Wesley, 1954.

Atkinson, R., & Shiffrin, R. Control processes in memory. In D. Norman, *Memory and attention* (2nd ed.), New York: Wiley, 1976.

Auerbach, M. *The conservative illusion*. New York: Columbia University Press, 1959.

Baddeley, A. *The psychology of memory*. New York: Harper & Row, 1976.

Baggaley, A. Countercultural and opposing values at a two-year college. *Multivariate Experimental Clinical Research*, 1976, *2*, 57–62.

Bagozzi, R., & Burnkrant, R. Attitude organization and the attitude-behavior relationship. *Journal of Personality and Social Psychology*, 1979, *37*, 913–929.

Bass, B. Development and evaluation of a scale for measuring social acquiescence. *Journal of Abnormal and Social Psychology*, 1956, *53*, 296–299.

Beale, H. *Are American teachers free?* New York: Scribner's, 1936.

Bell, J., & Miller, A. Congruence between educational attitudes and academic philosophies. *Psychology in the Schools*, 1979, *16*, 154–158.

Bem, D., & Funder, D. Predicting more of the people more of the time: Assessing the personality of situations. *Psychological Review*, 1978, *85*, 485–501.

Bentler, P. Semantic space is (approximately) bipolar. *Journal of Psychology*, 1969, *71*, 33–40.

Bentler, P. Multivariate analysis with latent variables: Causal modeling, *Annual Review of Psychology*, 1980, *31*, 419–456.

Bentler, P., & Speckart, G. Models of attitude-behavior relations. *Psychological Review*, 1979, *86*, 452–464.

Birenbaum, M., & Zak, I. Contradictory or complementary? Reassessment of two competing theories of the structure of attitudes. *Multivariate Behavioral Research*, 1982, *17*, 503–514.

Bishop, G. The effect of education on ideological consistency, *Public Opinion Quarterly*, 1976, *40*, 337–348.

Bittner, E. Radicalism. In D. Sills (Ed.), *International encyclopedia of the social sciences*. New York: Macmillan & Free Press, 1968.

Bledsoe, J. Validity and reliability of two brief scales of educational attitudes. *Perceptual and Motor Skills*, 1976, *42*, 1331–1334.

B'nai B'rith, Anti-Defamation League. The John Birch society. *Facts*, 1955, *51*, 616–623.

Bock, R., & Bargmann, R. Analysis of covariance structures. *Psychometrika*, 1966, *31*, 507–534.

Bower, G. Organizational factors in memory, *Cognitive Psychology*, 1970, *1*, 18–46.

Bradburn, N. *The structure of well-being*. Chicago: Aldine, 1969.

Brodbeck, M. Models, meaning, and theories. In M. Brodbeck (Ed.), *Readings in the philosophy of the social sciences*. New York: Macmillan, 1968.

Brown, R. *Words and things*. New York: Free Press, 1958.

Brubacher, J. *Modern philosophies of education* (3rd ed.). New York: McGraw-Hill, 1962.

Bruner, J., Goodnow, J., & Austin, G. *A study of thinking*. New York: Wiley, 1956.

Burke, E. *Reflections on the revolution in France*. Indianapolis: Liberal Arts Press, 1955 (1790).

Campbell, A., Converse, P., Miller, W., & Stokes, D. *The American voter*. New York: Wiley, 1960.

Cattell, R. *Factor analysis*. New York: Harper, 1952.

Cattell, R. Theory of fluid and crystallized intelligence: A critical experiment. *Journal of Educational Psychology*, 1963, *54*, 1–22.

Cattell, R., & Burdsal, C. The radial parcel double factoring design: A solution to the item vs. parcel controversy. *Multivariate Behavioral Research*, 1975, *10*, 165–179.

Cherlin, A., & Reeder, L. The dimensions of psychological well-being: A critical review. *Sociological Methods & Research*, 1975, *4*, 189–214.

Coan, R. Facts, factors, and artifacts: The quest for psychological meaning. *Psychological Review*, 1964, *71*, 123–140.

Cliff, N. Some cautions concerning the application of causal modeling methods. *Multivariate Behavioral Research*, 1983, *18*, 115–126.

Commager, H. *The American mind: An interpretation of American thought and character since the 1880's*. New Haven: Yale University Press, 1950.

Comrey, A. Comparison of personality and attitude variables. *Educational and Psychological Measurement*, 1966, *26*, 853–860.

Comrey, A., & Newmeyer, J. Measurement of radicalism-conservatism. *Journal of Social Psychology*, 1965, *47*, 357–369.

Constantinople, A. Masculinity-femininity: An exception to a famous dictum? *Psychological Bulletin*, 1973, *80*, 389–407.

Converse, P. The nature of belief systems in mass publics. In D. Apter (Ed.), *Ideology and discontent*. New York: Free Press, 1964.

Costa, P., & McCrae, R. Influence of extraversion and neuroticism on subjective well-being: Happy and unhappy people. *Journal of Personality and Social Psychology*, 1980, *38*, 668–678.

Couch, A., & Keniston, K. Yeasayers and naysayers: Agreeing response set as a personality variable. *Journal of Abnormal and Social Psychology*, 1960, *60*, 151–174.

Cremin, L. *The transformation of the school: Progressivism in American education, 1876–1957*. New York: Knopf, 1961.

Cronbach, L. Response sets and test validity. *Educational and Psychological Measurement*, 1946, *6*, 475–494.

Cronbach, L. Further evidence on response sets and test design. *Educational and Psychological Measurement*, 1950, *10*, 3–31.

Cronbach, L. Coefficient alpha and the internal structure of tests. *Psychometrika*, 1951, *16*, 297–334.

Cronbach, L., & Meehl, P. Construct validity in psychological tests. *Psychological Bulletin*, 1955, *52*, 281–302.

Crowne, D., & Marlowe, D. *The approval motive.* New York: Wiley, 1964.

Curti, M. *The social ideas of American educators.* New York: Scribner's, 1935.

de Tocqueville, A. *Democracy in America.* New York: Vintage Books, 1945.

Dewey, J. *The child and the curriculum.* Chicago: University of Chicago Press, 1902.

Dewey, J. *Democracy and education.* New York: Macmillan, 1916.

Dupuis, A. *Philosophy of education in historical perspective.* Chicago: Rand McNally, 1966.

Edwards, A. *The social desirability variable in personality assessment and research.* New York: Dryden Press, 1958.

Edwards, A., & Walsh, J. Response sets in standard and experimental personality scales. *American Educational Research Journal*, 1964, *1*, 52–61.

Eysenck, H. General social attitudes. *Journal of Social Psychology*, 1944, *19*, 207–227.

Eysenck, H. Primary social attitudes: 1. The organization and measurement of social attitudes. *International Journal of Opinion and Attitude Measurement*, 1947, *1*, 49–84.

Eysenck, H. Social attitudes and social class. *British Journal of Social and Clinical Psychology*, 1971, *10*, 210–212.

Eysenck, H. The structure of social attitudes. *British Journal of Social and Clinical Psychology*, 1975, *14*, 323–331.

Eysenck, H. Structure of social attitudes. *Psychological Reports*, 1976, *39*, 463–466.

Eysenck, H., & Wilson, G. *The psychological basis of ideology.* Lancaster, England: MTP Press, 1978.

Ferguson, L. Primary social attitudes. *Journal of Psychology*, 1939, *8*, 217–223.

Ferguson, L. Primary social attitudes of the 1960s and those of the 1930s. *Psychological Reports*, 1973, *33*, 655–664.

Festinger, L. A theory of social comparison processes. *Human Relations*, 1954, *7*, 117–140.

Festinger, L. *A theory of cognitive dissonance.* Stanford: Stanford University Press, 1957.

Fleming, D. Attitude: The history of a concept. In D. Fleming & B. Bailyn (Eds.), *Perspectives in American History* (Vol. I). Cambridge, Mass.: Charles Warren Center for Studies in American History, 1967.

Forster, A., & Epstein, B. *Danger on the right.* New York: Random House, 1964.

Free, L., & Cantril, H. *The political beliefs of Americans: A study of public opinion.* New Brunswick, NJ: Rutgers University Press, 1967.

Fruchter, B. Manipulative and hypothesis-testing factor-analytic experimental designs. In R. Cattell (Ed.), *Handbook of multivariate experimental psychology.* Chicago: Rand McNally, 1966.

Girvetz, H. *The evolution of liberalism.* New York: Collier Books, 1963 (1950).

Goldstein, K. *The organism.* New York: American Book Co., 1939.

Gough, H. *California Psychological Inventory.* Palo Alto, CA.: Consulting Psychologists Press, 1957.

Guilford, J. *Psychometric methods* (2nd ed.). New York: McGraw-Hill, 1954.

Guilford, J. The structure of intellect. *Psychological Bulletin*, 1956, *53*, 267–293.

Guilford, J. Three faces of intellect. *American Psychologist*, 1959, *14*, 469–479.

Guilford, J. *The nature of human intelligence.* New York: McGraw-Hill, 1967.

Guttman, L. "Best possible" systematic estimates of communalities. *Psychometrika*, 1956, *21*, 273–285.

Guttman, L. The first laws of attitude and intelligence. Address given at the meeting of the American Educational Research Association, San Francisco, April 1976.

Harman, H. *Modern factor analysis* (3rd ed.). Chicago: University of Chicago Press, 1976.

Hartz, L. *The liberal tradition in America*. New York: Harcourt, Brace & World, 1955.

Hebb, D. *The organization of behavior*. New York: Wiley, 1949.

Hendrickson, A., & White, P. Promax: A quick method for rotation to oblique simple structure. *British Journal of Statistical Psychology*, 1964, *17*, 65–70.

Henry, N. (Ed.). *Philosophies of education*. 41st Yearbook of the NSSE (Part I). Chicago: University of Chicago Press, 1942.

Hewitt, J., Eysenck, H., & Eaves, L. Structure of social attitudes after twenty-five years: A replication. *Psychological Reports*, 1977, *40*, 183–188.

Hicks, J., & Wright, J. Convergent-discriminant validation and factor analysis of five scales of liberalism-conservatism. *Journal of Personality and Social Psychology*, 1970, *14*, 114–120.

Hobhouse, L. *Liberalism*. New York: Henry Holt, n.d.

Hofman, J. *Attitudes toward education and the meaning of educational concepts: A study of consistency*. Unpublished doctoral dissertation, New York University, 1964.

Hofman, J. Dimensionality (structure) of educational attitude referents: Note on validity of a criterial referents theory of attitudes. *Psychological Reports*, 1970, *26*, 215–217.

Huba, G., & Bentler, P. On the usefulness of latent variable causal modeling in testing theories of naturally occurring events (including adolescent drug use): A rejoinder to Martin. *Journal of Personality and Social Psychology*, 1982, *43*, 604–611.

Humphreys, L. Number of cases and number of factors: An example where N is very large. *Educational and Psychological Measurement*, 1964, *24*, 457–466.

Humphreys, L., & Ilgen, D. Note on a criterion for the number of common factors. *Educational and Psychological Measurement*, 1969, *29*, 571–578.

Huntington, S. Conservatism as an ideology. *American Political Science Review*, 1957, *51*, 454–473.

Johnson, D., & Ahlgren, A. Relationship between student attitudes about cooperation and competition and attitudes toward schooling. *Journal of Educational Psychology*, 1976, *68*, 92–102.

Jöreskog, K. Statistical analysis of sets of congeneric tests. *Psychometrika*, 1971, *36*, 109–133.

Jöreskog, K. Analyzing psychological data by structural analysis of covariance matrices. In D. Krantz, R. Atkinson, R. Luce, & P. Suppes (Eds.), *Contemporary developments in mathematical psychology* (Vol. II): *Measurement, psychophysics, and information processing*. San Francisco: Freeman, 1974.

Jöreskog, K. Structural analysis of covariance and correlation matrices. *Psychometrika*, 1978, *43*, 443–477.

Jöreskog, K., & Sörbom, D. *LISREL-IV: Analysis of linear structural relationships by the method of maximum likelihood*. Chicago: National Educational Resources, 1978.

Jöreskog, K., & Sörbom, D. *Advances in factor analysis and structural equation models*. Cambridge, MA: Abt Books, 1979.

Jöreskog, K., & Sörbom, D. *LISREL-V: Analysis of linear structural relationships by maximum likelihood and least squares methods*. Uppsala: Dept. of Statistics, Univ. of Uppsala, 1981.

Kaiser, H. The varimax criterion for analytic rotation in factor analysis. *Psychometrika, 22*, 187–200, 1958.

Katz, D., & Stotland, E. A preliminary statement to a theory of attitude structure and change. In S. Koch (Ed.), *Psychology: A study of a science* (Vol. 3). New York: McGraw-Hill, 1959.

Kerlinger, F. The attitude structure of the individual: A *Q*-study of the educational attitudes of professors and laymen. *Genetic Psychology Monographs*, 1956, *53*, 283–329, (a)

Kerlinger, F. The origin of the doctrine of permissiveness in American education. *Progressive Education*, 1956, *33*, 161–165, (b)

Kerlinger, F. Progressivism and traditionalism: Basic factors of educational attitudes. *Journal of Social Psychology*, 1958, *48*, 111–135.

Kerlinger, F. Factor invariance in the measurement of attitudes toward education. *Educational and Psychological Measurement*, 1961, *21*, 273–285.

Kerlinger, F. Attitudes toward education and perceptions of teacher characteristics: A *Q* study. *American Educational Research Journal*, 1966, *3*, 159–168.

Kerlinger, F. Social attitudes and their criterial referents: A structural theory. *Psychological Review*, 1967, *74*, 110–122. (a)

Kerlinger, F. The first- and second-order factor structures of attitudes toward education. *American Educational Research Journal*, 1967, *4*, 191–205. (b)

Kerlinger, F. A social attitude scale: Evidence on reliability and validity. *Psychological Reports*, 1970, *26*, 379–383. (a)

Kerlinger, F. Comment on Zdep and Marco's "Commentary on Kerlinger's structural theory of attitudes." *Psychological Reports*, 1970, *26*, 289–290. (b)

Kerlinger, F. A *Q* validation of the structure of social attitudes. *Educational and Psychological Measurement*, 1972, *32*, 987–995. (a)

Kerlinger, F. *Q* methodology in behavioral research. In S. Brown & D. Brenner (Eds.), *Science, psychology, and communication: Essays honoring William Stephenson*. New York: Teachers College Press, 1972. (b)

Kerlinger, F. The structure and content of social attitude referents: A preliminary study. *Educational and Psychological Measurement*, 1972, *32*, 613–630. (c)

Kerlinger, F. *Foundations of behavioral research* (2nd ed.). New York: Holt, Rinehart and Winston, 1973.

Kerlinger, F. Similarities and differences in social attitudes in four Western countries. *International Journal of Psychology*, 1978, *13*, 25–37.

Kerlinger, F. *Behavioral research: A conceptual approach*. New York: Holt, Rinehart and Winston, 1979.

Kerlinger, F. Analysis of covariance structure tests of a criterial referents theory of attitudes. *Multivariate Behavioral Research*, 1980, *15*, 403–422. (a)

Kerlinger, F. Social attitudes of Dutch citizens and students. *Nederlands Tijdschrift voor de Psychologie*, 1980, *35*, 383–396. (b)

Kerlinger, F., & Kaya, E. The construction and factor analytic validation of scales to measure attitudes toward education. *Educational and Psychological Measurement*, 1959, *19*, 13–29.

Kerlinger, F., Middendorp, C., & Amón, J. The structure of social attitudes in three countries: Tests of a criterial referent theory. *International Journal of Psychology*, 1976, *11*, 265–279.

Kerlinger, F., & Pedhazur, E. *Multiple regression in behavioral research*. New York: Holt, Rinehart and Winston, 1973.

Kerr W. *Tulane factors of liberalism-conservatism: Manual of instructions*. Chicago: Psychometric Affiliates, 1946.

Kerr, W. Untangling the liberalism-conservatism continuum. *Journal of Social Psychology*, 1952, *35*, 111–125.

Kirk, R. *The conservative mind* (Rev. Ed.), Chicago: Henry Regnery, 1960.

Knitzer, H. Ideology and American political elites. *Public Opinion Quarterly*, 1978, *42*, 484–502.

Krech, D., & Crutchfield, R. *Theory and problems of social psychology*. New York: McGraw-Hill, 1948.

Ladd, E., & Lipset, S. Politics of academic natural scientists and engineers. *Science,* 1972, *176,* 1091–1100.

Laski, H. *The rise of European liberalism.* New York: Barnes & Noble, 1962.

Lazarsfeld, P. Latent structure analysis. In S. Koch (Ed.), *Psychology: A study of a science* (Vol. 3). New York: McGraw-Hill, 1959.

Lazarsfeld, P., & Henry, N. *Latent structure analysis.* Boston: Houghton Mifflin, 1968.

Luttbeg, N. The structure of beliefs among leaders and the public. *Public Opinion Quarterly,* 1968, *32,* 398–409.

Mannheim, K. Conservative thought. In P. Kecskemeti (Ed.), *Essays on sociology and social psychology.* New York: Oxford University Press, 1953.

Marjoribanks, K., & Josefowitz, N. Kerlinger's theory of social attitudes: An analysis. *Psychological Reports,* 1975, *37,* 819–823.

McAtee, W., & Punch, K. Progressivism and traditionalism in teachers' attitudes toward education. *Australian Journal of Education,* 1977, *21,* 268–276.

McClosky, H. Conservatism and personality. *American Political Science Review,* 1958, *52,* 27–45.

McGuire, W. The nature of attitudes and attitude change. In G. Lindzey & E. Aronson (Eds.), *The handbook of social psychology* (2nd ed., Vol. 3). Reading, Mass.: Addison-Wesley, 1969.

Messick, S. The perception of social attitudes. *Journal of Social and Abnormal Psychology,* 1956, *52,* 57–66.

Middendorp, C. *Progressiveness and conservatism: The fundamental dimensions of ideological controversy and their relationship to social class.* The Hague: Mouton, 1976.

Milholland, J. Theory and techniques of assessment. *Annual Review of Psychology,* 1964, *15,* 311–346.

Mill, J. *On liberty.* New York: Norton, 1975 (1859).

Montanelli, R., & Humphreys, L. Latent roots of random data correlation matrices with squared multiple correlations on the diagonal: A Monte Carlo study. *Psychometrika,* 1976, *41,* 341–348.

Morris, V. *Philosophy and the American school.* Boston: Houghton Mifflin, 1961.

Morrison, D. *Multivariate statistical methods.* New York: McGraw-Hill, 1967.

Mulaik, S. *The foundations of factor analysis.* New York: McGraw-Hill, 1972.

Myers, A., & Gonda, G. Utility of the masculinity-femininity construct: Comparison of traditional and adrogyny approaches. *Journal of Personality and Social Psychology,* 1982, *43,* 514–522.

National Society for the Study of Education. *Modern philosophies and education.* 54th Yearbook. Chicago: University of Chicago Press, 1955.

Neisser, U. *Cognition and reality.* San Francisco: Freeman, 1976.

Newcomb, T. *Personality and social change.* New York: Dryden, 1943.

Newcomb, T. Autistic hostility and social reality. *Human Relations,* 1947, *1,* 69–86.

Newcomb, T. *Social psychology.* New York: Dryden, 1950.

Newcomb, T., Koenig, K., Flacks, R., & Warwick, D. *Persistence and change: Bennington College and its students after twenty-five years.* New York: Wiley, 1967.

Newcomb, T., Turner, R., & Converse, P. *Social psychology.* New York: Holt, Rinehart and Winston, 1965.

Nisbet, R. Preface. *Journal of Contemporary History,* 1978, *13,* 629–634.

Nunnally, J. *Psychometric theory* (2nd ed.). New York: McGraw-Hill, 1978.

Oliver, R., & Butcher, H. Teachers attitudes to education. *British Journal of Social and Clinical Psychology,* 1962, *1,* 56–69.

Orton, W. *The liberal tradition.* New Haven: Yale University Press, 1945.

Overall, J. Note on the scientific status of factors. *Psychological Bulletin,* 1964, *61,* 270–276.

Pedhazur, E. The Wilson-Patterson attitude inventory. In O. Buros (Ed.), *The eighth mental measurement yearbook* (Vol. I). Highland Park, NJ: The Gryphon Press, 1978.

Peterson, D. Scope and generality of verbally defined personality factors. *Psychological Review*, 1965, *72*, 48–59.

Postman, L., Bruner, J., & McGinnies, E. Personal values as selective factors in perception. *Journal of Abnormal and Social Psychology*, 1948, *43*, 142–154.

Rambo, W. Measurement of broad spectrum social attitudes: Liberalism-conservatism. *Perceptual and Motor Skills*, 1972, *35*, 463–477.

Robertson, A., & Cochrane, R. The Wilson-Patterson conservatism scale: A reappraisal. *British Journal of Social and Clinical Psychology*, 1973, *12*, 428–430.

Robinson, J., Rusk, J., & Head, K. *Measures of political attitudes*. Ann Arbor: Institute for Social Research, University of Michigan, 1968.

Robinson, J., & Shaver, P. *Measures of social psychological attitudes*. Ann Arbor: Institute for Social Research, University of Michigan, 1969.

Rokeach, M. *The open and closed mind*. New York: Basic Books, 1960.

Rokeach, M. *Beliefs, attitudes, and values*. San Francisco: Jossey-Bass, 1968.

Rokeach, M. *The nature of human values*. New York: Free Press, 1973.

Rorer, L. The great response-style myth. *Psychological Bulletin*, 1965, *63*, 129–156.

Rosch, E. Natural categories. *Cognitive Psychology*, 1973, *4*, 328–350.

Rosch, E. Cognitive reference points. *Cognitive Psychology*, 1975, *7*, 532–547.

Rosch, E. Classification of real-world objects: Origins and representations in cognition. In P. Johnson-Laird & P. Wason (Eds.). *Thinking: Readings in cognitive science*. Cambridge: Cambridge University Press, 1977.

Rosch, E., & Lloyd, E. (Eds.). *Cognition and categorization*. New York: Lawrence Erlbaum Associates, 1978.

Rossiter, C. *Conservatism in America* (2nd ed.). New York: Vintage, 1962.

Rossiter, C. Conservatism. In D. Sills (Ed.), *International encyclopedia of the social sciences*. New York: Macmillan & Free Press, 1968.

Sanai, M. A factorial study of social attitudes. *Journal of Social Psychology*, 1950, *31*, 167–182. (a)

Sanai, M. An experimental study of politico-economic attitudes. *International Journal of Opinion and Attitude Research*, 1950, *4*, 563–577. (b)

Sanai, M. An experimental study of social attitudes. *Journal of Social Psychology*, 1951, *34*, 235–264.

Saris, W., de Pijper, W., & Zegwaart, P. Detection of specification errors in linear structural equation models. In K. Schuessler (Ed.), *Sociological Methodology: 1979*. San Francisco: Jossey-Bass, 1979.

Scheffé, H. A method for judging all contrasts in the analysis of variance. *Biometrika*, 1953, *40*, 87–104.

Shaw, M., & Wright, J. *Scales for the measurement of attitudes*. New York: McGraw-Hill, 1967.

Sherman, R., & Ross, L. Liberalism-conservatism and dimensional salience in the perception of political figures. *Journal of Personality and Social Psychology*, 1972, *23*, 120–127.

Skinner, B. Behaviorism at fifty. *Science*, 1963, *140*, 951–958.

Smith, D. Liberalism. In D. Sills (Ed.), *International encyclopedia of the social sciences*. New York: Macmillan & Free Press, 1968.

Smith, I. *The invariance of educational attitudes and their relation to social attitudes: An inverse factor analytic study*. Unpublished doctoral dissertation, New York University, 1963.

Sontag, M., & Pedhazur, E. Dimensions of educational attitudes: Factorial congruence of two scales. *Journal of Educational Measurement*, 1972, *9*, 189–198.

Stagner, R. Fascist attitudes: An exploratory study. *Journal of Social Psychology*, 1936, *7*, 309–319.

Stephenson, W. *The study of behavior*. Chicago: University of Chicago Press, 1953.

Summers, G. (Ed.). *Attitude measurement*. Chicago: Rand McNally, 1970.

Tatsuoka, M. *Multivariate analysis: Techniques for educational and psychological research*. New York: Wiley, 1971.

Thurstone, L. Primary mental abilities. *Psychometric Monographs*, No. 1, 1938.

Thurstone, L. *Multiple-factor analysis*. Chicago: University of Chicago Press, 1947.

Thurstone, L. *The measurement of values*. Chicago: University of Chicago Press, 1959.

Thurstone, L., & Chave, E. *The measurement of attitude*. Chicago: University of Chicago Press, 1929.

Thurstone, L., & Thurstone, T. *Factorial studies of intelligence*. Chicago: University of Chicago Press, 1941.

Viereck, P. *Conservatism revisited* (Rev. ed.). New York: Collier Books, 1962.

Warr, P., Barter, L., & Brownbridge, G. On the independence of positive and negative affect. *Journal of Personality and Social Psychology*, 1983, *44*, 644–651.

Watkins, F. *The political tradition of the West: A study in the development of modern liberalism*. Cambridge, Mass.: Harvard University Press, 1957.

Wiley, D. Schmidt, W., & Bramble, W. Studies of a class of covariance structure models. *Journal of the American Statistical Association*, 1973, *68*, 317–323.

Williams, R., & Wright, C. Opinion organization in a heterogeneous adult population. *Journal of Abnormal and Social Psychology*, 1955, *51*, 559–564.

Wilson, G. (Ed.). *The psychology of conservatism*. London: Academic Press, 1973.

Wilson, G., & Patterson, J. A new measure of conservatism. *British Journal of Social and Clinical Psychology*, 1968, *7*, 264–269.

Wolfe, M., & Engel, J. Dimensions of opinion about teacher-pupii relations. *Journal of Experimental Education*, 1978, *46*, 41–45.

Wonderlic, E. *Wonderlic personnel test*. Northfield, Ill.: E. F. Wonderlic, 1961.

Woodmansee, J., & Cook, S. Dimensions of verbal racial attitudes: Their identification and measurement. *Journal of Personality and Social Psychology*, 1967, *7*, 240–250.

Wray, J. Comment on interpretations of early research into belief systems. *Journal of Politics*, 1979, *41*, 1173–1181.

Zak, I. Dimensions of Jewish-American identity. *Psychological Reports*, 1973, *33*, 891–900.

Zak, I. Structure of ethnic identity of Arab-Israeli students. *Psychological Reports*, 1976, *38*, 239–246.

Zak, I., & Birenbaum, M. Kerlinger's criterial referents theory revisited. *Educational and Psychological Measurement*, 1980, *40*, 923–930.

Zdep, S., & Marco, G. A commentary on Kerlinger's structural theory of social attitudes. *Psychological Reports*, 1969, *25*, 731–738.

Ziegler, M., & Atkinson, T. Information level and dimensionality of liberalism-conservatism. *Multivariate Behavioral Research*, 1973, *8*, 195–213.

Author Index

Subject Index

DATE DUE

JAN 1 1 199?			
MAR 2 6 1991			
JUN 1 0 199?			